Central and Eastern Europe in the EU

Since the onset of the global financial crisis in 2008, the EU has been in almost permanent crisis mode. It is witnessing new dimensions of internal differentiation among its member states, and the migration crisis has shown that the Central and Eastern European countries (CEEs) in particular are slowly but certainly transforming themselves from predominantly passive policy-takers towards becoming more active players in the process of shaping the EU's governance agenda.

This edited volume offers the first comprehensive and critical insight into how the CEEs position themselves in the EU's changing internal and external environment, their stance towards the European integration process under current crisis conditions, and what political and economic strategies they prioritize.

Christian Schweiger is Visiting Professor and Chair for Comparative European Governance Systems at Chemnitz University of Technology, Germany.

Anna Visvizi is Head of Research at the Institute of East-Central Europe (IESW) and Associate Professor at Deree College – The American College of Greece.

Routledge Studies in the European Economy

For a full list of titles in this series, please visit www.routledge.com/series/SE0431

40 Labour and Social Transformation in Central and Eastern Europe
Europeanization and Beyond
Edited by Violaine Delteil and Vassil Kirov

41. The Contemporary Crisis of the European Union
Prospects for the future
Ivan T. Berend

42. Ageing, Lifestyles and Economic Crises
The New People of the Mediterranean
Edited by Thierry Blöss
In Collaboration with Isabelle Blöss-Widmer, Elena Ambrosetti, Michèle Pagès and Sébastien Oliveau

43. When Ideas Fail
Economic Thought, the Failure of Transition and the Rise of Institutional Instability in Post-Soviet Russia
Joachim Zweynert

44. Economic Crisis and Structural Reforms in Southern Europe
Policy Lessons
Edited by Paulo Manasse and Dimitris Katsikas

45. Crisis in the European Monetary Union
A Core-Periphery Perspective
Giuseppe Celi, Andrea Ginzberg, Dario Guarascio and Annamaria Simonazzi

46. Rethinking Economic and Monetary Union in Europe
A Post-Keynesian Alternative
Philip B. Whyman

47. Central and Eastern Europe in the EU
Challenges and Perspectives Under Crisis Conditions
Edited by Christian Schweiger and Anna Visvizi

Central and Eastern Europe in the EU

Challenges and Perspectives Under Crisis Conditions

Edited by
Christian Schweiger and Anna Visvizi

Routledge
Taylor & Francis Group
LONDON AND NEW YORK

First published 2018 by Routledge

2 Park Square, Milton Park, Abingdon, Oxon, OX14 4RN
605 Third Avenue, New York, NY 10017

Routledge is an imprint of the Taylor & Francis Group, an informa business

First issued in paperback 2020

British Library Cataloguing in Publication Data
A catalogue record for this book is available from the British Library

Library of Congress Cataloging in Publication Data
Names: Schweiger, Christian, 1972- author. | Visvizi, Anna, 1976- editor.
Title: Central and Eastern Europe in the EU : challenges and perspectives under crisis conditions / Christian Schweiger and Anna Visvizi.
Description: 1 Edition. | New York : Routledge, 2018. | Series: Routledge studies in the European economy ; 47
Identifiers: LCCN 2017056520 | ISBN 9781138714021 (hardback) | ISBN 9781351863704 (pdf) | ISBN 9781351863698 (epub) | ISBN 9781351863681 (mobi)
Subjects: LCSH: European Union. | Europe--Economic integration. | Europe, Eastern--Economic integration. | Europe, Central--Economic integration.
Classification: LCC HC241 .S3653 2018 | DDC 337.1/420943--dc23
LC record available at https://lccn.loc.gov/2017056520

ISBN: 978-1-138-71402-1 (hbk)
ISBN: 978-0-367-73447-3 (pbk)

Typeset in Bembo
by Taylor & Francis Books

To the people of Central and Eastern Europe who made the peaceful transition to democracy in 1989/90 possible.

Contents

Illustrations

Figures

Tables

Contributors

Attila Ágh is Professor in the Political Science Department at Budapest Corvinus University. He was the founder and the former Head of Department of Political Science at the University, the Director of the Research Centre 'Together for Europe' and also the President of the Central European Political Science Association (CEPSA). He was a visiting professor at many universities across the world including Aarhus, Vienna, New Delhi and Los Angeles. His major research interest is comparative politics with special regard to the EU developments, focusing the Europeanization and Democratization in the New Member States. He has published more than twenty books and dozens of papers in international journals.

Krisztina Arató is Professor and Deputy Director of Political Science Institute at ELTE University Faculty of Law in Budapest, Hungary. She has been the president of the Hungarian Political Science Association since 2015, and member of the Collegium of the Hungarian Research Fund since 2014. Her teaching and research activities include the history of European integration, cohesion policy of the European Union, characteristics of the Visegrád cooperation as well as civil society and social dialogue in Hungary and Europe. She is author and editor of a number of books and articles, among others 'The Voyage of Europe. History of European integration' (2015, Gondolat, in Hungarian with Boglárka Koller) and *Myths and Countermyths of the European Union* (University of Strathclyde 2014).

Will Bartlett is Visiting Senior Fellow at the Research Unit on South East Europe (LSEE) at the London School of Economics and Political Science. His research interests focus on economic and social development in South East Europe. From 2009 to 2015 he was Senior Research Fellow in the Political Economy of South East Europe at LSEE, where he established the LSEE Research Network on Social Cohesion in South East Europe. His publications include the monograph *Croatia: between Europe and the Balkans* (Routledge, 2003) and *Europe's Troubled Region: Economic Development, Institutional Reform and Social Welfare in the Western Balkans* (Routledge, 2008), as well as numerous articles in refereed journals including 'Interdependence Between Core and peripheries of the European Economy:

Secular Stagnation and growth in the Western Balkans' with Ivana Prica (*European Journal of Comparative Economics*, 2017). Since September 2017 he has been a Visiting Research Fellow at the International Inequalities Institute of the LSE, where he is pursuing research on inequality and social welfare in the successor states of former Yugoslavia.

Tomas Bekišas is an attaché at the Lithuanian Ministry of Foreign Affairs and alumnus of the Institute of International Relations and Political Science. He is primarily interested in European Union (EU) decision-making, EU institutions, EU policies and their effect on the EU Member States, especially their party systems. Tomas Bekišas contributed to this book in his personal capacity. The views expressed are his own and do not necessarily represent the views of the Ministry of Foreign Affairs of the Republic of Lithuania.

Mihnea Cătuţi is a PhD candidate at the University of York and has obtained degrees from the University of Bristol and the Central European University. His research concentrates on European integration and enlargement, with a focus on energy and environmental policies. He also worked as a research intern at the Centre for European Policy Studies (CEPS) in Brussels.

Maciej Duszczyk is Vice-Rector for Research at the Institute of Social Policy and Board Member of the Centre of Migration Research, University of Warsaw. From 2008 to 2011 he was on the Board of Strategic Advisers to the Prime Minister of Poland. Currently he is a member of the Council of the National Congress of Science and Higher Education and an external collaborator for the International Labour Organization, European Commission and International Organization for Migration. He has received scholarships from the Jean Monnet Project, Carl Duisburg Gesellschaft and the Polish Committee for Scientific Research. Duszczyk specialises in topics within the labour market, social policy and economic migration.

Beáta Farkas is Professor and Head of the Institute of Finance and International Economic Relations at the University of Szeged, Hungary. She joined the university after obtaining degrees in both Law and Economics, and now holds a PhD in Economics. She was the founding Dean of the Faculty of Economics and Business Administration.

Zsolt Gál is Assistant Professor at the Department of Political Science, Faculty of Arts at Comenius University in Bratislava, Slovakia. He holds an MA degree in Political Science from this department and a PhD degree in Economics from Corvinus University in Budapest, Hungary. His research interests include public finances, economic aspects of European integration, economic transformation and international migration. Zsolt teaches several courses in these fields at Comenius University. He is the author of the book *The 2007–2009 Financial Crisis. What Went Wrong and What Went Different?* (Univerzita Komenského, Bratislava 2011) and numerous other publications.

Liutauras Gudžinskas is Associate Professor at the Political Theory department in the Institute of International Relations and Political Science at Vilnius University (IIRPS VU), and the editor-in-chief of the Baltic Journal of Political Science. He focuses on the post-communist transformation and Europeanization of the Baltic states and other countries in Central and Eastern Europe (CEE). Among issues of quality of democracy and governance in the region, Liutauras Gudžinskas is particularly interested in such topics as the reforms of welfare policies and the functioning of political institutions. Most recently, together with colleagues from the IIRPS VU, he published a book on the public confidence in government institutions in Lithuania and other CEE states. Until 2009, Liutauras Gudžinskas worked at the EU policy analysis division at the Office of the Government of the Republic of Lithuania and for a few years acted as head of the division.

Boglárka Koller is Associate Professor, Dean and Head of the Department of European Studies in the Faculty of International and European Studies at the National University of Public Service. She is a Board Member of the Hungarian Political Science Association. Her research focuses on the Central-Eastern European region in the EU, particularly the Visegrád cooperation. Recent publications include 'European and National Agendas in the 2014 EP Elections in Hungary' in Ruxandra et al (eds) *Political Communication and European Parliament Elections in Times of Crisis: Perspectives from Central and South-Eastern Europe* (London: Palgrave MacMillan) and 'Identity Patterns in East-Central Europe in a comparative perspective', *Journal of Comparative Politics* 9 (2): 85–98.

Nicole Lindstrom is Senior Lecturer in the Department of Politics at the University of York. Her research and teaching interests lie in comparative and international political economy and public policy, with a particular focus on political economic transformations in the enlarged European Union. Before coming to York in 2007, she was a member of the Departments of International Relations and European Studies and Political Science at Central European University in Budapest. She held a visiting position in the Graduate Program of International Affairs at The New School for Social Research and was a visiting fellow at the Centre for the Study of Globalisation and Regionalisation at the University of Warwick. Her current research focuses on a number of different EU policy areas, including service liberalization, higher education policy, financial services regulation, and state aid policy. Recent publications include 'Wither Diversity of Post-Socialist Welfare Capitalist Cultures?: Crisis and Change in Estonia and Slovenia', *European Journal of Sociology* 56 (1): 119–139 (2015) and the monograph The Politics of Europeanization and Post-Socialist Transformations (Basingstoke: Palgrave MacMillan 2015).

Darina Malová is Professor at the Department of Political Science, Comenius University in Bratislava, Slovakia. She specializes in Slovak and Central

European politics and European integration, especially the Eastern enlargement of the EU. In 2009 she established the Center of Excellence for Social Innovation at Comenius University that studies new ideas and good practices, including deliberative democracy, social and gender equality in Slovakia and the European Union. Her publications include *Governing New Democracies* (with Jean Blondel and Ferdinand Mueller-Rommel, Palgrave 2007) and *From Listening to Action: New Member States in the European Union* (Devin 2010).

András Máté-Tóth is Professor and Head of the Department for the Study of Religions at the University of Szeged. He has a PhD in Practical Theology from the University of Vienna, Austria and a PhD in Science of Communication from the University of Pécs, Hungary. He is Privatdozent for Practical Theology at the University of Vienna and Doctor of the Hungarian Academy of Science. His main research interest is the societal and religious transformations in Central and Eastern Europe after the system change of 1990 around new religious movements. Recent publications include 'Not an Extraordinary Group – Scientologists in Hungary and Germany – Comparative Survey Data', in James R Lewis and Kjersti Helles (eds) *Handbook of Scientology. Focus on Religion in Central and Eastern Europe: A Regional View.* Berlin: De Gruyter Verlag, 2016. 204 p. (Religion and Society; 68.)

Anna Molnár is Associate Professor at the National University of Public Service in Budapest. She is a member of the Executive Academic Board of the European Security and Defence College (ESDC) and of the Committee on International and Development Studies at the Hungarian Academy of Sciences. Her research concentrates on EU security and defence policy, neighbourhood policy and external relations, the Visegrád defence cooperation and Euroscepticism in the comparative context. Recent publications include 'Economic Crisis and Euroscepticism: A Comparative Study of the Hungarian and Italian Case (1990–2013)', Politics in Central Europe 12 (3): 51–82 (2016) and 'Towards an EU Strategy for the Adriatic and Ionian Macro-Region', in A. Agh et al (eds) *10 Years After: Multi-Level Governance and Differentiated Integration in the EU* (Budapest: Blue Ribbon Research Centre).

Christian Schweiger is Visiting Professor and Chair for Comparative European Governance Systems at Chemnitz University of Technology, Germany. His research concentrates on the comparative study of political systems, economies and welfare states of the member states of the European Union (particularly the UK, Germany and transformation in the CEE countries), the political economy of the EU Single Market, economic globalisation and transatlantic relations. His most recent publications include the jointly edited collection with José M. Magone and Brigid Laffan *Core-periphery Relations in the European Union: Power and conflict in a dualist political economy* (Routledge, 2016) and the monograph *Exploring the EU's Legitimacy Crisis: The Dark Heart of Europe* (Edward Elgar, 2016).

Tomáš Strážay works as a Senior Research Fellow at the Research Center of the Slovak Foreign Policy Association (RC SFPA), where he heads the program Central and Southeastern Europe. He is a co-founder and leading expert in the project Think Visegrad – V4 Think Tank Platform and editor of the International Issues and Slovak Foreign Policy Affairs quarterly. He received his PhD from the Institute of Political Studies of the Polish Academy of Sciences in Warsaw, Poland.

Zoltán Szenes is Professor of Security and Defence Studies and Professor in the Department for International and Security Studies at the National University of Public Service in Budapest. He was previously Hungarian Chief of Defence and a member of the Advisory Team on Foreign and Security Policy to the Hungarian Prime Minister (2007–2009). His research and teaching focuses on security studies, defence policy, NATO studies and defence management. He is also Adjunct Professor in the Baltic Defence College and former Chairman of the Military Science Committee of the Hungarian Academy of Sciences. He co-authored the first Hungarian Military Strategy and was involved in the new NATO Strategic Concept preparation work as a member of the MFA Expert Group in Hungary.

Anna Visvizi is Head of Research at the Institute of East-Central Europe (IESW) and Associate Professor at Deree College – The American College of Greece. A political scientist and economist, editor and research consultant, with extensive experience in academia and the think-tank sector, Dr. Visvizi presented her work in many forums across Europe and the US, including Capitol Hill. A practiced team-worker, researcher, analyst and lecturer, Dr. Visvizi's expertise spans the following interrelated areas of research: political economy; migration; smart cities; innovation, competitiveness and policy-making, with the geographical focus of her research defined by the EU, China, and the Arab World.

Acknowledgements

We would like to thank Christiana Gransow for her help with the final editing process of the book.

1 Introduction

The EU under crisis conditions: Central and Eastern European perspectives

Christian Schweiger and Anna Visvizi

Arguably, since the onset of the global financial crisis in 2008, the EU has operated in permanent crisis mode. The EU leaders have been preoccupied with managing the eurozone crisis. As a result, although a diversity of novel governance mechanisms has been established these do not uniformly apply to the 28 EU member states. Consequently, the EU witnesses new dimensions of internal differentiation among its member states. The Central and Eastern European countries (CEEs) are particularly affected by the multidimensional horizontal (in terms of membership of different groupings) and vertical (in terms of the level of political integration) differentiation, which has manifested itself both within the eurozone and in the wider EU. The refugee and migration crises have shown that the CEEs are slowly but certainly turning from predominantly passive policy-takers into member states adopting a more active role in the process of shaping the EU's governance agenda. At the same time, several developments on their respective domestic political scenes trigger earnest questions about the CEE stance towards the European integration process. In light of this, the question of the CEEs' evolution to policy-makers on the EU scene acquires a new angle.

Over the past few years, the developments in the CEEs have been influenced by a variety of domestic and external challenges. This volume maps these challenges, examines the dynamics that they trigger in the CEEs, and traces the projection thereof on the EU's internal dynamics in terms of political deliberation at supranational and intergovernmental levels. Specifically, through the lens of the CEEs' political and economic transformation, the objective of this volume is to examine their quest for more active engagement in the EU policy-making process and its implications.

The global financial crisis and the subsequent sovereign debt crises in the eurozone have had severe economic and political repercussions, not only for the euro area but also for the EU as a whole, the CEEs included. The eurozone crisis exposed a profound leadership void in the EU (Nugent 2017: 183). That void resulted from the fact that all countries in the group of larger member states, with the exception of Germany, suffered severe economic implications from the crisis and, hence, became preoccupied with domestic economic consolidation efforts. Germany was subsequently pushed into adopting the position of semi-hegemonic leader in the EU (Bulmer and Paterson 2013). However, as new crises, including the economic recession and the twin refugee and migration crises, continued unfolding, Germany's role became increasingly contested, exacerbating the paralysis of political cooperation at the EU level. In those circumstances, existing internal divisions in the EU have become more tangible and – what previously had manifested itself predominantly in the dichotomy between the euro core group and the outsiders – had acquired multiple new dimensions. The CEEs are the most apparent manifestation of that. That is, the sovereign debt crisis has resulted not only in the growing internal division of the eurozone between the creditor and the debtor economies, but it has also made the euro insider-outsider dichotomy more complex (Laffan 2016: 28). This volume attests to that.

The eurozone sovereign debt crisis

The emergence of multiple layers of governance mechanisms in the EU Single Market and the eurozone represents a departure from the traditional community method of collective integration. At present, the coordinative policy mechanisms divide the 28 EU member states horizontally into a eurozone core, including 19 member states, a semi-periphery euro plus group and a small outer periphery (Schweiger 2014: 74–75). Each of these groups are currently characterised by descending levels of vertical policy coordination. The eurozone core group is in the process of moving towards deeper political integration. The eurozone outsiders in the factually dormant Euro Plus Pact and the Fiscal Compact are to a greater or lesser extent associated with this process. The outer periphery group, which is currently represented by the Czech Republic and the outward-bound United Kingdom, remains detached from it. The CEE member states, which are represented in all of the EU's internal cleavages, have shown that these groups are not static but subject to fluctuations.

A number of countries from the CEE region have been joining the euro core since 2007, even during the adverse conditions of the sovereign debt crisis. Individual CEE countries have also started to move between the semi-periphery and the outer periphery group, with the Czech Republic in the process of adopting the Fiscal Compact, and Hungary and Poland becoming more detached from eurozone policy coordination. Possibly, their drifting away from the EU's core may in itself be the direct outcome of the multiple crises that the EU has faced recently. Research suggests that the question of the euro adoption is in fact a matter of political choice rather than a country's ability to fulfil the Maastricht nominal convergence criteria (Tokarski and Visvizi 2015). Like the rest of the EU, the CEE member states were confronted with the economic implications of the euro area crisis. However, they have managed to steer themselves through relatively intact, with Poland having been the only country in the EU that did not slide into recession during the crisis. The fact that Poland did so outside the main euro core has contributed to the recent weakening of the former Polish political resolve to adopt the euro under the new

Law and Justice (PiS) government (Visvizi and Tokarski 2014: 460). This has to be considered in the overall context of the tendency of 'democratic backsliding' in the region towards a new form of authoritarianism. This trend has particularly affected countries outside the euro core, especially Hungary and Poland, but also Bulgaria and Romania (Birdwell et al 2013: 20). This is not just the result of the decreasing attraction of the post-crisis eurozone. From the perspective of the outsiders the crisis has turned the euro-19 core into a permanent financial transfer union from the richer to the poorer economies (Haughton 2017: 258), which is symbolised by the institutionalised financial solidarity that current euro members have to exercise under the newly created European Stability Mechanism (ESM). At the same time, there is a growing concern amongst the outsiders that they could be permanently left out from the deepening euro core – firmly under Germany's ordoliberal diktat (Funk 2015) and end up at the outside periphery of the EU in a 'two-tier club' (Visvizi 2012: 32).

Brexit

The CEE countries have traditionally been close allies of the United Kingdom in the EU. Arguably, the CEEs not only share the British emphasis on accelerating the liberalisation of the Single Market and avoiding the return to domestic protectionist policies but also are keen to maintain the principle of subsidiarity (Schweiger, Markovic and Nagy 2016). Consequently, the decision by a slim majority of the British public to opt for exit from the EU in the June 2016 referendum not only took the countries in the region by surprise, but also created a source of profound political and economic concerns. Indeed, the impending Brexit will fundamentally alter the power balance within the EU (Csaba 2016). It is far from certain if, without the UK, the remaining EU-27 will be able to resolve their internal differences and build consensus in major policy areas, such as asylum and migration, security, economic and social reform. The CEE members consequently are in a process of losing an important partner at a time when relations with their so far closest ally, i.e. Germany, for several reasons, have started to turn sour under the leadership of the chancellor Angela Merkel (Schweiger 2017). Brexit, hence, poses both a challenge and an opportunity for the region. On the one hand, the CEEs have the opportunity to fill the leadership gap in the EU that has already emerged as a result of the UK's preparation for Brexit. Neither will Germany be able to continue its recent increasingly less semi- and more fully hegemonial leadership style in the EU (Schweiger 2016: 120), nor will it be sufficient for the former Franco-German leadership axis to be revived. In the larger EU-27, which is characterised by a multiplicity of interests, only a more comprehensive leadership constellation is likely to be able to achieve tangible results. In particular Poland has the potential to step into this void, either individually, by re-engaging in the Weimar Triangle Cooperation with Germany and France, or as part of the semi-institutionalised cooperation of the Visegrád Group, including, apart from Poland, the Czech Republic, Hungary and Slovakia. On the other hand, there is a real risk that the tendency towards authoritarian backsliding will deepen and spread across the region if the persistent economic and social peripheralisation of the region is accompanied by a growing political marginalisation. This could occur if the already patchy cleavage between the EU mainstream political agenda, mainly defined by Germany and France, and the illiberal populism of the Orbán government in Hungary and the Szydlo government in Poland manifests itself as a wider feature of a permanent East–West divide.

The refugee crisis and the migration challenge

In this respect the refugee and migration crises, which peaked over the period 2015–2016, and continue to serve as a reminder of the EU member states' inability to navigate the challenges they inflicted, pose a major challenge for the future of relations within the EU, with the relationship among the 'old' members in the West and the 'newcomers' in the East becoming particularly contested. As other major players amongst the EU-15 are substantially weakened by domestic economic and political challenges, Germany has emerged as the quasi leader of the EU. A limited input from the economically frail France is to be recognised in this respect, even if France struggles to regain its former confidence under the leadership of the newly elected president Emanuel Macron. The German government's insistence on the implementation of binding refugee distribution quotas for the whole of the EU has met fierce resistance from the CEE countries. The V4 group became the main advocates for the wider CEE position on this issue, which has been illustrated by their firm joint opposition to the EU distribution quotas. Ultimately the failure to jointly resolve this crucial problem in a cooperative manner tells a lot about the nature of Germany's increasingly self-centred and uncompromising leadership (Meiers 2015: 49). Similarly, it mirrors the increasingly self-confident and uncompromising stance of the CEE member states who are today less concerned about acting as 'good Europeans' (Dimitrov 2012: 308) than during the first decade following accession.

Positioning the CEEs in a changing environment

There has been a tendency in the literature to examine the CEE region by focusing on domestic transformation processes in these countries. In that context, the CEEs used to be seen as passive policy-takers preoccupied with adopting the EU's acquis. The role of the CEEs as possible agenda-setters in the EU has thus been largely neglected in the literature on the region. This volume seeks to address this issue. More than a decade after their accession to the EU, the categorisation as passive, compliant member states no longer adequately reflects the domestic political developments in many of these countries. Under the persistent crisis conditions in the EU, the CEEs have become more self-assured in defending their national interests. This volume traces and examines these developments in detail. The refugee and migration crises, and the German-influenced way of addressing them, serve as one of the most recent examples of the V4 countries establishing and defending a joint opposition at the EU level.

This volume highlights and explains the logic behind this emerging trend and its likely implications for the future of the EU. Considering what has been dubbed in the literature as an 'illiberal turn' in certain countries of the region (Ágh 2013; Ágh 2014), this volume identifies the likely sources of that turn and dwells on the question of how it may affect the CEEs stance towards the European integration process under conditions of multiple crises that the EU is faced with. The book presents a comprehensive range of contributions from experts on the CEE region. It is based on a series of conferences and public events which were organised by authors contributing to this volume in the framework of a research network geared towards the examination of the ongoing multidimensional domestic political, economic, social and cultural transformation processes in the wider CEE region.

The selection of chapters offers the most comprehensive analysis on the market of the challenges that the wider CEE region has been facing under the conditions of growing internal and external crisis in the EU. As such, each of the chapters adds to the analysis and, step-by-step, contributes to the construction of an insightful and complete analysis of the CEE region today and its role in shaping the EU's future. The book offers the first comprehensive and critical insight into how the CEEs position themselves in the EU's changing internal and external environment and what political and economic strategies they prioritise. The analyses presented here therefore offer a rare opportunity to reflect on the follow-up of the economic, political and social transformation processes that the CEEs embarked on in the early 1990s. Special emphasis is put on the role of the Visegrád Group (V4), i.e. cooperation between the Czech Republic, Hungary, Poland and Slovakia and its increasingly dynamic role in the broadly conceived region of East and Central Europe.

The individual contributions included in the volume sketch a picture of the CEE members as (i) representing a region that is full of contradictions with regard to the level of social inclusion, economic growth and performance, political orientation and foreign policy priorities; (ii) a group of countries some of which still have not found their way to sustainable growth and political stability; and still, (iii) a group of countries that have successfully built their presence on the EU scene.

That variability is approached in the volume from three perspectives. The chapters included in the first part of the volume address the broad question of the sources and likely implications of the gradual re-positioning of the CEEs on the EU scene. Here the notion of multiple crises that the EU has endured constitutes an important context of the analysis. In chapter 2 **Schweiger** examines how the CEE member states have been affected by the growing complexity of the EU's internal differentiation. The chapter also examines the prospects for these countries to use the opportunity of the recalibration of the EU's internal leadership constellation after Brexit to emerge from their role as predominantly passive policy-takers. **Farkas** and **Máté-Tóth** dedicate chapter 3 to the neglected shadows of the multidimensional transition process in the region through the application of modernisation theories. Both authors detect a distinct

CEE model of capitalism in the framework of the varieties of socio-economic developments in Europe. In chapter 4 **Visvizi** examines how the persistent internal crisis conditions in the EU and the impact of the wider geopolitical framework have resulted in a new 'normalcy' which is distinctive for the region. In chapter 5 **Farkas** analyses whether the recent crises in the EU undermine the political and economic status quo in the region and what this means for the future influence of the CEE countries in the EU.

As if through a magnifying glass, the second part of the volume offers a detailed insight into country-specific developments that have been inflicted by the crisis situation in the EU. Here political, economic and strategic considerations that shape CEEs' domestic political scene weigh in the analysis. Chapter 6 by **Duszczyk** considers which route Poland will take in the crisis-ridden EU which he describes as standing at a crossroads. Duszczyk outlines the recent changes in Poland's European policy under the Law and Justice (PiS) government elected in 2015 and asks what these mean for the country's future position as a potential regional leader within the V4 and leadership partner for Germany and France after Brexit. This is followed by a three-level game approach to the analysis of Hungary's position in the Visegrád Group presented by **Arató** and **Koller** in chapter 7. The authors examine the threefold dimension of Hungary's engagement in the V4 in terms of the domestic institutional polity, concrete policy-making and the wider political environment. In chapter 8 **Gál** and **Malová** critically examine Slovakia's status as a predominantly passive policy-taker, which has only recently emerged as a more active force within the V4 in the context of the refugee crisis. The authors emphasise in this respect that Slovakia's success in terms of economic integration and joining the euro has not been matched by a wider Europeanisation of domestic norms and values. **Lindstrom** takes a similar approach in chapter 9 with regard to Bulgaria's and Romania's positions in the EU. **Lindstrom** argues that in spite of limited institutional resources Bulgaria and Romania have developed strategies to pursue their policy preferences and explains how this was possible under an *asymmetrical* relationship with the EU.

In chapter 10 **Gudžinskas** and **Bekišas** look at the transformation process in the Baltic states and examine the major objectives of their policies towards the EU in terms of differences and joint interests. **Bartlett** in chapter 11 considers Croatia as the latest and to this day last country that recently joined the EU. The chapter examines the political dimension of Croatia's integration into the EU, which has witnessed unresolved challenges but overall also noticeably positive developments.

Against the background of those findings, the third part of the volume examines how the variability of challenges and crises-inflicted dynamics and differentiation that concern the CEEs influences the functioning of the V4. The interesting observation here is that the V4 turns into a hub of influence both in the Central-Eastern European region and in the EU as a whole. In chapter 12 **Strazay** analyses the internal and external factors on which the V4 cooperation as an informally institutionalised initiative is based. He argues that the V4 have managed to set their own priorities in spite of overall lingering scepticism about the purpose of the cooperation. **Ágh** considers what he terms the 'dual crisis' that has significantly affected the V4 – the Ukraine and refugee crisis – in chapter 13. From his perspective both crises have managed to strengthen the V4 in the context of their particular regionalised identity, which he outlines in the chapter and examines in terms of its long-term perspective. In chapter 14 **Molnár** and **Szenes** conclude the third part of the book with an examination of new initiatives in the V4 group, particularly the joint battle-group in the wider context of military cooperation within the framework of the EU's defence and security policy.

There has been a tendency in the literature to examine the CEE region by focusing on domestic transformation processes in these countries. In that context, the CEEs used to be seen as passive policy-takers preoccupied with adopting the EU's acquis. The role of the CEEs as possible agenda-setters in the EU has thus been largely neglected in the literature on the region. This volume seeks to address this issue. More than a decade after their accession to the EU, the categorisation as passive good citizens no longer adequately reflects the domestic political developments in many of these countries. Under the persistent crisis conditions in the EU, the CEEs have become more self-assured in defending their national interests. This volume traces and examines in detail these developments. The migration crisis and the German-influenced way of addressing it serves as one of the most recent examples of the V4 countries establishing and defending a joint opposition at the EU level. Certainly, other instances exist. This volume highlights and explains the logic behind this emerging trend and its likely implications for the future of the EU.

Twenty-seven years after the collapse of communism, the CEE region is not what the stereotypical idea of the region once was. Profound political, economic and social transformations have changed the countries in question beyond the expected. Today, at a moment of ideational uncertainty in the region, faced with multiple crises undermining the trust in the European integration process, the need to reach out to a broader audience and to assist them in understanding the specificity of the CEE region is more crucial than ever. The aim of this volume is to contribute to this process in an EU that has to recalibrate its leadership constellation and to regain a sense of direction and political purpose under the conditions of the deepening internal legitimacy crisis and the United Kingdom's impending exit from the EU.

References

Ágh, A. (2013) The Triple Crisis in Hungary: The 'Backsliding' of Hungarian Democracy after Twenty Years. *Romanian Journal of Political Science* 13(1), pp. 25–51.

Ágh, A. (2014) Decline of Democracy in East-Central Europe: The Last Decade as the Lost Decade in Democratization. *Journal of Comparative Politics* 7(2), pp. 4–33.

Birdwell, J., Feve, S., Tryhorn C. and Vibla, N. (2013) *'Democracy in Europe Can No Longer be Taken For Granted': Backsliders.* London: Demos.

Bulmer, S., Paterson, W.E. (2013) Germany as the EU's Reluctant Hegemon? Of Economic Strength and Political Constraints. *Journal of European Public Policy* 20(10), pp. 1387–1405.

Csaba, L. (2016) The EU at Sixty: A Watershed Or Business as Usual? (Comparing Grexit to Brexit), *Acta Oeconomica* 66(1), pp. 61–75.

Dimitrov, V. (2012) The Central and East European Countries: From Weak Latecomers to Good Citizens of the Union. In: Hayward, J. and Wurzel, R. (eds) *European Disunion: Between Sovereignty and Solidarity*. Basingstoke: Palgrave MacMillan, p. 308.

Funk, L. (2015) Towards a Resilient EMU? The German-Inspired Response to the Euro Crisis Assessed. In: Ryan, J. (ed.) *Towards a Resilient Eurozone: Economic, Monetary and Fiscal Policies*. Peter Lang: Frankfurt/Main, pp. 31–67.

Haughton, T. (2017) Central and Eastern Europe: The Sacrifices of Solidarity, the Discomforts of Diversity, and the Vexations of Vulnerabilities. In: Dinan, D., Nugent N. and Paterson, W.E. (eds) *The European Union in Crisis*. London: Palgrave, pp. 253–268.

Laffan, B. (2016) Core-Periphery Dynamics in the Euro Area: From Conflict to Cleavage? In: Laffan, B., Magone, J.M. and Schweiger C. (eds) *Core-Periphery Relations in the European Union: Power and Conflict in a Dualist Political Economy*. London: Routledge, pp. 19–34.

Meiers, F.J. (2015) The Stress Test of German Leadership. *Survival* 57(2), pp. 47–55.

Nugent, N. (2017) The Crisis and the EU's Institutions, Political Actors, and Processes. In: Dinan, D., Nugent, N. and Paterson W.E. (eds) *The European Union in Crisis*. London: Palgrave, pp. 167–187.

Schweiger, C. (2014) *The EU and the Global Financial Crisis: New Varieties of Capitalism*. Cheltenham: Edward Elgar.

Schweiger, C. (2016) *Exploring the EU's Legitimacy Crisis: The Dark Heart of Europe*. Cheltenham: Edward Elgar.

Schweiger, C. (2017) East-Central Europe between German Semi-Hegemony and Brexit.

Yearbook of the Institute of East-Central Europe (YIESW) 15(2), pp. 7–25.

Schweiger, C., Markovic, F. and Nagy T.A. (2016) *The Dire Straits of Brexit: Potential implications for the EU, UK and V4*. Bratislava: Central European Policy Institute, 19

February. [ONLINE] Available from: http://www.europeanpublicaffairs.eu/the-dire-straits-of-brexit-potential-implications-for-the-eu-uk-and-the-v4/

Tokarski, P. and Visvizi, A. (2015) Poland's Winding Road to the Euro Area: From Cost-benefit

Analysis to Risk Aversion. *The Polish Quarterly of International Affairs* 40(3), pp. 65–84.

Visvizi, A. (2012) The Eurozone Crisis in Perspective: Causes and Implications. *Yearbook of the Institute of East-Central Europe* 10(5), pp. 13–32.

Visvizi, A. and Tokarski, P. (2014) Poland and the Euro: Between Lock-In and Unfinished

Transition. *Society and Economy* 36(4), pp. 445–468.

Part I

Central and Eastern Europe in the EU's changing internal and external dimension

2 Positioning the CEE region in the EU's core–periphery divide

Christian Schweiger

Introduction

The accession of eight new member states from the Central-Eastern European region, as well as Cyprus and Malta as two additional Southern European countries, in 2004 was widely classified as the 'big bang' enlargement, which represented an unprecedented large-scale widening of the European Union. Never before since the onset of the process of institutionalised European integration in the 1950s had such a large group of countries joined at once. Combined with the delayed accession of Bulgaria and Romania in 2007 a total of ten countries had joined the EU, who shared experience of almost four decades of rigid authoritarian state planning under communism.

Against the background of their common past as countries of the Soviet-dominated communist bloc the CEE member states faced similar challenges as they entered the EU. All of them had to make substantial efforts to transform their authoritarian state structures to equip them for the implementation of the EU's complex legal acquis. At the same time they had to abandon the legacy of centrally planned economic development, which had characterised the Council for Mutual Economic Assistance (COMECON), in preparation for the open market competition in the Single European Market. The former demanded to challenge the widespread culture of corruption and cronyism which had emerged during the communist area. The latter led to the implementation of the liberalisation principles of the Washington consensus. In some cases, most notably the Baltic states, this resulted in a neoliberal 'shock therapy' with rapidly increasing dependence on foreign direct investment and ultimately to worsening social inequality in most countries (Myant and Drahokoupil 2011: 186 and 303).

This chapter investigates the extent to which the CEE members have managed to integrate themselves into the EU's ever more complex political architecture, which has been characterised by the growing deepening internal differentiation under Germany's expanding and increasingly contested (semi-)hegemonial leadership.

EU accession and 'adaptive Europeanisation' through conditionality

The EU became the leading agent for the transition efforts in the region through the strict conditionality it applied in assessing the membership applications of the CEE applicants (Tomini 2016: 8). The EU-15 countries had numerous concerns regarding the accession of countries which had only limited experience with Western-style liberal democracy and economic liberalism. For the eastward enlargement the EU consequently developed the concise Copenhagen membership criteria, which determined that all applicants must be able to show a functioning liberal democracy based on the rule of law and the respect for human rights, a competitive market economy and the ability to integrate smoothly into the EU's legal acquis, including economic and monetary union. The Copenhagen conditionality applied towards the CEE applicants resulted in a detailed EU monitoring regime of their transition progress on all levels of state activity (Grabbe 2011: 1015). In the case of Bulgaria and Romania this resulted ultimately in their exclusion from the first accession group, as the European Commission assessment of their preparation for EU membership was deemed unsatisfactory. Concerns that were raised mainly concentrated on the lack of transition towards good governance with corruption, institutional inefficiency and crime remaining prominent in both countries, in addition to the insufficient protection of minorities (Bojkov 2004; Noutcheva and Bechev 2008). Amongst the first group of accession countries some of the EU-15 countries, particularly Germany and France, were most concerned about Poland. Here the general low wage culture in the region in combination with a comparatively high unemployment rate of 20 per cent resulted in the 'Polish plumber' debate. It illustrated the widespread concerns in the EU-15 on the effects of a potential race to the bottom on wage levels and employment standards caused by the eastward enlargement (Barysch 2005: 7). The result was the implementation of temporary restrictions on the freedom of movement for citizens from the 2004 CEE-8 accession group in the EU. All EU-15 countries, apart from Ireland, the United Kingdom and Sweden, imposed transitional periods on the freedom of CEE-8 workers to enter their labour markets (Dobson and Sennikova 2007: 124). Germany and Austria even maintained these restrictions until 2011, the final deadline for transitional periods on the freedom of movement for CEE-8 countries, which could only be negotiated individually with the Commission on the basis of the expectation of 'serious disturbances' in the labour market of the receiving countries (CESifo Group Munich).

The transitional periods were just one indicator of the fact that the CEE countries had little choice but to accept their status as passive policy takers. The EU-15 governments were unwilling to give their Eastern neighbours the same benefit of the doubt they had applied during previous enlargement rounds (Lippert, Hughes, Grabbe and Becker 2001: 74). The CEE governments hence focused strongly on compliance with the EU's conditionality and quickly established themselves as 'good citizens' in the EU (Dimitrov 2012). This was reflected by the CEE's performance in implementing the EU's legal acquis. With the exception of the Czech Republic and Poland, it was substantially better than the EU-15 average and especially than that of the Southern European member states (Börzel and Sedelmeier 2017: 202). The second indicator for the CEE's status as not just passive policy-takers but in fact second class members (Aslund 2010) could be found in the strict application of the eurozone stability and growth pact (SGP) criteria. The founding members of the eurozone, including France and Germany, had granted themselves the luxury of repeatedly breaking the SGP criteria (Dyson 2017: 68). In the case of Greece and Italy both countries were permitted to join the euro at its foundation in 2002, in spite of the fact that their structural deficits were above 100 per cent of their annual GDP and hence way beyond the required 60 per cent limit (Schweiger 2014: 161). Conditionality within the existing eurozone hence remained substantially weak before the crisis as the budgetary rules were practically not enforced (de la Porte and Heins 2017: 151).

In contrast the CEE countries were kept waiting in line and had to make substantial efforts to not only meet the SGP three per cent annual deficit limit and the 60 per cent overall structural debt limits in relation to their GDP. Their eurozone applications were also strictly assessed on the basis of the SGP inflationary targets. In spite of this strict conditionality the eurozone enlarged exclusively eastwards between 2007 and 2015. This was even more striking as the CEE countries Slovenia, Slovakia, Estonia, Latvia and Lithuania joined during a period of instability and ultimately of a systemic crisis in the eurozone.

For the CEE countries who managed to join the eurozone fiscal austerity hence became a precondition of their success. It is therefore not surprising that the CEE euro members have been the most ardent supporters of the German chancellor Merkel's concept of the euro as a stability union and the strict implementation of fiscal austerity in the Southern European crisis countries, especially in the most ailing euro member Greece. In this respect the CEE euro insiders have been strongly supportive of Merkel's categoric rejection of the notion of a transfer union and made substantial efforts to maintain a good performance on the euro SGP criteria (Handl and Paterson 2013: 332).

The attempt of the Slovakian centre-right government under prime minister Iveta Radičova to block financial support for Greece by vetoing the European Financial Stability Facility (EFSF) in 2011 however illustrated the growing unease of the euro members in the region with the lack of reforms in the Southern periphery of the eurozone (Haughton 2017: 258). The creation of the EFSF and its successor, the permanent European Stability Mechanism (ESM), has been regarded with mounting scepticism in the CEE countries. From their perspective the ESM symbolises the undesired institutionalised financial solidarity with the Southern European members who failed to make efforts towards greater economic competitiveness and showed little budgetary responsibility (Busch 2014: 203). This explains why the remaining outsiders the Czech Republic, Hungary, Poland and more recently even Bulgaria and

Romania have lost much of their initial enthusiasm towards joining the eurozone. Latest Eurobarometer data shows that support for the euro has substantially cooled amongst the general public in the CEE-5 euro outsider group. The clearest majority in favour of the euro can still be found in Romania (60 per cent). Even in Hungary a slim majority is still in favour of the euro, which is surprising given the fierce and persistent eurosceptic rhetoric of the Fidesz government led by populist prime minister Viktor Orbán. In contrast opposition towards the euro has hardened in Bulgaria (47 per cent against) and even more substantially in Poland (61 against) and the Czech Republic (77 per cent) (European Commission 2017: 34).

The CEE group's internal division is representative of the EU's overall trend towards increasing differentiation along multiple core–periphery lines. Horizontally the CEE division into euro core group members and outsiders reflects the current division of the EU into the euro-19 core group led by Germany and seven countries who remain outside the single currency (High Level Reflection Group 2014: 39). Until the Brexit decision the interests of the latter group to protect their monetary sovereignty and greater scope for domestic economic and fiscal policies were informally represented by the UK. Now Poland as the largest remaining country in the group under the eurosceptic Law and Justice government (PiS) of prime minister Beata Szydlo looks most likely to advocate the interests of the outsider group. Andrzej Duda, the Polish president who is also from the PiS recently sent a warning to Berlin and Paris that support for the EU in Poland and other countries outside the euro could substantially weaken if the core-19 group deepens and makes decisions without consulting the outsiders. Duda warned of the risk of 'more Brexits' to come if the political core–periphery divide in the EU deepens further (EURACTIV 2017a). The CEE members are also collectively part of the EU's growing economic and social core–periphery divide, which is now represented by an ever more obvious gap between living standards and levels of social provision between the richer economies in the North and the laggards in the South-Eastern periphery (Galgoczi 2015).

The failure of the process of 'adaptive Europeanisation' (Ágh 2014: 33) through conditionality to achieve substantial improvements in the levels of social cohesion in the CEE region explains why it has been lacking domestic ownership. The resulting shallow levels of Europeanisation which have emerged in some of the CEE member states, most noticeably through backtracking on political reforms in Hungary, Poland and Romania, could be part of a wider long-term trend which eventually risks deepening the political peripherilisation of the region in the EU (Ágh 2014: 63; Ganev 2013). The main risk here lies in the combination of the trend towards backsliding on progressive democratic transformation with potentially growing public euroscepticism. 'Authoritarian backsliding' is generally defined as a process of increasing the state's executive power over the political process and the freedom of public debate in hybrid regimes with underdeveloped or missing civil society structures (Dresden and Howard 2016: 1124). In the CEE region these developments can be witnessed most noticeably in Hungary and Poland, where the populist centre-right governments of Fidesz and the Justice and Law Party (PiS) are combining authoritarian domestic reforms with nationalistic euroscepticism which openly questions the EU's values and challenges the authority of the European Commission. This is not only fuelled by the populist centre-right governments in Hungary and Poland but also by Germany's increasingly uncompromising stance on crucial issues such as the eurozone governance and the management of the lingering migration crisis (Hellmann 2016: 19; Meiers 2015: 126).

The process of adaptive Europeanisation in the CEE region ultimately lacked domestic ownership and consequently resulted in the more recent tendency towards growing opposition to the EU's political agenda. Initially the CEEs were among the group of countries who strongly supported a liberal agenda for the Single European Market with an emphasis on welfare reform, in addition to a business-friendly regulatory and tax environment. Although the individual economic and social transition process in each of the CEE countries has been markedly different, they generally supported liberally minded countries such as Ireland and the United Kingdom in their successful lobbying for swift market liberalisation and deregulation in the EU (Schweiger, Marcovic and Nagy 2016). The background to this was the success of the Irish and the British economy at the time of the CEE accession to the EU in the early 2000s. By that time Ireland had transformed itself from the economic poorhouse of Europe towards a dynamic and investment-orientated Celtic Tiger economy. The UK under prime minister Tony Blair's New Labour government had successfully implemented its *third way* economic agenda, which combined the Thatcherite focus on financial services-driven economic growth with targeted investment in education. At the same time the EU's traditional economic powerhouse Germany had fallen into recession and recorded record levels of unemployment and was consequently considered to have become the 'sick man of the euro' (The Economist 1999).

Against the background of the German (and French) economic weakness in the early 2000s the Blair government managed to successfully upload their third way reform agenda to the EU's Lisbon Strategy. Blair was substantially supported in this by German chancellor Gerhard Schröder, who had previously openly expressed his sympathies for third way economics in the joint paper with Blair in 1999 (Schweiger 2015). After the CEE-8 group had joined they were strongly supportive of the joint efforts by Blair and the newly appointed reformist Commission president Barroso to revise the Lisbon Strategy and to introduce a target-driven open method of national policy coordination. The Visegrád Group issued a joint statement in June 2004 in which it emphasised that 'EU enlargement will foster the principal goal of the Lisbon Strategy – the transformation of the European economy into the world's most competitive' (Visegrád Group 2004). In this respect they matched the expectation that they had 'become impatient with the EU's slow progress with structural reform' (Barysch and Grabbe 2002: 35). The result was a move towards a more streamlined focus on encouraging member states to implement economic and welfare state reforms. These were aimed at stimulating growth and increasing employment figures by increasing means-testing for welfare (especially unemployment) benefits and creating opportunities for people to take up low-paid (often precarious) employment in the deregulated services sector (Vaughan-Whitehead 2015: 17–20; Schweiger 2014: 32). The CEE members consequently played their part in promoting a pro-liberalisation agenda in the EU which has resulted in predominantly 'negative' integration, i.e. the weakening of existing national economic, political and welfare structures with the aim of removing trade barriers in the Single Market.

What emerged is today's stable pattern of 'negative' without 'positive' integration, in which cross-border markets and market freedoms increasingly overlay and suspended

the legal systems, political power structures and democratic processes of the national states (Streeck 2017: 105).

Declining EU legitimacy and transition "backsliding"

The effects of the EU's failure to match the economic liberalisation agenda with the establishment of common social standards and support mechanisms has generally had an adverse effect on the levels of social cohesion in the member states of the Single Market. The social effects of the global financial crisis and the eurozone sovereign debt crisis continue to be felt across the EU and have substantially contributed to the process of alienation between political elites and the general public. This process has been adequately described as the neoliberal 'de-politicization' of the Single Market governance and ultimately also the 'de-democratization of European politics' (Giannone 2015: 104 and 109). The effects of this agenda are clearly evident in the CEE region, where rapid economic transformation has profoundly weakened the social fabric of societies and ultimately risks undermining the fragile process of political transformation. In this respect it has been observed in recent studies on the transformation process in the CEE member states that there is a tendency of societies in the region bordering on the brink of social anarchy, which is reflected by rising levels of individual and state-level corruption, in combination with organised crime:

> The weakening of the macro-social economic and political integration in the course of the reforms caused destabilization of micro-social interaction patterns. On its turn, the destabilization of the normative framework of everyday interactions caused macro-social instabilities. Both processes mutually amplified each other and jointly brought about the effects of acute normlessness (anomie). Disenchantment, escapism and aggression are phenomena that characterize this social situation.
>
> (Genov 2010: 201)

The link between the social transition costs and the deepening dissatisfaction with the democratic process in the CEE region has also been highlighted by the Progress Report on the first two decades of social and political development in the new member states since the fall of communism. The report points out that already during the first decade the rapid economic transition resulted in widespread '"economic" demobilisation', which manifested itself in social exclusion of large parts of society. The losers of the transition process have subsequently been turning towards a new political wave of populism with a nationalist undertone, which has in recent years started to undermine the fragile democratisation process in some countries in the region:

> The destabilization effects have appeared in various social sectors, and step by step they have been cumulated into the deconsolidation process concerning the foundation of the democratic system. Thus, after a decade of social destabilization caused by the socio-economic demobilization, the next decade arrived with an increasing political deconsolidation caused by the populist remobilization of the relative and/or absolute losers.
>
> (Ágh 2013: 31)

The domestic political developments in the various member states, which are outlined in detail in the individual country studies presented in the second part of this book, are a testimony to the advance of populist politics in the CEEs. As Gál and Malová outline in chapter 8, even in a core euro country like Slovakia populism has now become an essential feature of the mainstream political discourse, which was particularly obvious during the Slovak parliamentary election in March 2016. The election was overshadowed by the refugee crisis and the attempts to implement a binding distribution quota system across the EU, driven by Germany. Social democratic prime minister Robert Fico positioned his party SMER-SD in clear opposition to the quotas and adopted an anti-immigration tone which many considered as strongly populist and unnecessary because voters were more concerned about issues related to their personal economic security (Cunningham 2016). The elections also saw the far-right Slovak National Party (SNS) and the Kotleba (People's Party Our Slovakia – LSNS) enter parliament with both having gained just over eight per cent of the votes at a time when Slovakia was preparing to take over the EU's six-month presidency (Gabrizova 2016). These are worrying developments given the fact that both Hungary and Poland are already governed by profoundly populist parties with a two-thirds majority, which allows them to implement profound domestic constitutional changes. The Hungarian prime minister Orbán has in recent years deliberately positioned himself in opposition to the EU's mainstream political agenda and promoted the 'illiberal' state as a specific new form of governance in the CEE region:

> The new state that we are building is an illiberal state, a non-liberal state. It does not deny foundational values of liberalism, as freedom, etc. But it

> does not make this ideology a central element of state organization, but applies a specific, national, particular approach in its stead.
>
> (Orbán 2014)

In his 2017 annual address to the Hungarian nation Orbán was even bold enough to compare his eurosceptic and nationalist agenda to that of the freedom fighters who had risen against Soviet oppression in Hungary in 1956:

> it was good to see – precisely on the sixtieth anniversary of the 1956 Revolution – what a great thing freedom still is in the world (…) In our community, the European Union, this means that we, the sovereign nations, stand in opposition to the federalists, and the voters stand in opposition to the Brussels bureaucrats.
>
> (Orbán 2017)

Orbán has followed this up with two parallel and intrinsically connected public campaigns. One is directed against the founder of the private Central European University (CEU) in Budapest, George Soros, whom Orbán accuses of secretly backing the EU´s 'liberal' migration policy. As a result the Hungarian PM has threatened the closure of CEU as part of an 'anti-Soros' law which restricts civil society groups and educational bodies which are supported by foreigners (EURACTIV 2017b). Parallel to this Orbán has initiated a new public consultation on major EU policy areas entitled 'Állitsuk Meg Brüssyelt!' (Let's Stop Brussels). Under the campaign the government has sent a survey with six questions ranging from immigration to taxation to all Hungarian households, which they can respond to in writing until May 2020 (Byrne 2017). The survey is clearly an attempt to repeat the 2016 public referendum on the refugee quotas in Hungary, which had failed due to low turnout below the 50 per cent threshold (Kingsley 2016). More recently Orbán has brought both campaigns together by accusing the European Commission to represent the interests of Soros as a result of 'political inception' (EURACTIV 2017b).

This confident populism is echoed by the populist right-wing Law and Justice (PiS) government of Beata Szydlo, who is following Orbán's autocratic approach through similar domestic constitutional reforms that weaken the democratic scrutiny of the executive and the independence of the media from state interference. Here a supposed shared legitimacy of the foundations of liberal democracy has recently been challenged in an increasingly polarised domestic political climate (Tomini 2016: 34). The classification of political systems in the CEE region as 'hybrid' and in some cases even as 'flawed' democracies reflects the concrete negative effects this political polarisation has had on the shallow process of democratisation (Economist Intelligence Unit 2016).

It also illustrates the limitations of Europeanisation through conditionality. Based on the historical institutionalist logic of path-dependence the lock in of institutional change in the context of Europeanisation is usually most stable under the favourable conditions of the 'increasing returns', i.e. lasting positive effects which are particularly linked to 'cost-efficiency'. If these positive effects are fading or even leading to adverse effects (i.e. higher costs) domestic resistance is likely (Sedelmeier 2012: 23). There is clearly a danger that the growing public disillusionment with the democratic process in the CEE countries sooner or later results in a more widespread populist turn and consequently a move towards a new form of illiberal authoritarianism. The key to prevent this would lie in the EU to offer a viable alternative to the nationalist and eurosceptic political agenda, a task at which it currently clearly fails, as Debeuf points out: 'If the EU is not able to work out solutions to its challenges, people will turn even more to populist parties. This tribalization of Europe is a vicious cycle that hasn't ended yet' (Debeuf 2016).

In this respect the EU's approach under German leadership towards the 2015 refugee crisis has been extremely problematic. It allowed the populist governments in Hungary and Poland to organise opposition across the CEE region against the EU approach. Like Orbán, the Polish PiS government of Beata Szydlo determined its fundamental opposition to EU refugee quotas, which they branded as a potential 'ticking time bomb' for the country (Cienski 2017). Both countries have led the way in uniting the Visegrád Group in firm opposition to the refugee quotas and to Germany's leadership over this issue. That this was possible is remarkable, given the frequent difficulties in keeping the cooperation going in the past (Törö, Butler and Gruber 2014), and even more so because of the current political divide of the V4 between two right-wing (in Hungary and Poland) and two centre-left social democratically led governments (in the Czech Republic and Slovakia – even though the Slovakian government coalition contains the far-right Slovak National Party SNS). The frequently dormant and divided V4 group has consequently been invigorated as a result of the failure of the German government led by Angela Merkel to use its dominant position in the EU since the financial crisis to build a broad policy consensus against the refugee quotas. The V4 have firmly rejected the quotas as an attempt to instil solidarity measures which they consider as 'unacceptable' (Visegrád Group 2015).

The poisoned chalice of German leadership in the EU

Under Angela Merkel Germany's leadership approach in the EU has been gradually transformed from semi-hegemonial, uninspiring and technocratic crisis management during the initial phase of the eurozone sovereign debt crisis; towards uncompromising exclusive decision-making which has become increasingly contested (Meiers 2015). Merkel's 'self righteous' (Streeck 2016) approach was shown during the final phase of the eurozone crisis (based on the mantra 'there is no alternative') and the more recent refugee/migration crisis (promoting a liberal stance towards refugees as a 'moral imperative') (Schweiger 2017). Merkel however clearly misjudged her own leverage on imposing a collective solution on an issue which is considered as politically sensitive in other countries who do not necessarily share Germany's cosmopolitan outlook (Bulmer and Paterson 2017: 224). The electoral success of the eurosceptic anti-immigration Alternative für Deutschland (AfD) at the October 2017 national election in Germany, when it entered parliament with 12.6 per cent of votes, shows that Merkel's liberal refugee policy has also become controversial in Germany, especially (but not exclusively) in the Eastern parts of the country (Mudde 2017). Moreover, Merkel showed little sensitivity for the domestic policy pressures and national perspectives of countries who should be considered as Germany's natural partners, with whom close relations are extremely relevant for the future of the EU (Handl and Paterson 2013). In this respect the revival of the V4 group, not as a vehicle for enhanced cooperation with, but in opposition to Germany's leadership should be a grave cause of concern for Berlin.

Conclusion: avoiding the permanent peripheralisation of the CEEs

The future role of the countries that are still characterised as the newcomers in the EU stands at a crucial crossroads more than a decade after their accession. How they position themselves in years to come will also substantially influence the direction of the Union. The main problem in this respect is the recent tendency to allow them to drift off into an ever more peripheral position, not just in economic and social but increasingly also in political terms. The growing alienation from the political mainstream, which is significantly determined by Germany's strategic interests, risks allowing the CEE region to retreat into self-proclaimed political isolation. This does not have to happen and there are still positive signs that it can be avoided. In spite of the recent crises and the declining acceptance of Germany's leadership, an overwhelming majority of citizens in the CEE member states continue to support EU membership (from 59 in Slovakia to 80 per cent in Poland and Romania) and even consider the EU to be 'a good thing' (from 52 in Croatia and Slovakia to 78 per cent in Poland). The exception is the more eurosceptic Czech Republic with modest figures of 41 and 35 per cent on both questions (Milo, Klingová and Hajdu 2017: 13). This is a positive signal but it is counterweighed by the feeling in some CEE countries that they do not fully belong to the EU and are 'somewhere in between' East and West (Milo, Klingová and Hajdu 2017: 11).

The absence of a counterweight to Germany's expanding power base in the EU is symbolised by the United Kingdom's impending exit and France's weakened economic position. The renewed German grand coalition government emerging from the recent national elections continues to be led by Merkel on the basis of a variety of domestic and European policy interests between the parties involved. If the new coalition fails to engage in an open dialogue with the CEE members, it is most likely that more governments will follow Orban's and Szydlo's eurosceptic path. Demands for political opt outs from major policy areas, such as justice and home affairs (in response to the EU approach over migration and asylum policy), could then become a realistic possibility (Hokovský 2016).

The refugee/migration problem has illustrated that in a larger EU, which consists of a variety of national cultures and interests, common solutions cannot be imposed through top-down, one-size-fits-all approaches. Instead (and to stop the split over the migration crisis from becoming systemic) the EU's future policy agenda has to emerge from a process of intensive and permanent multilateral consultation and dialogue. In this context Germany has a major role to play in ensuring that it offers predictable and more inclusive leadership (Bulmer and Paterson 2017: 230) and the opportunity for the CEE members (especially Poland and the V4 group) to become partners in leadership. At the same time the CEE governments, including those in Budapest and Warsaw, need to constructively engage and stop the populist tendency to use the EU as a permanent scapegoat for domestic problems. Differentiated levels of integration between the CEEs and the EU will remain important to maintain scope for political and economic diversity. A permanent core–periphery cleave between the euro centre and the Central-Eastern periphery would however indeed pose the risk of more Brexits, to echo the recent warning from the Polish presidential palace issued in the direction of Berlin and Paris. (EURACTIV 2017a).

References

Ágh, A. (2013) *Progress Report of the New Member States: 20 Years of Social and Political Developments.* Budapest: College of Communication and Business.

Ágh, A. (2014) Ten Years of Catching-Up in the European Union: Differentiated Integration and Multilevel Governance in ECE. In: Ágh, A., Kaiser, T. and Koller, B. (eds) *10 Years After: Multi-Level Governance and Differentiated Integration in the EU.* Budapest: Blue Ribbon Research Centre, pp. 31–61.

Aslund, A. (2010) *The Last Shall Be the First: The East European Financial Crisis.* Washington: Peter G. Peterson Institute for International Economics.

Barysch, K. (2005) East versus West? The European Economic and Social Model after Enlargement. *Progressive Politics* 4(3) (March), pp. 6–13.

Barysch, K. and Grabbe, H. (2002) *Who's Ready for EU Enlargement.* November. London: Centre for European Reform.

Bojkov, V.D. (2004) Neither Here, nor There: Bulgaria and Romania in Current European Politics. *Communist and Post-Communist Studies* 37(4), pp. 509–522.

Börzel, T.A. and Sedelmeier, U. (2017) Larger and More Law Abiding? The Impact of Enlargement on Compliance in the European Union. *Journal of European Public Policy* 24(2), pp. 197–215.

Bulmer, S. and Paterson, W.E. (2017) Germany and the Crisis: Asset or Liability? In: Dinan, D., Nugent, N. and Paterson W.E. (eds) *The European in Crisis.* London: Palgrave, pp. 188–211.

Busch, A. (2014) Germany and the Euro. In: Padgett, S., Paterson, W.E. and Zohlnhöfer, R. (eds) *Developments in German Politics 4.* Basingstoke: Palgrave MacMillan, pp. 188–210.

Byrne, A. (2017) *Defiant Orban Encourages Hungarians to Say No to Brussels. Financial Times.* 15 May. [ONLINE] Available from: https://www.ft.com/content/f60dfd26-34c4-11e7-bce4-9023f8c0fd2e (accessed 7 October 2017).

CESifo Group Munich *Free Movement of Labour in the EU.* [ONLINE] Available from: https://www.google.de/url?sa=t&rct=j&q=&esrc=s&source=web&cd=3&cad=rja&uac t=8&ved=0ahUKEwjV5P3xneHVAhXREVAKHcbqDkkQFgg6MAI&url=https %3A %2F%2Fwww.cesifo-group.de%2FifoHome%2Ffacts%2FDICE%2FMigration%2FMigration%2FLabour-Migration%2Fdice-rep-free-mov-labour%2FfileBinary%2Fdice-rep-free-mov-labour.pdf&usg=AFQjCNFRLkrZOjvc5xxA-ZbeMVV9tPcoJA (accessed: 18 August 2017).

Cienski, J. (2017) *Why Poland Doesn't Want Refugees. Politico.* 21 May. [ONLINE] Available from: http://www.politico.eu/article/politics-nationalism-and-religion-explain-why-poland-doesnt-want-refugees/ (accessed 7 October 2017).

Cunningham, B. (2016) '*We Protect Slovakia': Voters Worry about Jobs and Health Care – But the PM Is Obsessed with Non-Existent Migrants. Politico* 2 October. [ONLINE] Available from: http://www.politico.eu/article/slovakia-fico-migrants-refugees-asylum-crisis-smer-election/ (accessed 7 October 2017).

Debeuf, Koert (2016) *Response to Judy Dempsey's Question: Will Populist Parties Run Europe? Carnegie Europe.* 9 March. [ONLINE] Available from: http://carnegieeurope.eu/strategiceurope/?fa=62990 (accessed 7 October 2017).

Dimitrov, V. (2012) The Central and East European Countries: From Weak Latecomers to good citizens of the Union. In: Hayward, J. and Wurzel, R. (eds) *European Disunion: Between Sovereignty and Solidarity.* Basingstoke: Palgrave MacMillan, pp. 298–313.

Dobson, J.R. and Sennikova, I. (2007). From Fundamental Freedom to Political and Economic 'Hot Potato' in 50 Years: Labour Mobility and Migration within the EU. *Journal of Business Economics and Management* VIII (2), pp. 123–146.

Dresden, J.R. and Howard, M.M. (2016) Authoritarian Backsliding and the Concentration of Political Power. *Democratization* 23(7), pp. 1122–1143.

Dyson, K. (2017) Playing for High Stakes: The Eurozone Crisis. In: Dinan, D., Nugent, N. and Paterson, W.E. (eds) *The European Union in Crisis.* London: Palgrave, pp. 16–32.

Economist Intelligence Unit (EIU) (2016) *Democracy Index 2016: Revenge of the 'Deplorables'*. [ONLINE] Available from: http://www.eiu.com/public/thankyou_download.aspx?activity=download&campaignid=DemocracyIndex2016 (accessed 7 October 2017).

Economist, The (1999) The Sick Man of the Euro. 3 June. [ONLINE] Available from: http://www.economist.com/node/209559 (accessed 6 October 2017).

EURACTIV (2017a), *Poland Warns Multi-Speed Europe Could Spawn 'More Brexits'.* 6 September. [ONLINE] Available from: http://www.euractiv.com/section/future-eu/news/poland-warns-multi-speed-europe-could-spawn-more-brexits/ (accessed 18 September 2017).

EURACTIV (2017b) *Orban Says Brussels Bureaucrats Under Soros Influence.* 6 October. [ONLINE] Available from http://www.euractiv.com/section/freedom-of-thought/news/orban-says-brussels-bureaucrats-under-soros-influence/ (accessed 7 October 2017).

European Commission (2017) *Standard Eurobarometer 87 Spring 2017.* [ONLINE] Available from: http://ec.europa.eu/commfrontoffice/publicopinion/index.cfm/ResultDoc/download/DocumentKy/79565 (accessed 3 September 2017).

Gabrizova, Z. (2016) *Slovakia Turns Unpredictable Ahead of its EU Presidency. EURACTIV.* 7 March 2016. [ONLINE] Available from: http://www.euractiv.com/section/elections/news/slovakia-turns-unpredictable-ahead-of-its-eu-presidency/ (accessed 7 October 2017).

Galgoczi, B. (2015) The Tale of Two Peripheries in a Divided Europe. In: Schweiger, C. and J.M. Magone (eds) *The Effects of the Eurozone Sovereign Debt Crisis: Differentiated Integration Between the Centre and the New Peripheries of the EU*. London: Routledge, pp. 103–111.

Ganev, V.I. (2013) Post-Accession Hooliganism: Democratic Governance in Bulgaria and Romania after 2007, *East European Politics and Societies and Cultures* 27(1), pp. 26–44.

Genov, N. (2010) *Global Trends in Eastern Europe*. London and New York: Routledge.

Giannone, D. (2015) Suspending Democracy? The Governance of the EU's Political and Economic Crisis as a Process of Neoliberal Restructuring. In: Demetriou, K.N. (ed.) *The European Union in Crisis: Explorations in Representation and Democratic Legitimacy*, pp. 101–122.

Grabbe, H. (2011) How Does Europeanization Affect CEE Governance? Conditionality, Diffusion and Diversity. *Journal of European Public Policy* 1(1), p. 1013–1031.

Handl, V. and W.E. Paterson (2013), The continuing relevance of Germany's engine for CEE and the EU. *Communist and Post-Communist Studies* 46, p. 327–337.

Haughton, T. (2017), *European Disunion: Between Sovereignty and Solidarity*. Hayward, J. and Wurzel, R. (eds). Basingstoke: Palgrave MacMillan, pp. 253–268.

Hellmann, G. (2016) Germany's World: Power and Followership in a Crisis-Ridden Europe. *Global Affairs* 2(1), pp. 3–20.

High Level Reflection Group (2014) *Central Europe Fit for the Future: Visegrád Group Ten Years After Accession*. Bratislava: Central European Policy Institute and Demos Institute.

Hokovský, R. (2016) How Migrants Brought Central Europe Together. *Politico*. 16 July. [ONLINE] Available from: http://www.politico.eu/article/how-migrants-brought-central-europe-together-visegrad-group-orban-poland/ (accessed 7 October 2017).

Kingsley, P. (2016) Hungary's Refugee Referendum Not Valid After Voters Stay Away. *The Guardian*. 2 October. [ONLINE] Available from: https://www.theguardian.com/world/2016/oct/02/hungarian-vote-on-refugees-will-not-take-place-suggest-first-poll-results (accessed 7 October 2017).

Lippert, B., Hughes, K., Grabbe, H. and Becker, P. (2001) *British and German Interests in EU Enlargement: Conflict and Cooperation*. London: Chatham House.

Meiers, F.J. (2015) *Germany's Role in the Euro Crisis: Berlin's Quest for a More Perfect Monetary Union*. London: Springer.

Milo, D., Klingová, K. and Hajdu, D. (2017) *GLOBSEC Trends 2017: Mixed Messages and Signs of Hope from Central and Eastern Europe*. GLOBSEC Policy Institute [ONLINE]

Available from: https://www.globsec.org/wp-content/uploads/2017/08/globsec_trends_2017.pdf (accessed 7 October 2017).

Mudde, C. (2017) What the Stunning Success of AfD Means for Germany and Europe. *The Guardian*. 24 September 2017. [ONLINE] Available from: https://www.theguardian.com/commentisfree/2017/sep/24/germany-elections-afd-europe-immigration-merkel-radical-right (accessed 7 October 2017).

Myant, M. and Drahokoupil J. (2011) *Transition Economies: Political Economy in Russia, Eastern Europe, and Central Asia*. Hoboken: Wiley.

Noutcheva, G. and Bechev, D. (2008), The Successful Laggards: Bulgaria and Romania's Accession to the EU. *East European Politics & Societies* 22(1), pp. 114–144.

Orbán, V. (2014) *Speech at Baile Tusnad (Tusnádfürdö)*. 26 July. [ONLINE] Available from: https://budapestbeacon.com/full-text-of-viktor-Orbáns-speech-at-baile-tusnad-tusnadfurdo-of-26-july-2014/ (accessed 7 October 2017).

Orbán, V. (2017) *Prime Minister Viktor Orbán's State of the Nation Address.* 14 February. [ONLINE] Available from: http://www.kormany.hu/en/the-prime-minister/the-prim e-minister-s-speeches/prime-minister-viktor-orban-s-state-of-the-nation-address-20170214 (accessed 7 October 2017).

Porte, C. de la and Heins, E. (2017) The Aftermath of the Eurozone Crisis: Towards Fiscal Federalism? In: Dinan, D., Nugent, N. and Paterson, W.E. (eds) *The European Union in Crisis.* London: Palgrave, pp. 149–166.

Schweiger, C. (2014) *The EU and the Global Financial Crisis: New Varieties of Capitalism.* Cheltenham: Edward Elgar.

Schweiger, C. (2015) National Interests and Differentiated Integration in the EU under Crisis Conditions: The Cases of Germany, Britain and France. In: Schweiger, C. and J.M. Magone (eds) *The Effects of the Eurozone Sovereign Debt Crisis: Differentiated Integration Between the Centre and the New Peripheries of the EU.* London: Routledge, pp. 59–71.

Schweiger, C. (2017) The Legitimacy Challenge. In: Dinan, D., Nugent, N. and Paterson W.E. (eds) *The European in Crisis.* London: Palgrave, pp. 212–232.

Schweiger, C., Markovic, F. and Nagy T.A. (2016) The Dire Straits of Brexit: Potential implications for the EU, UK and V4. Bratislava: Central European Policy Institute, February. [ONLINE] Available from: http://www.europeanpublicaffairs.eu/the-dire straits-of-brexit-potential-implications-for-the-eu-uk-and-the-v4/ (accessed 7 October 2017).

Sedelmeier, U. (2012) Is Europeanisation Through Conditionality Sustainable? Lock-In of Institutional Change after EU Accession. *West European Politics* 35(1), pp. 20–38.

Streeck, W. (2016) Scenario for a Wonderful Tomorrow. *London Review of Books* 38(7) 31 March, pp. 7–10. [ONLINE] Available from: https://www.lrb.co.uk/v38/n07/wolfgang-streeck/scenario-for-a-wonderful-tomorrow (accessed 7 October 2017).

Streeck, W. (2017) *Buying Time: The Delayed Crisis of Democratic Capitalism.* London: Verso. 2nd edition

Tomini, L. (2016) Reassessing Democratic Consolidation in Central and Eastern Europe and the Role of the EU. In: Coman, R. and Tomini, L. ed. *The State of Democracy in Central and Eastern Europe.* Abingdon: Routledge, pp. 7–39.

Törö, C., Butler, E. and Gruber, K. (2014). Visegrád: The evolving pattern of coordination and partnership after EU enlargement. *Europe-Asia Studies* 66(3), pp. 364–394.

Vaughan-Whitehead, D. (2015) The European Social Model in Times of Crisis: An Overview. In: Whitehead-Vaughan, D. (ed.) *The European Social Model in Crisis: Is Europe Losing its Soul?* pp. 1–65.

Visegrád Group (2004) Joint Statement Adopted During the 11th Meeting of the Chairmen of the Foreign Affairs Committees, Defence and Security Committees and European Union Affairs Committees of the Parliaments of the Czech Republic, Slovakia, Poland and Hungary. Warsaw, 21–22 June. [ONLINE] Available from: http://www.visegradgroup.eu/2004/joint-statement-adopted (accessed 6 October 2017).

Visegrád Group (2015) Joint Statement of the Heads of Governments of the Visegrad Group of Countries in Prague. 4 September. [ONLINE] Available from: http://www.visegradgroup.eu/calendar/20150904-v4-joint (accessed 7 October 2017).

3 A rift in European integration?

Neglected shadows of the Central and Eastern European transformation

Beáta Farkas and András Máté-Tóth

Introduction

The Visegrád countries fiercely oppose the migration policy followed by the European Union and especially by Germany. Profound differences in attitudes and values have been revealed which may seem surprising considering the successful political and economic integration of the Central and Eastern European (CEE) countries in the past decade.

In this chapter, we investigate the social background of the attitudes in the CEE countries which have transpired in recent debates. We have built a systematic interdisciplinary framework for our analysis. After reconstructing some crucial elements of the historical legacy of CEE countries, we describe the institutional setting of the CEE economies as a distinct model of capitalism. This model can be deemed successful in historical comparison but is very far from ordinary people's expectations, which has resulted in disappointment and frustration. As a consequence, the phenomenon of woundedness caused by the traumas of wars, genocides and the socio-economic system change prevails in the region even if there are significant differences among the countries in question. A frequent response to frustration and woundedness is to take the role of a victim as an individual or as a nation. The self-understanding as a victim distorts and hinders social and economic development. We conclude that an understanding of the social background behind economic and political processes in the CEE countries is of vital importance in avoiding a rift in the European integration process.

Conceptual framework

The CEE transformation of the past 25 years can be interpreted as systemic change from the viewpoints of sociology, political science and economics in the framework of institutional analysis. There are long-lasting debates on methodological issues between new institutional economics and historical neo-institutionalism in sociology and in political science. Economists base their investigation on rational choice theory and methodological individualism, often assuming that the actors' profit maximizing decision-making leads to an optimal equilibrium. In contrast, sociologists and political scientists apply a holistic and historical approach, conceiving of institutions as structural frames and organizational solutions. They place an emphasis on the role of norms, values, and beliefs. However, recently the approaches of institutionalist economists, sociologist, and political scientists have got closer to each other, which is reflected in both the *Handbook of Comparative Institutional Analysis* and *Handbook of New Institutional Economics* (Ménard 2005; Morgan et al 2010). While it has been accepted that the institutions became identified with the rules of the game, providing stability and meaning to social life, the nature of these rules is interpreted in different dimensions. Institutions have a structural dimension encompassing formal and informal rules and an ideational dimension including normative and cognitive patterns. The notion that institutions do not necessarily embody efficient and rational solutions has also gained acceptance. Furthermore, institutions are products of human action and, at the same time, constraints on actors, which is expressed by the term 'path dependency' (Djelic 2010). We follow a consensus also when we consider actors and institutions as being mutually interdependent and reflexively intertwined with each other (Jackson 2010).

In order to understand the results of institutional analysis, we need a comprehensive theoretical background. We can assess the current position of the CEE countries if we conceptualize their transformation in the framework of a modernisation theory. Similarly, to classical sociologists, we consider modernity and modernisation as cultural and institutional factors and constellations, which come together in Europe. The western living standards, styles and patterns shape people's references and expectations, serving as reference points in CEE throughout the centuries of modernisation. We assume that modernisation has core values and institutions that are evolutionary universals like the notion of human rights, democracy and the resource allocation via contract-based, free cooperation of economic actors (that is, via market mechanisms) instead of a command economy. However, we accept some aspects of the theory of multiple modernities (Eisenstadt 1999, Eisenstadt 2000), especially the understanding that modernisation is not of a teleological or linear nature. Eisenstadt's essential claim is the following: 'what we witness in the contemporary world is the development – certainly not always peaceful and indeed often confrontational – of multiple modernities' (Eisenstadt 1999: 284). Although globalization determines hard constraints, various elements of modernity in the arenas of economy, politics or family do not converge in societies, but they are still elaborating their autonomous dimensions and features. Following Eisenstadt's logic, we are able to interpret the processes, tensions, and contradictions of CEE transformation if we pay more attention to the impact of the geopolitical status of the region, and we consider this transformation in the framework of a particular constellation of modernisation. Eisenstadt himself reflects on the special position of Central and Eastern Europe speaking about the tradition of transposition of western values, institutions and rules to the non-western part of Europe and to non-European societies. These societies react to the transposition activity of western culture with a double reaction: on the one hand, with 'center-formation' (Eisenstadt 1973: 6; 1999: 289) and, on the other hand, with protest.[1]

Another important protagonist for rethinking modernity, Bauman (2013b) introduces the category of 'liquid modernity' in his publications. As Eisenstadt, he reflects the fundamental dimensions of globality and globalization on the one hand and uncertainty and tentativeness of the post-modern thinking on the other hand. Bauman signifies important characteristics of contemporary societal perceptions and hermeneutics for the analysis of the CEE region. The main aspect of liquid modernity is a shift from the taken-for-granted dimensions and skills of the past decades into paradigmatic challenges and adventures of uncertainty. Challenges are definitively faster than the capacity of understanding; therefore, people and societies find themselves in a permanent time lag and miss the certainty of being able to control proceedings.

After outlining the conceptual framework, we have to clarify the territorial boundaries of our investigation. The geographical unit called Central and Eastern Europe is not a self-evident unit in a geographical, topographical, historical or even a political sense but a created space, a constructed area. 'Traditional area studies boundaries are defined in a way that are theoretically and empirically arbitrary' (Hanson 2009: 170). To explain the characteristic features of CEE transformation, we can successfully use the notion of 'the lands in between' and 'in-betweenness' (that is, between east and west), applying the theories of Delanty (2012), Szűcs (1983) and Tismaneanu (1992), which focus on Central or East Central Europe. In the theories of European historical regions, the latter generally includes Poland, Hungary, the Czech Republic, Slovakia, and Slovenia. However, the period of the communist system, the transformation from a command to a market economy, and the preparation for and/or the accession to the EU carry the common legacy of the past seven decades. Thus, we extend the geographical boundaries towards the Baltic states and the Western Balkan countries, even if the South Eastern countries show distinctive features as a subgroup within the region and we use the term Central and Eastern Europe to refer to the whole area.

The historical legacy of 'in-betweenness'

Since the collapse of the Soviet Union the region of post-socialist countries is usually handled as a single area in the political and economic analyses of transformation, e.g. in the reports of the European Bank of Reconstruction and Development (EBRD). However, this does not 'justify grouping Tajikistan and Slovenia in the same typological category – two decades after the collapse of communism in East-Central Europe' (Hanson 2009: 170). We have to use a double approach. On the one hand, we bid farewell to the concept of a divided Europe that emerged after World War II and is still routinely used. On the other hand, we still have to keep in mind the long legacy of a divided Europe including the impact of this bipolarity on the diverse concepts of regional identity.

East Central European intellectuals never consider their countries as a part of a homogenous Soviet or Post-Soviet area. After the Cold War and the east–west division of Europe, scholarly interest in CEE increased three times. The first wave was the *Mitteleuropa* debate in the 1980s, led by dissident writers and philosophers represented, among others, by Adam Michnik, György Konrád and Václav Hável. The main goal of this debate was the demarcation of the region Central Europe from the rest of the Soviet zone called Eastern Europe (Bugge 1999). In his famous essay, 'The three historical regions of Europe' written in 1981, Jenő Szűcs had the same aim when he described Central Europe, the region between the Baltic and Adriatic, as 'the lands in between', that is, between the western zone of expansion and the Russian zone of expansion to the east, from the Middle Ages on. In civilization terms, 'these lands in between' were formed by western Christianity and followed western cultural patterns and institutional settings.

The second wave occurred at the turbulent time of the collapse of communism around 1990 (Mason 1992). In the quite often enthusiastic approach of the time, the leading motive was to give a clear 'yes' to Europe as a future and a 'no' to the Soviet past. Thirdly, interest in the region peaked at the time of the first round of EU enlargement in 2004. The main issue of debates was the fulfilment of EU membership conditions, that is, both democratic and economic aspects of the Copenhagen criteria (see, for example, Henderson 2005; Schimmelfennig and Sedelmeier 2005).[2] Spohn (2005) has expected that European identity in CEE would preserve its typically ambivalent *gestalt.* Despite the EU integration results in the social structural convergence with Western European societies, the peripheral dependency and related cultural ambivalences remain an integral part of Eastern European identities.

Although the approaches outlined above were different and inspired by actual challenges, the western analysts' assessment of socio-economic features of the region has been similar since the systemic change. As Longworth stated, 'it is not the Third World, but it is certainly not the Western world either' (Longworth 1992: 3–4). For most approaches, societies of the region are located between the two idealistic value sets of West and East. The West symbolizes democracy, freedom, market economy, civil society, and human rights, whereas the East symbolizes oligarchy, late feudalism, a weak civil society, limited freedom, and a limited acceptance of human rights (Tismaneanu 1992: xii). The benchmark for the description and assessment of the region was and still remains taking the 'West' for granted. However, recent investigations place more and more emphasis on the discrepancy between the structural compliance with western standards and a cultural disharmony or different mentality (Boatcă 2006; Boatcă and Spohn 2010; Jordan 2005; Spohn 2010, 2015).

The enlargements of the EU in 2004 and 2007 extended the membership not only to East Central Europe but also to the Baltic states and two South Eastern European countries, Bulgaria and Romania, labelling them as new member states. Western influences were stronger in East Central Europe than in areas to the south in the Balkans and to the north where Russia exerted more influence (Delanty 2012; Mason 1992; Szűcs 1983). The East Central European countries can be seen as part of European modernity. Their political heritage provided the basis of a weak democratic tradition. In the case of South Eastern European countries, the Byzantine–Orthodox civilizational background was determinant. For much of their history these countries were located between the Habsburg and Ottoman Empires. Although the Baltic states were ruled by Russia and the Soviet Union for a long time, they belong to western Christianity, and the German, Swedish, and Polish influences were also strong over several centuries (Delanty 2012). We see later in this chapter that these historical and cultural differences are clearly reflected in the quality of governance to date.

To sum up, the entire region is a borderland, which is culturally influenced to a different extent by western and eastern Christian culture and by the Ottoman-Islamic world. Furthermore, a large Jewish population, which lived in diaspora, contributed to its multi-ethnic diversity and modernisation. In the twentieth century, the region was profoundly transformed by the impact of German fascism from the west and by the several-decade Soviet occupation and communism from the east.

The attitudes, preferences and expectations with which people entered the political and economic transformation after the fall of communism were formed by the experiences of dictatorship (Delanty 2012).

The first CEE cross-country survey on people's attitudes and expectations was conducted in 1991 when societies already experienced the economic recession accompanying the transition. Therefore, we have only anecdotal evidence from before, on enthusiasms and feelings of velvet revolutions, as prominent politicians expressed it. For example, Polish Prime Minister Tadeusz Mazowiecki said '[we] bring Poland back into the stream of human progress' (cited in Bartmanski 2011: 214). The Czech president, Václav Havel, summed up the dilemmas back in 1990: 'People have passed through a very dark tunnel at the end of which there was a light of freedom. Unexpectedly they passed through the prison gates and found themselves in a square. They are now free and they don't know where to go' (cited in Cichocka and Jost 2014: 7). Social scientists noticed back in the early 1990s that the citizens of the post-communist European countries nursed many illusions after the breakthrough of 1989. They observed utopian tendencies, especially with regard to a semi-imaginary West, capitalism and democracy, whose close link to the free market was assumed. Furthermore, impossibly high hopes were placed on the free market economy (Arnason 2005; Bartmanski 2011).

With the mounting difficulties of political and economic transition, disillusionment replaced high expectations. The overall picture shows that throughout the years between 1991 and 1998 approximately 60–70 per cent of CEE households felt their economic situation to be worse than before 1989. Despite the economic difficulties, the supporters of a communist restoration remained in a minority of between 5 and 30 per cent (Haerpfer 2002: 7, 18, 59).

The model of capitalism in Central and Eastern Europe

At the beginning of economic transition all countries suffered from a severe recession. There were several elements which influenced the scale of the economic downturn. The countries which had been part of a larger economy – like the Baltic states in the Soviet Union, the Western Balkan countries in Yugoslavia – had to cope not only with structural change but also with very radical changes in economic relations after the dissolution of the Soviet Union and Yugoslavia. The Balkan wars deepened the economic crisis in the 1990s. The progress in market-oriented reform was more rapid and sustained in the countries which were preparing for EU membership. Having no historical experience on the transition from command economy to market economy, the adaptation and implementation of EU legal regulation ensured an anchor for the ten countries that joined the EU in 2004 and 2007. As a result of transformation, the post-socialist EU member states have become fully functioning market economies measured by the transition indicators elaborated in the reports of the European Bank for Reconstruction and Development (EBRD). Due to the eligibility of EU accession, many more institutional reforms have been achieved even in the EU member candidate Western Balkan countries than in the European members of the Commonwealth of Independent States (EBRD 2013: 109). The EU member states have reached a substantial economic convergence towards the EU-28 average measured in GDP per capita. The northern countries of the region seem to be more successful than the southern ones. Although the 2008 global crisis caused an immediate, dramatic fall in the GDP of the Baltic states, recovery was also extremely quick. The economic performance of Poland and Slovakia is also impressive. The less dynamic economy of the Czech Republic started from the second highest GDP level among the post-socialist countries. In Hungary, the average growth rate has been low over the last decade, and the economies of Slovenia and Croatia have been diverging from the EU-28 since the 2008 crisis. The other Western Balkan countries hardly reach one third of the EU-28 average GDP (Table 3.1).

The unique feature of transformation among the post-socialist EU members is the outstanding role of foreign direct investment (FDI) in modernisation (Gill and Raiser 2012; Medve-Bálint 2014). Although the economic performance indicates significant catching-up, the socio-economic model that resulted from the transformation is ambiguous.

On the one hand, these countries have benefited from the integration in global supply chains, especially the Visegrád countries from being part of German supply chain in machinery and transport equipment sectors. FDI inflows have led to technology transfers and export growth in knowledge-intensive sectors, and, furthermore, they have supplemented domestic savings. Here we do not have space to provide a detailed and complex analysis of the differences in the impact of FDI in the individual countries according to the sectoral composition of FDI inflows or the quality of institutions in the host

Table 3.1 Economic performance of the CEE countries, in percentages

	Real GDP1989=100	*GDP per capita in purchasing power standards (PPS) EU-28=100*				*Averagegrowth rate*	
	2003	*2004**	*2008*	*2009*	*2016*	*2004–2016*	*2010–2016*
EU Member States							
Estonia	104.9	55	69	64	75	2.8	3.2
Latvia	87.9	47	59	52	65	3.0	2.3
Lithuania	86.7	50	63	56	75	3.3	3.2
Poland	134.5	49	55	60	68	3.9	3.1
Czech Republic	107.4	79	84	85	88	2.7	1.9
Slovakia	114.2	56	71	71	77	4.0	3.0
Hungary	115.3	62	63	64	67	1.6	1.8
Slovenia	119.5	86	90	85	83	1.8	0.9
Croatia	91.2	57	63	62	60	1.1	0.1
Romania	92.6	34	49	50	58	3.4	2.2
Bulgaria	87.0	35	43	44	47	3.3	1.8
Western Balkan countries							
Montenegro	50.1	30	41	39	42	:	:
Former Yugoslav Republic of Macedonia	81.4	27	32	34	37	3.4	2.6
Albania	123.6	22	25	27	29	:	2.3
Serbia	50.1	32	36	37	37	2.5	0.8
Bosnia and Herzegovina	:	24	30	31	32	:	1.6

Source: Eurostat, UNECE 2004: 80.*Note:* *Data are available for Montenegro, the Former Yugoslav Republic of Macedonia, Albania, Serbia and Bosnia and Herzegovina from 2005.

economy etc. (see, for example, Estrin and Uvalic 2013). In general, we can say that the only viable option to restructure and modernize transition economies was FDI. The richest economy of the region, Slovenia, attempted to follow a distinct path keeping up the high ratio of domestic (that is, state) ownership and restricting FDI inflows. Under the pressure of the 2008 global crisis, the typical efficiency problems of state ownership and intervention have come to light (Stanojević 2012, Stanojević 2014), and Slovenia has been forced to modify the economic policy toward a more liberalized, privatized market economy.

On the other hand, during the last two decades it has become obvious that FDI has limits in boosting economic growth and productivity. The technology and knowledge transfer, in effect spill-over effects, were expected to help the domestic companies to develop an internationally competitive indigenous economy. The literature on FDI spill-overs shows significant positive productivity effects in the case of domestic suppliers (that is, in vertical, backward linkages). General horizontal spill-over effects seem to be weak in the overwhelming majority of empirical investigations (see, for example, Bijsterbosch and Kolasa 2010; Gorodnichenko et al 2014; Hanousek et al 2011; Rugraff and Hansen 2011). The difference in productivity between large (typically foreign-owned) companies and small and medium sized (typically domestic) enterprises is much greater than in the advanced EU member states.

The multinational companies located their assembly activities in CEE, and due to lower wages they could strengthen their competitiveness through their flexibility in offshoring. From the viewpoint of CEE countries, assembly activities are at the low end of global value chains, and these are low value-added activities. There are possibilities of upgrading along the value chain for both subsidiaries and domestic suppliers, but the outlook on upgrading experiences in CEE is very mixed (see, for example, Éltető et al 2015).

The development of the innovation system can foster upgrading within a global value chain. The European Commission assesses the innovation performance of each member state and classifies them as innovation leaders, followers, moderate and modest innovators. Slovenia is the only innovation follower; all three modest innovators are CEE countries, and the remaining seven CEE countries form the group of moderate innovators together with the Mediterranean member states. Based on several indicators, the innovation performance is expressed by one composite index. Prior to the crisis some convergence was observable among the member states which fluctuated during the crisis years and reversed in 2012, reaching the differences of 2008, and convergence continued in 2014 again (European Commission 2015).

The lower productivity resulting from the underdeveloped domestic economy and the lower added value of the production conducted at the foreign corporations allow for relatively low wages and not only in volume but, in relative terms, a low level of investment in human capital, both in education and in social protection. While the EU-28 average of public expenditure on education was 5.1 per cent of the GDP, in the CEE EU members the average figure was 4.3 per cent in 2014. The expenditures on social protection as a percentage of GDP ranged between 14 and 20 per cent in the latter countries with the exception of Slovenia, while the EU-average was 28.7 per cent in 2014.[3] This makes the residual welfare state durable, and limits the development of R&D and innovation systems, which in turn maintains the lower productivity. This institutional arrangement, which has evolved in the CEE countries, can reproduce itself (Farkas 2016).

Overall, the capitalism model of the CEE countries undoubtedly led to successes. However, it is also clear that the features of the current CEE model do not support the thinking that prevails in the EU or IMF documents, namely, that the new, post-socialist member states are on a development path that only differs from the North Western core countries in quantitative terms, and that convergence is only a matter of time. The present institutional frameworks are only adequate for a development path that perpetuates asymmetric mutual dependency between the North Western and CEE countries (Epstein, 2014; Farkas, 2016). It is an essential insight because the most important promise of the change of political system was that the CEE countries, which were left out of the mainstream of development after World War II, could converge with the more fortunate western countries within a historically foreseeable time frame.

In addition, convergence prospects have worsened since the 2008 global crisis. In Table 3.1 the simple average growth rate indicates significantly slower economic development after the decline in 2009 than the average rate of the decade 2004–14. The more favourable data of the Baltic states are due to the fact that the fall of GDP was two to three times larger than in other CEE countries, resulting in very low baseline data for the subsequent years. The results of econometric models forecast unanimously a slowdown in economic convergence in the medium and long run (Borsi and Metiu 2015; Kaitila 2013; Podkaminer et al 2015). It appears that halving the current distance from the EU-28 average can be expected to take about 28–30 years or more for the CEE member states (Podkaminer et al. 2015: 5). Several factors are behind the slowdown. The productivity increase during the transition from a planned economy to a market economy was a non-recurrent effect. Furthermore, paradoxically, the weak economic growth in the euro area also slowed down the convergence of the export-oriented CEE countries. In the coming years the speed of population ageing will increase in CEE, impeding growth. Besides the low fertility rate, free movement of labour in the EU has increased emigration in the majority of CEE countries, and it is uncertain what proportion will be only temporary migrants.[4]

Societal embeddedness of economic transformation

Social inequities have increased substantially since the political system change. Although the value of the 1989 Gini index is quite uncertain, the 2014 Gini index is obviously higher in each country.[5] As a consequence, the rise of income is less perceptible under the circumstances of growing inequalities. Empirical research suggests that preferences for redistribution are not declining in CEE: instead, they are increasing (Okulicz-Kozaryn 2014). Furthermore, individuals' evaluation depends not only on their current income. Living standards are forcefully influenced by the accumulated physical and human assets of wider society (i.e. through the development of infrastructure, social skills etc.) Convergence in these areas is naturally slower than in current income and is measurable only with difficulty. However, the differences in living standards, conditions, and opportunities are clearly reflected in the differences in the social climate index,[6] which was created in Eurobarometer surveys and available only for member states but not for candidate countries. The negative values express dissatisfaction, and the CEE countries are in the lower half of the EU members in the Eurobarometer ranking (Table 3.2). It is remarkable that the ten countries with positive social climate indices are Northern and North Western countries plus Malta (European Commission 2014: 9). These data support the view that the living standards and conditions of the Northern and North Western countries are sought by countries throughout the EU.

Economic forecasts always assume that the institutional arrangement will not change. In this case, this means that movement upwards in global value chains, the strengthening of the indigenous growth drivers, improvement in the quality of institutions, and the development of education and of the innovation system could accelerate economic convergence. However, institutional changes would

Table 3.2 Overall social climate index

		2009	*2010*	*2011*	*2012*	*2013*	*2014*
EU-28 average		**-0.7**	**-0.7**	**-0.6**	**-0.8**	**-0.9**	**-1.0**
Ranking	**Country**						
11	Estonia	-0.4	0.0	-0.3	-0.4	-0.5	0.1
12	Czech Republic	-0.3	-0.1	-0.9	-0.6	-0.7	-0.9
15	Lithuania	-2.5	-3.1	-2.9	-2.4	-1.6	-1.4
16	Latvia	-2.2	-2.3	-2.7	-1.9	-1.4	-1.7
17	Poland	-1.3	-1.4	-1.7	-2.6	-2.0	-1.8
18	Slovenia	-0.5	-0.9	-1.3	-1.4	-2.0	-1.9
19	Slovakia	-1.6	-0.8	-1.7	-1.8	-2.0	-2.1
21	Hungary	-3.7	-3.4	-3.6	-3.8	-2.4	-2.3
24	Croatia	–	–	–	–	-3.5	-3.3
26	Romania	-2.4	-4.5	-4.4	-3.8	-4.0	-3.4
27	Bulgaria	-3.6	-3.1	-3.0	-2.9	-3.3	-3.6

Source: Authors' construction based on European Commission 2014: 9.

require very complex adaptation, and certain historical legacy in the region is a stronger obstacle to development than the limited financial resources, which has become apparent in the functioning of European cohesion policy. The latest report on cohesion demonstrates the close relationship between the effectiveness of cohesion policy and the quality of governance and institutional system in lagging countries or regions (European Commission 2017a).

In the current economic understanding of competitiveness, it is generally accepted that good governance, legal certainty and high-quality regulations including competition and procurement policy, the absence of corruption and an independent and efficient judicial system are essential for a stable business environment. These criteria are incorporated in the first, 'Institutions' pillar of the Global Competitiveness Index of World Economic Forum. According to this sub-index, Estonia is the only CEE country which is close to the North and North Western EU members (Schwab and Sala-i-Martin 2015: 10–11).

The World Bank also has a research dataset, 'Worldwide Governance Indicators' (WGI) focusing on good governance in terms of both efficiency and rule of law. These data are converted into a percentile ranking of all countries, and the Northern and North Western EU members are above 90 per cent. The average value of the indicators of six broad dimensions of governance[7] is between 70–80 per cent in the Central Eastern European countries and below 60 per cent in the Southeast European countries. There is a very strong correlation between the WGI ranking and economic development measured in GDP per capita (Figure 3.1).

Eurobarometer surveys show the low levels of trust in formal political institutions, especially in political parties in the EU members year by year, but in the CEE countries this is consistently lower even than in Northern and North Western countries (see *Standard Eurobarometers*, the latest issue: European Commission 2017b). Considering these investigations, it is not surprising that the level of system legitimation is significantly lower in post-communist countries than in traditionally capitalist ones. However, some consolidation in system justification has recently been observed (Cichocka and Jost 2014; Pop-Eleches and Tucker 2011). The weaknesses detailed in this section, in the performance of political systems, public administration and social capital, constrain not only the economic perspectives of the CEE countries but the reality that they will be able to achieve the desired patterns of daily life in North Western Europe.

Woundedness and victimization

After the transformation, CEE societies – at least the EU members – found themselves in a historically familiar situation, between the core countries and Eastern European peripheral countries, and they experienced progress and failed expectations at the same time. Whereas in the first period of modernisation and industrialization, Western European culture and way of living provided a reference point of urbanized bourgeoisie and intelligentsia, in the age of mass democracy and mass media it is a reference point for the entire society.

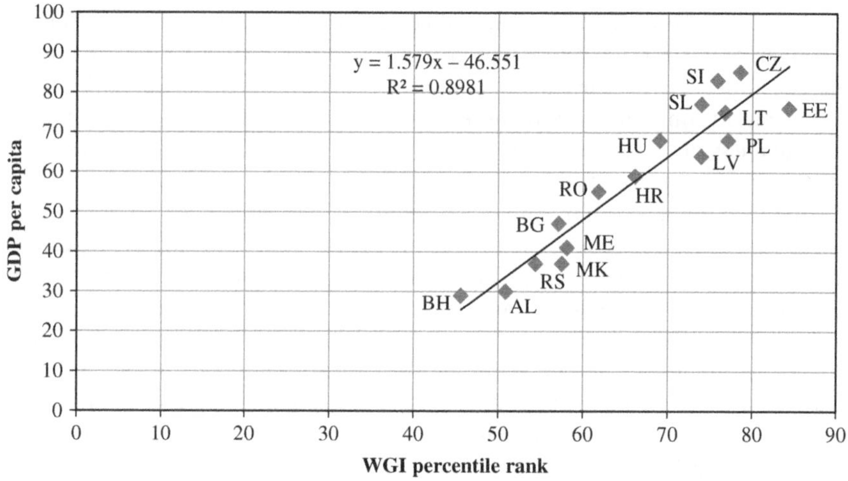

Figure 3.1 Correlation between GDP per capita (in PPS, EU-28=100) and WGI ranking in the CEE countries

Notes: EE=Estonia, LV=Latvia, LT=Lithuania, PL=Poland, CZ=Czech Republic, SL=Slovakia, HU=Hungary, SI=Slovenia, HR=Croatia, RO=Romania, BG=Bulgaria, ME=Montenegro, MK=Former Yugoslav Republic of Macedonia, RS=Serbia, AL=Albania, BH=Bosnia and Herzegovina

Source: Authors' calculation based on the Worldwide Governance Indicators (Kaufmann and Kraay, 2015) and Eurostat

However, the development in CEE and the results of convergence to Western Europe were demolished by the series of external shocks over centuries, such as for example the Ottoman and Russian invasions, the two World Wars, and the imposition of a Soviet regime. This turbulent history may be a reason that social norms have supported pessimism and cynicism and 'the cultures of complaining' have been prevalent in CEE for a long time (Cichocka and Jost, 2014). In addition to the repeated interruption of development, the genocides of the twentieth century have burdened the future of these societies, and the region can be characterized as a post-genocide region.

Since the fall of the Berlin Wall, societies in CEE have been challenged to create a new societal identity. Deep traumas, which impregnate their history and their memory, play a crucial role in the formation of contemporary societal identities (Alexander et al 2004; Eder and Spohn 2005; Spohn 2005; Sztompka 2004). Horrors of genocide and many other historical intersections and cross-cutting experiences are present through narrations of these traumas. Therefore, the identity of the region should be named and understood as a post-traumatic narrative identity (Lacapra 1999; Vollhardt and Bilewicz 2013).

Several phenomena demonstrate the importance of the past in the contemporary national identities of CEE. The presence of public memorials is overemphasized and newer ones have been raised permanently. Furthermore, historical facts and their contemporary interpretations trigger very hot public debates, which are related to the deep divisions of societies. As a part of the recreation of national identities, new hero cults are born and the national canon of classic literature and music have been reformed (Povedák et al 2014; Tismaneanu 2009).

Transformation recession, rapid change in social, political and economic structures caused further traumas in the region – especially for the losers of the new system. Additionally, the CEE transformation has taken place in the age of liquid modernity, which shifts the responsibility onto the shoulders of individuals. Governments or traditional social institutions like the educational system or banking sector have not assured clear cultural and economic orientation. 'The virtue proclaimed to serve the individual's interests best is not conformity to rules (which at any rate are few and far between, and often mutually contradictory) but flexibility ...' (Bauman 2013a: 4).

As a result of intertwined layers of traumas and challenges, woundedness has become a fundamental element of identity, and in the prevalent self-understanding, people consider themselves as victims. The perception of one's own position as a victim emerges in both internal relations (between political parties, between state and citizens or entrepreneurs etc.) and external relations (between the given country and a neighbouring country, the multinationals, the IMF, Brussels etc.). In the political rhetoric of governments in CEE, on the one hand, metaphors of battle against hostile and foreign actors and interest constellations predominate – not infrequently going as far as conspiracy theories.[8] On the other hand, victimization serves as an explanation of failed plans and projects.

The self-understanding as a victim, a strong emphasis on national identity, and the intense focus on the past often paralyze social actors and institutions, impeding efficient management of challenges and discovery of novelties. Instead of finding new proceedings and alternative solutions for structural and cultural problems, social actors in CEE are inclined to generate new dichotomies, to name and blame enemies, and to make outside factors and players responsible for unsolved problems. The more insecurity is caused by global and regional economical transformations and by hystericized public opinion, the more important are strong identities and clear demarcation lines inside and outside particular societies.

Frustration and trauma accompanying transformation has been reflected in the phenomenon of post-communist nostalgia, the different aspects of which are analysed by Todorova and Gille (2010). We do not address the interpretation of post-communist nostalgia but we use it as a proxy to measure the level of woundedness and its paralyzing effect. We assume that if somebody chooses the contemporary period when people are the happiest, they feel capable of coping with both the burden of the past and current challenges. According to the comparative survey Aufbruch (New Departures), about half of the population in the CEE countries consistently stated in 1997 and in 2007 that people were happier between 1945 and the political change of 1989–90 than before World War II or after the political change of 1989–90 (Tomka and Zulehner 2007: 28, 222).

This nostalgia is a particular type of memory, which is based on lived experience, but there is no hope or even desire for its return because of exhausted options and some improvement. It is linked to the trauma of transformation (Creed 2010). Data clearly show that there is a strong age bias, elderly people have more nostalgia for communist times (Ekman and Linde 2005; Tomka and Zulehner 2007). People who neither enjoyed special advantages nor suffered from persecution during the communist era remember these decades simply as their youth. Nevertheless, the post-communist nostalgia refers to a high level of discontent. It does not pose a direct threat to democracy in post-communist Europe today, but one should not disregard the nostalgia for communism as a desire for an undemocratic political culture (Ekman and Linde 2005).

As Tables 3.1 and 3.2 as well as Figure 3.1 indicate, there are significant differences among the CEE countries in their economic and governance performance and social climate, which refer to the different levels of woundedness. The ranking of the countries suggests a North–South division. There is no space here to provide a detailed analysis of each country. Thus, we point only to one element that influenced the level of woundedness. In the Baltic states and Slovakia the establishment of an independent nation state provided impetus to accept the severe difficulties caused by the transformation. Baltic societies tolerated the very harsh austerity measures after the 2008 global crisis as well, and they were willing to introduce the euro at any price. Finally, state independence was accompanied by economic progress. During the transformation recession and the 2008 global crisis people sought individual solutions and found jobs abroad instead of striking and demonstrating.

As we have seen above, the South Eastern European countries have brought a less advantageous historical legacy to set up a market economy. Nevertheless, the deep woundedness of Western Balkan societies has been rooted in the Balkan Wars, which accompanied the break-up of Yugoslavia. Unlike in the Baltic states and Czechoslovakia, nationalism did not promote state building there but led to ethnic conflicts, genocides and devastation, which were accompanied by an economic decline.

Conclusion

Our comprehensive analysis reveals that after the collapse of the communist system, the CEE countries have returned to the old development path of in-betweenness. We have seen that there are serious endogenous constraints, which impede the switch from path dependency to a new trajectory that would ensure catching up with the Western European countries. In addition, there is a real danger that – as so many times in the past – exogenous shocks, like the growing costs of climate change or of managing the migration influx may slow down or interrupt the CEE region's convergence to Western Europe. Furthermore, CEE politicians often amplify the fears, disappointments, and false expectations of the societies for their own purposes instead of facing reality.

Two factors control whether the consequences of ambiguous CEE transformation lead to the derailment of integration. On the one hand, the different historical and social background has to be taken into account in EU policy formation. For example, the independent, culturally more or less homogenous, Christian rooted nation state has a different meaning for the societies enjoying independence for the first time (e.g. Slovakia) or almost the first time (e.g. Estonia and Latvia) in their history or for societies which had experienced increased ethnic diversity and suffered the loss of two-thirds of the country (Hungary at the end of World War I) than for societies which have lived in sovereign states over centuries.

One the other hand, without a critical self-perception and realistic expectations, past traumas and current challenges paralyze the CEE societies. After a brief period of enthusiasm, the CEE countries encountered the fact that they could not simply copy the patterns of Western European modernity. However, post-communist nostalgia or other forms of protest are not viable alternative solutions. Some countries of catching-up modernisation (e.g. Finland and Japan) could use the special features of their cultures to promote their development. A similar way would be a desirable option for the CEE societies.

Finally, an understanding of the social mechanism that creates the self-perception of woundedness and victimization is essential because recently similar phenomena have emerged in Western European countries and the USA. Victimization was a central topic in the Brexit referendum, the presidential elections in both the USA and Austria and it is on the agenda of every anti-elite party (in Italy, France etc.).

Notes

1 'Thus, various groups and elites in Central and Eastern Europe and in Asian and African societies were able to refer to both the tradition of protest and the tradition of center-formation in these societies, and to cope with problems of reconstructing their own centers and traditions in terms of the new setting. From this perspective the most important aspect of the expansion of these themes beyond Western Europe and of their appropriation by different groups in the non-Western European societies may be seen in the fact that it allowed for the possibility to rebel against the institutional realities of the new modern civilization in terms of its own symbols and premise.' Eisenstadt (1999: 289).

2 In addition, the CEE applicants faced stricter conditionality than previous accession rounds (Goetz 2005).

3 Eurostat online database (accessed 19 January 2018).

4 Since 2000, the Baltic state depopulation has been about 7–13 per cent (OECD 2013). Furthermore, population decline is very severe problem in Hungary, Croatia, Serbia, Bosnia and Herzegovina, Romania and Bulgaria (Eurostat online database, Lukic et al 2012).

5 Eurostat online database and UNU-WIDER 'World Income Inequality Database (WIID3c)', September 2015, https://www.wider.unu.edu/project/wiid-world-income-inequality-database (accessed 3 February 2016).

6 The social climate index of Eurobarometer is composed of the evaluation of individuals' life and circumstances: satisfaction with life, the healthcare system, the pension

system, unemployment benefits, the cost of living, relations between people from different cultural or religious backgrounds or nationalities, the way inequalities and poverty are addressed, energy and housing prices, the way public administration runs, the situation of the economy, the personal job situation, the financial situation of individuals' household, and the employment situation.

7 The Worldwide Governance Indicators project constructs aggregate indicators of six broad dimensions of governance: voice and accountability, political stability and absence of violence/terrorism, government effectiveness, regulatory quality, rule of law, control of corruption.

8 'If you cannot see that today terrorist danger is a fact that can hurt every country in Europe and you think that Poland should not defend itself, you are going hand in hand with those who point this weapon against Europe, against all of us.' (Beata Szydlo's comment to Manchester terror attack 27 May 2017, http://www.express.co.uk/news/world/809779/Poland-prime-minister-Beata-Szyd-o-rage-Europe-EU-leaders-Manchester-bombing)

'Hungary is of course advancing its own interests, because of this and because of our friendship, the inquisition's attack on Poland will never succeed; we will always bear solidarity with the Poles,' – Viktor Orbán Prime Minister of Hungary in Brussels criticized EU-commission's sanctions against Poland. (Financial Times 22, July 2017 https://www.ft.com/content/b1bd2424-6ed7-11e7-93ff-99f383b09ff9)

'I have to say that in Brussels an alliance has been forged against the opinion of the people. The members of this alliance are the Brussels bureaucrats and their political elite, and the system that may be described as the Soros Empire.' (Viktor Orbán's speech at the 28th Bálványos Summer Open University and Student Camp 22 July 2017, http://www.kormany.hu/en/the-prime-minister/the-prime-minister-s-speeches/viktor-orban-s-speech-at-the-28th-balvanyos-summer-open-university-and-student-camp)

References

Alexander, J.C., Smelser, N.J., Sztompka P., Eyerman, R. and Giesen, B. (eds) (2004) *Cultural Trauma and Collective Identity*. Berkeley, CA: University of California Press.

Arnason, P. J. (2005) Introduction: Demarcating East Central Europe. *European Journal of Social Theory* 8(4), pp. 387–400.

Bartmanski, D. (2011) Successful Icons of Failed Time: Rethinking Post-communist Nostalgia. *Acta Sociologica* 54(32), pp. 213–231.

Bauman, Z. (2013a) *Liquid Times: Living in an Age of Uncertainty*. Cambridge UK: Polity Press.

Bauman, Z. (2013b) *Liquid Modernity*. Cambridge UK: Polity Press.

Bijsterbosch, M. and M. Kolasa (2010) FDI and productivity convergence in Central and Eastern Europe: an industry-level investigation. *Review of World Economics* 145(4), pp. 689–712.

Boatcă, M. (2006) 'Die zu Ende gedachte Moderne – Alternative Theoriekonzepte in den Latein-amerikanischen und Osteuropäischen Peripherien'. In: Schwinn, T. (ed.) *Die Vielfalt und Einheit der Moderne: Kultur- und strukturvergleichende Analysen*. Wiesbaden: VS Verlag für Sozialwissenschaften, pp. 281–304.

Boatcă, M. and W. Spohn (eds) (2010) *Globale, Multiple und Postkoloniale Modernen*. München: Rainer Hampp Verlag.

Borsi, M. T. and N. Metiu (2015) The Evolution of Economic Convergence in the European Union. *Empirical Economics* 48(2), pp. 657–681.

Bugge, P. (1999) Central Europe: A Tool for Historians or a Political Concept? *European Review of History* 6(1), pp. 15–35.

Cichocka, A. and J.T. Jost (2014) Stripped of illusions? Exploring System Justification Processes in Capitalist and Post-Communist Societies. *International Journal of Psychology* 49(1), pp. 6–29.

Creed, G.W. (2010) 'Strange Bedfellows. Socialist Nostalgia and Neoliberalism in Bulgaria'. In: Todorova, M.N. and Gille, Z. (eds) *Post-Communist Nostalgia*. New York: Berghahn Books, pp. 29–45.

Delanty, G. (2012) The Historical Regions of Europe: Civilizational Backgrounds and Multiple Routes to Modernity. *Historická sociologie (Historical Sociology)* 1(1–2), pp. 9–24.

Djelic, M.-L. (2010) Institutional Perspectives – Working towards Coherence or Irreconcilable Diversity. In: Morgan, G., Campbell J., Crouch C., Pedersen O.K. and Whitley, R. (eds) *The Oxford Handbook of Comparative Institutional Analysis*. Oxford: Oxford University Press, pp. 15–40.

EBRD (2013) *Stuck in Transition? Transition Report 2013*. London: European Bank for Reconstruction and Development.

Eder, K. and W. Spohn (eds) (2005) *Collective Memory and European Identity: The Effects of Integration and Enlargement*. Aldershot: Ashgate.

Eisenstadt, S.N. (1973) Post-Traditional Societies and the Continuity and Reconstruction of Tradition. *Daedalus* 102(1), pp. 1–27.

Eisenstadt, S.N. (1999) Multiple Modernities in an Age of Globalization. *The Canadian Journal of Sociology* 24(2), pp. 283–295.

Eisenstadt, S.N. (2000) Multiple Modernities. *Daedalus* 129(1), pp. 1–29.

Ekman, J. and J. Linde (2005) Communist Nostalgia and the Consolidation of Democracy in Central and Eastern Europe. *Journal of Communist Studies and Transition Politics* 21(3), pp. 354–374.

Éltető, A., A. Magasházi and A. Szalavetz (2015) Global Value Chains and Upgrading. *Competitio* 14(1), pp. 5–22.

Epstein, R. (2014) Overcoming 'Economic Backwardness' in the European Union. *Journal of Common Market Studies* 52(1), pp. 17–34.

Estrin, S. and M. Uvalic (2013) Foreign Direct Investment into Transition Economies: Are the Balkans Different? LSE 'Europe in Question' Discussion Paper Series No. 64.

European Commission (2014) *Social Climate. Special Eurobarometer 418.*

European Commission (2015) *Innovation Union Scoreboard 2015.*

European Commission (2017a) *7th Report on Economic, Social and Territorial Cohesion.*

European Commission (2017b) *Standard Eurobarometer 88: Autumn 2017.*

Farkas, B. (2016) *Models of Capitalism in the European Union: Post-crisis Perspectives.* Basingstoke, New York: Palgrave Macmillan.

Gill, I. S. and M. Raiser (2012) *Golden Growth: Restoring the Lustre of the European Economic Model.* Washington: The World Bank.

Goetz, K.H. (2005) The New Member States and the EU: Responding to Europe. In: S. Bulmer and C. Lequesne (eds) *The Member States of the European Union.* Oxford University Press, p. 256.

Gorodnichenko, Y., J. Svejnarand, K. Terrell (2014) When Does FDI Have Positive Spillovers? Evidence from 17 Transition Market Economies. *Journal of Comparative Economics* 42(4), pp. 954–969.

Haerpfer, C. (2002) *Democracy and Enlargement in Post-Communist Europe: The Democratisation of the General Public in 15 Central and Eastern European Countries, 1991–1998.* London: Routledge.

Hanousek, J., E. Kočenda and M. Maurel (2011) Direct and Indirect Effects of FDI in Emerging European Markets: A Survey and Meta-analysis. *Economic Systems* 35(3), pp. 301–322.

Hanson, S.E. (2009) Area Studies. In: T. Landman and N. Robinson (eds) *The SAGE Handbook of Comparative Politics*. London: Sage Publications, pp. 159–174.

Henderson, K. (2005) *Back to Europe: Central and Eastern Europe and the European Union*. London: Routledge.

Jackson, G. (2010) Actors and Institutions. In: G. Morgan, J. Campbell, C. Crouch, O. K. Pedersen and R. Whitley (eds) *The Oxford Handbook of Comparative Institutional Analysis*. Oxford: Oxford University Press, pp. 63–86.

Jordan, P. (2005) Großgliederung Europas nach kulturräumlichen Kriterien. *Europa Regional* 13(4), pp. 162–173.

Kaitila, V. (2013) Convergence, Income Distribution, and the Economic Crisis in Europe. ETLA Working Papers No. 14.

Kaufmann, D. and A. Kraay (2015) Worldwide Governance Indicators. [ONLINE] Available at: http://www.govindicators.org (accessed 8 February 2016).

Lacapra, D. (1999) Trauma, Absence, Loss. *Critical Inquiry* 25(4), pp. 696–727.

Longworth, P. (1992) *The Making of Eastern Europe*. Basingstoke: Macmillan.

Lukic, T., R. Stojsavljevic, B. Durdev, I. Nad and B. Dercan (2012) Depopulation in the Western Balkan Countries. *European Journal of Geography* 3(2), pp. 6–23.

Mason, D.S. (1992) *Revolution in East Central Europe: The Rise and Fall of Communism and the Cold War*. Boulder, CO: Westview Press.

Medve-Bálint, G. (2014) The Role of the EU in Shaping FDI Flows to East Central Europe. *Journal of Common Market Studies* 52(1), p. 35–51.

Ménard, C. (ed.) (2005) *Handbook of New Institutional Economics*. Dordrecht: Springer.

Morgan, G., J. Campbell, C. Crouch, O.K. Pedersen and R. Whitley (eds) (2010) *The Oxford Handbook of Comparative Institutional Analysis*. Oxford: Oxford University Press.

OECD (2013) *Coping with Emigration in Baltic and East European Countries*. Paris: OECD Publishing.

Okulicz-Kozaryn, A. (2014) Winners and Losers in Transition: Preferences for Redistribution and Nostalgia for Communism in Eastern Europe. *Kyklos* 67(3), pp. 447–461.

Podkaminer, L., S. Richter, A. Adarov, V. Astrov, S. Çiçek and M. Holzner (eds) (2015) *A Time of Moderate Expectations: Economic Analysis and Outlook for Central, East and Southeast Europe*. Vienna: The Vienna Institute for International Economic Studies.

Pop-Eleches, G. and J.A. Tucker (2011) Communism's Shadow: Postcommunist Legacies, Values, and Behavior. *Comparative Politics* 43(4), pp. 379–408.

Povedák, I., V. Voigt and J. Santino (2014) *Heroes and Celebrities in Central and Eastern Europe*. Szeged: Department of Ethnology and Cultural Anthropology.

Rugraff, E. and M.W. Hansen (eds) (2011) *Multinational Corporations and Local Firms in Emerging Economies*. Amsterdam: Amsterdam University Press.

Schimmelfennig, F. and U. Sedelmeier (2005) *The Europeanization of Central and Eastern Europe*. Ithaca: Cornell University Press.

Schwab, K. and X. Sala-i-Martin (eds) (2015) *The Global Competitiveness Report 2013–2014*. Geneva: World Economic Forum.

Spohn, W. (2005) National Identities and Collective Memory in an Enlarged Europe. In: K. Eder and W. Spohn (eds) *Collective Memory and European Identity: The Effects of Integration and Enlargement*. Aldershot: Ashgate, pp. 1–14.

Spohn, W. (2010) Political Sociology: Between Civilizations and Modernities. A Multiple Modernities Perspective. *European Journal of Social Theory* 13(1), p. 49–66.

Spohn, W. (2015) 'Europäisierung, Nation und Religion – Zur Transformation kollektiver Identitäten in einem sich erweiternden Europa. In: Schützeichel, R. and Jordan, S. (eds) *Prozesse*. Wiesbaden: Springer, pp. 435–461.

Stanojević, M. (2012) The Rise and Decline of Slovenian Corporatism: Local and European Factors. *Europe-Asia Studies* 64(5), pp. 857–877.

Stanojević, M. (2014) Conditions for a Neoliberal Turn: The Cases of Hungary and Slovenia'. *European Journal of Industrial Relations* 20(2), pp. 97–112.

Sztompka, P. (2004) The Trauma of Social Change: A Case of Postcommunist Societies. In: Jeffrey, C.A., Smelser, N.J., Sztompka, P., Eyerman R. and Giesen, B. (eds) *Cultural Trauma and Collective Identity*. Berkeley, CA: University of California Press, pp. 149–189.

Szűcs, J. (1983) The Three Historical Regions of Europe: An Outline. *Acta Historica Academiae Scientiarum Hungaricae* 29(2–4), pp. 131–184.

Tismaneanu, V. (1992) *Reinventing Politics: Eastern Europe from Stalin to Havel*. New York, Toronto: Free Press, Maxwell Macmillan Canada.

Tismaneanu, V. (2009) *Fantasies of Salvation: Democracy, Nationalism and Myth in Post-Communist Europe*. Princeton, N.J.: Princeton University Press.

Todorova, M.N. and Z. Gille (eds) (2010) *Post-Communist Nostalgia*. New York: Berghahn Books.

Tomka, M. and PM. Zulehner (2007) *Aufbruch 2007*. Vienna: Tabellenband.

UNECE (2004) Economic Survey of Europe, No. 2. Statistical Appendix. [ONLINE] Available at: http://www.unece.org/fileadmin/DAM/ead/pub/042/042appendix.pdf (accessed 3 February 2016).

Vollhardt, J.R. and M. Bilewicz (2013) After the Genocide: Psychological Perspectives on Victim, Bystander, and Perpetrator Groups. *Journal of Social Issues* 69(1), p. 1–15.

4 Perpetual crises, the return of geopolitics and the emergence of a new normalcy in Central Europe

Anna Visvizi

Introduction

The multiple and interconnected crises, including the global financial crisis, the euro area crisis, the twin migration and refugee crises, and other traditional and nascent risks to safety and security have had a profound impact on the dynamics of developments in the European Union (EU) over the past few years. Arguably, very specific dynamics were, thus, induced into the EU-level decision-making process as well as into domestic political deliberation in the EU member states. As a result, a substantial revamp of the system of checks and balances pertinent to EU-level politics had taken place, therefore supporting arguments of progressive differentiation in the EU (Magone, Laffan and Schweiger 2016). For instance, the euro area crisis and the EU economic governance reforms deepened the divide between countries that have adopted the euro and those that have not. Similarly, the degree of exposure to the implications of the unprecedented wave of migration that Europe experienced in 2015–2016 revealed how difficult it is to build and communicate consensus among the EU member states. Consequently, another line of division amongst the EU member states emerged. Also, the annexation of Crimea and war in Eastern Ukraine exposed a considerable lack of understanding among the EU stakeholders and, implicitly, divergence of their affiliations and loyalties. The evolving nature of transatlantic relations, as well as the implications of the Brexit referendum have only exacerbated tensions simmering under the surface of the EU political debate. It is in this complex context that it is necessary to place the case of the Central and Eastern European countries, most specifically Poland, Hungary, the Czech Republic and Slovakia, if their transformation from best pupils of European integration to *les enfants terribles* is to be understood.

Indeed, until recently lauded as success stories of Europeanization and EU-level socialization, Poland, Hungary, the Czech Republic and Slovakia, the – as it seems – permanently 'new' EU member states, in several respects disappoint today. Given the political, economic and symbolic weight of countries located in Central-Eastern Europe, it is necessary to rethink the developments in the region in the most possibly neutral manner. Considering the weight of the democratic liberal tradition that countries in the region had proudly supported throughout communism, it is imperative that these experiences are fed into the decision-making process in the EU today. This chapter muses about the economic and political performance of Poland, the Czech Republic, Hungary and Slovakia. By placing these developments in the broader context of processes shaping the EU and its external environment, it seeks to rescue the academic, political and popular debates on Central-Eastern Europe from falling into reductionism and bias. With this in mind, in the first section, the key developments and issues influencing the dynamics of the context in which Poland, the Czech Republic, Slovakia and Hungary are embedded, are examined. In the next two sections, the empirical focus of the analysis narrows to elaborate on country specific developments in the fields of economics and politics, respectively. Conclusions follow.

Placing the V4 in an increasingly fragile context

The geopolitical location of Central-Eastern Europe has always had grave implications for the respective countries' security and political options at their disposal. Today too, the external environment in which Poland, Hungary, the Czech Republic and Slovakia operate is increasingly fragile, thus serving as a source of new risks, threats and challenges, both traditional and new. The euro area crisis and its social and economic implications, as well as its political toll, exacerbated the nascent divisions at the EU supranational and intergovernmental levels. The implications of the Euro area crisis for Central-Eastern Europe, and especially for these EU members that have not adopted the single currency, have been largely neglected in the literature (Visvizi 2012). Nevertheless, their prolonged domestic, social and economic implications did not pass unnoticed. The war in Ukraine and the annexation of Crimea, followed by the exodus of more than one million Ukrainian citizens to seek work and a better life in neighbouring Poland, only added to the perception of instability and imminent threat of inter-state conflict in the region. The information warfare in the Baltic states, i.e. countries particularly vulnerable to the influence of Russian propaganda, has left neither Poland, the Czech Republic, Slovakia nor Hungary intact. The twin refugee and migration crises may have had different direct implications for Poland and Hungary, yet, as a result both countries acquired the badge of those EU member states which are unwilling and, perhaps, unable to act in the spirit of solidarity at the EU level (Pachocka 2016; Visvizi 2017). In this context, the role of the Visegrád Group (V4) consisting of Poland, Hungary, the Czech Republic and Slovakia, has become more pronounced. While several factors contributed to that it is possible to argue that the V4 members acquired a sense of understanding that the forum may indeed be employed as a useful tool of policy-coordination and policy-projection at the EU level.

From a different angle, the prospect of Brexit raises serious concerns regarding the likely future economic, social, and political implications, including uncertainty related to the legal status of Polish, Czech, Slovak, Hungarian nationals employed in the UK; possible future pressures on home country labour markets, if today's emigrants return, and their socio-economic implications; decrease in remittances. For instance, only in 2015 the value of remittances sent home by Polish and Czech workers in the UK amounted to 1.144 million USD and 209 million USD respectively. This equates to approximately 1.4 and 1.5 per cent of GDP 2015 in both countries respectively (World Bank 2016). In addition, prospective Brexit will change the distribution of power in the Council of the EU, to the disadvantage of Poland. Also, Brexit will have an imminent impact on the size of the EU budget and so on the value of structural funds, which have been fundamental for fuelling Polish growth success. The 2016 US elections served as an additional trigger of uncertainty in the region. Today, it seems the Trump administration may be offering the region of Central-Eastern Europe the support it needs. It remains to be seen how Poland, the Czech Republic, Slovakia and Hungary will fit into the new transatlantic relation as it consolidates. All things considered, the context in which the V4 countries operate is pregnant with viable risks to safety and threats to security, whereby the political context at the EU level only exacerbates them. Developments on the domestic economic and political scenes add to the complexity of the status quo. The following sections elaborate on it.

V4 and their economic performance: catching up and backsliding

Poland, the Czech Republic, Hungary and Slovakia form the group of four countries that were the first ones to embark on the processes of systemic transition and economic transformation following the collapse of communism in 1989 (Żukrowska 2010). For this reason alone, the economic performance of these countries is frequently viewed explicitly through the lens of transition. Moreover, the same four countries paved the way towards eastern enlargement of the EU. From this angle, these countries' economic performance is frequently linked exclusively to their membership in the EU. As a result, a tendency consolidates in the literature to simplify and to link all weaknesses discernible through the analysis of socio-economic indicators in these countries to the ills of transition. At the same time, economic growth and rising economic convergence are attributed to membership of the EU. As ever, there are several ways of explaining the story of the region's success in terms of socio-economic growth and development attained over the past nearly 30 years. What puzzles today is the return of a disbelief and unwillingness to recognize the success of transition and transformation (Visvizi 2010). Indeed, already in the early 1990s, 'the dilemma of simultaneity' (Offe 1991) captured the same feeling of scepticism that re-building the state and the nation, democratizing, and restructuring the economy simultaneously was possible (Merkel 2008). As a result, transition and transformation are discussed in negative terms. Essentially, they are blamed for social inequalities present in the V4 countries today; also, an implicit link is established between the condition of troubled democratic order in those countries and transition. As these arguments fit squarely in the broader critique of capitalism, it could be that they simply reflect an overall disillusionment with the world, an attempt to be say something new, to provoke and to be seen. Driven by, among others, Piketty (2014) and his followers, the critique of capitalism has taken enormous dimensions, essentially rendering capitalism the source of all inequalities, evil and suffering in the world. A much more balanced voice in the same debate has taken the shape of the varieties of capitalism (VoC) debate. Here Bohle and Greskovits (2012) for instance offered a captivating insight into the meanders of capitalism in Europe's periphery. Clearly, although substantial work in this respect has been done (Csaba 2007; Farkas 2016), more careful consideration needs to be given to the political economy of transition if the complex causal feedback effects between the specific trajectories of transition each country in the region followed (Żukrowska 2012) and their performance today are to be understood (Visvizi 2010).

To sum it up, even if advantages of transition have not been spread evenly across society in the region, frequently leaving rural areas and the periphery in general at a disadvantage, it is important to stress the unprecedented leap forward that the V4 countries achieved in a period of less than 30 years. It is equally important to remember that the goal of transition and transformation was to re-establish democracy and economic freedom. Democracy, through its recognition of the rights of the individual, including the right to private property, and the resultant reforms aimed at deregulation and, in fact, establishment of market institutions, e.g. the stock market, did create equal opportunities for all, rather than equality in misery specific to communism (Visvizi 2016). Following the collapse of communism, a massive reallocation of factors of production had taken place, enabling the region to record massive foreign direct investment (FDI) flows and spectacular growth rates, which resulted in a phenomenal catch up (Gill and Raiser 2012: 44). Poland, Hungary, the Czech Republic and Slovakia followed different trajectories of transition, and therefore, considering also their country specific circumstances such as market size, population dynamics, availability of resources etc.; 30 years since the free June 4, 1989 elections in Poland (Hornik 2014), differences among these countries exist. As the following paragraphs indicate, nevertheless, the countries discussed here display a rather stable macroeconomic performance, even if challenges are in sight. The following discussion offers some broader support for these points.

Poland is the largest country in both size and population in the region of Central-Eastern Europe. It has recorded uninterrupted growth rates since 1992, thus serving as a good case for the value of Balcerowicz's 'shock therapy' (Visvizi 2010). Since its entry to the EU it has enjoyed stable growth rates placing Poland among the top performers in the EU. Following the global financial crisis and fiscal easing policies recommended by the European Commission, Poland's fiscal balance worsened, and – similarly as other EU member states – Poland was subdued by the Excessive Deficit Procedure (EDP) in 2009. Notably, in 2015, Poland's GDP per capita expressed in purchasing power standards reached 69 per cent of the EU average, up from 53 per cent in 2007. As the European Commission (2017b) observes, 'rising incomes and living standards have been accompanied by gains in employment, which reached an all-time high reducing unemployment to a record low'. Economic growth in Poland has been driven in equal shares by exports and domestic consumption. As traditional sources of competitiveness are dwindling, it is necessary that new sources of efficiency gains are identified (Riedel 2017). Given recent regulatory changes in Poland, especially those related to social expenditure, it remains to be seen how fast and to what extent these measures will affect the gains attained as a result of bold economic reforms and fiscal prudence implemented in Poland since 1991.

It is impossible to compare the cases of Poland and Hungary as the starting points of their transition and transformation were different. Today, the performance of the Hungarian economy is stable, although Hungary did experience dramatic fall in growth rates and a fiscal imbalance. Today, growth in Hungary remains stable, even if debt to GDP levels are above the symbolic 60 per cent threshold. Hungary's problem is high unemployment, especially hidden unemployment. The statistics are further affected by the massive reverse brain drain that Hungary experienced over the past years. It is estimated that more than 400,000 highly-skilled Hungarians migrated to other EU countries recently, thus reaching historical records of emigration (Serdült 2016). As far as investment levels are concerned, Hungary experienced a temporary decline in EU-funded

Table 4.1 Poland: macro-economic indicators 2004–2016

Poland	*2004*	*2009*	*2013*	*2014*	*2015*	*2016*
GDP growth (%, year on year)	5.1	2.8	1.4	3.3	3.8	2.7
Gross public debt (% GDP)	45.0	49.4	55.7	50.2	51.1	54.4
Central government deficit	-3.9	7.3	4.1	3.5	2.6	2.4
Current account balance	-5.5	-4.0	-1.3	-2.1	-0.6	-0.3
Unemployment	19.1	8.1	10.3	9.0	7.5	6.2

Source: Eurostat.

Table 4.2 Hungary: macro-economic indicators 2004–2016

Hungary	*2004*	*2009*	*2013*	*2014*	*2015*	*2016*
GDP growth (%, year on year)	5.0	-6.6	2.1	4.0	3.1	2.0
Gross public debt (% GDP)	58.5	77.8	76.6	75.7	74.7	74.1
Central government deficit	-5.4	4.6	2.6	2.1	1.6	1.8
Current account balance	-8.5	-0.8	3.8	2.1	3.3	4.8
Unemployment	6.1	10.0	10.2	7.7	6.8	5.1

Source: Eurostat

investment in 2015 and 2016, but expansive fiscal policy is likely to accelerate growth to around 3.5 per cent as of 2017 (European Commission 2017a).

The Czech Republic is a small but robust economy. The main driver of growth has been domestic demand. Following a recession in 2009, the Czech economy has since recorded stable growth. As disposal income growth was recorded, household consumption continued growing too:

> High investment growth in 2015, which translated into high overall GDP growth that year, was mainly due to the accelerated drawdown of available EU funds at the end of the last programming period. A significantly lower rate of drawdown in 2016, at the start of the new programming period, is expected to have contributed to a fall in investment and impacted negatively on headline economic growth.
>
> (European Commission 2017d)

Slovakia is the only country in the region of Central-Eastern Europe that is a member of the Euro area. Having adopted the euro in 2009, on the brink of the Greek sovereign debt crisis and the Euro area crisis, Slovakia payed a dire price for its commitment to the European project. Today, the Slovak economy is very stable, enjoying economic expansion at one of the fastest rates in the EU. See Table 4.4. Slovakia's growth is to be attributed to an increase in net exports, stable domestic private consumption and labour market recovery (European Commission 2017c: 4).

In the discussion on the V4's economic performance it is necessary to shed some light on their competitiveness. Considering that reallocation of resources enabled a major productivity boost in those countries in the early 1990s, today, it is necessary that new sources of competitive advantage are enhanced in the region. Table 4.5 presents the V4's competitiveness and ease of doing business rankings for 2016. Figure 4.1 also offers a detailed insight into factors enhancing or constraining these countries' competitiveness.

Table 4.3 The Czech Republic: macro-economic indicators 2004–2016

The Czech Republic	*2004*	*2009*	*2013*	*2014*	*2015*	*2016*
GDP growth (%, year on year)	4.9	-4.8	-0.5	2.7	5.3	2.6
Gross public debt (% GDP)	28.5	34.1	44.9	42.2	40.3	37.2
Central government deficit	-3.0	5.5	1.2	1.9	0.6	0.6
Current account balance	-3.7	-1.9	-0.5	0.2	0.2	1.1
Unemployment	8.3	6.7	7.0	6.1	5.1	4.0

Source: Eurostat

Table 4.4 The Slovak Republic: macro-economic indicators 2004–2016

The Slovak Republic	*2004*	*2009*	*2013*	*2014*	*2015*	*2016*
GDP growth (%, year on year)	5.30	-5.40	1.50	2.60	3.80	3.30
Gross public debt (% GDP)	40.60	36.30	54.70	53.60	52.50	51.90
Central government deficit	-3.1	5.9	15.1	5.4	2.9	1.8
Current account balance	-10.10	-3.40	1.90	1.10	0.20	-0.70
Unemployment	18.40	12.10	14.20	13.20	11.50	9.60

Source: Eurostat.

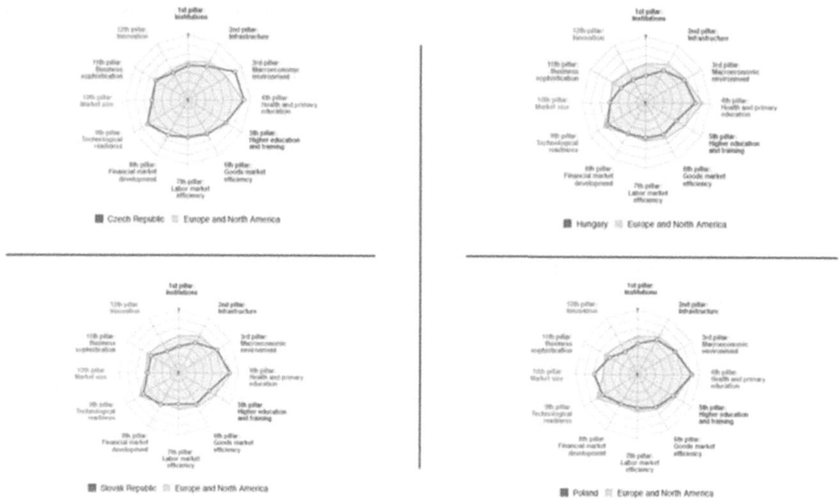

Figure 4.1 Competitiveness in the region
Source: WEF, 'Country/Economy Profiles', *The Global Competitiveness Report 2017–2018*, Geneva: World Economic Forum (WEF), 2017.

In other words, the prospect of these four countries' sustained and sustainable growth and development depends on their ability to innovate. In this context, education and education systems are crucial, especially the capacity to move towards smart education (Visvizi, Lytras and Daniela 2018). This issue is particularly important given the connection between smart education and innovation. As Figure 4.1 demonstrates, whereas technological readiness in the region is high, innovation and business sophistication remain largely unexploited drivers of competitiveness. In contrast, as Table 4.5 demonstrates, differences exist among the four countries discussed here as regards their business friendliness. The latter is an indispensable factor when attracting and maintaining FDI flows.

Table 4.5 Competitiveness and business friendliness in the region

	Poland	*Hungary*	*The Czech Republic*	*Slovakia*
Ease of doing business ranking 2017	24	41	27	33
Global competitiveness ranking (out of 137 countries)	39	60	31	59

Source: WB (2017) Ease of Doing Business rankings, Washington, D.C.: World Bank (WB) http://www.doingbusiness.org/rankings; WEF (2017) The Global Competitiveness Index 2017–2018 edition, Geneva: World Economic Forum (WEF), http://reports.weforum.org/global-competitiveness-index-2017-2018/countryeconomy-profiles/

An equally important aspect conditioning the V4's economic performance as well as political options and considerations is that of energy dependency. Energy dependency shows the extent to which an economy relies upon imports in order to meet its energy needs. Table 4.6 offers a glimpse into this issue. Notably, in 2015, Russia remained the single largest source of crude oil imports for Poland (96.8 per cent), the Czech Republic (97.8), Slovenia (89.4), and Hungary (93.2). The same applies to natural gas imports, hence positioning these countries in a very uncomfortable position vis-à-vis Russia. A more detailed examination of the infrastructure networks in these four countries, including the existing and non-existent infrastructure in diverse energy markets, makes this picture more complex and highlights opportunities and limitations vis-à-vis the options all four countries have in the field of securing alternative sources of energy supply. Given the infrastructure development process underway in Europe, e.g. Nord Stream 2 and its political and strategic intricacies, energy security is a source of strategic concern in the region. Plans are underway in Poland to limit Polish dependence on gas delivery from Russia. By 2022, following the construction of the Norway gas pipeline connection, Poland should be able to stop gas imports from Russia (EnergyMarketPrice 2016). In this way, other countries in the region will be enabled to lessen their

Table 4.6 Energy dependency: crude oil and natural gas dependency in 2015, as a percentage of total imports

	Total imports of energy sources	*Crude oil (%)*	*Natural gas (%)*	*Solid fuels (%)*
EU 28 average	54.0	88.8	69.1	42.8
Poland	29.3	96.8	72.2	-11.6
Czech Republic	31.9	97.8	95.1	-1.8
Hungary	53.4	93.2	69.7	34.0
Slovenia	48.7	89.4	99.6	18.9

Source: The author's compilation, based on Eurostat, Energy Dependence, http://ec.europa.eu/eurostat/tgm/table.do?tab=table&init=1&language=en&pcode=tsdcc310&plugin=1 (accessed 6 October 2017).

dependence on gas imports from Russia. It is worth noting that the year 2022 delimits also the end of so-called 'Yamal lng contract' signed in 2010 with Gazprom. This contact has been a source of ongoing tensions, e.g. in June 2017 Poland temporarily halted gas deliveries due to poor quality of the gas (Goettig 2017). Overall, energy security represents a very important factor that needs to be taken into consideration in any discussion on the region in question and the resulting policy-options or the lack of them.

Visegrád 4: political turmoil

Poland and Hungary, and to a lesser extent, Slovakia and the Czech Republic have been discussed as troubled democracies over the past few years (Hanley and Dawson 2017; Pap 2018). With the Hungarian prime minister Victor Orban best known for his 'illiberal democracy' phrase and Poland's government for the infamous judiciary reform of 2017, the perception of Central-Eastern Europe changed dramatically – for worse – recently. The following paragraphs offer an overview of the most recent indicators of political freedom in the region. As details concerning the developments in each of the countries concerned have been examined in their respective chapters in this volume, in this chapter only some general issues will be highlighted.

Overall, a deterioration of the political climate in the region has been recorded over the past decade. Whereas in Hungary the onset of Orban's government made many predict today's developments, the political turn in Poland took many observers by surprise. The countries in question continue to be characterized as free, still substantial losses in specific categories of liberties are taking place. Hungary is performing the worst in this respect; the Czech Republic seems to be most free country in this group of four. Specifically, Hungary's political rights rating declined from two to three due to government practices that curtailed the ability of the opposition to freely and meaningfully participate in the formal political system, as well as continuing impunity for high-level corruption (Freedom House 2017b). What is really worrying is what is not captured by the rankings and statistics. Civil society activists and opposition party members report that they witness the gradual shrinking of the free

Table 4.7 Freedom in the world scores 2017

	Freedom status	*Aggregate score 0–100*	*Freedom rating 1–7*	*Political rights 1–7*	*Civil liberties 1–7*
Czech Republic	free	94/100	1	1	1
Hungary	free	76/100	2.5	3	2
Poland	free	89/100	1.5	1	1
Slovakia	free	89/100	1	1	1

Source: Freedom House (2017) Freedom in the World ReportLegend: 0–100 where 0 indicates 'least free', 100 'most free'; 1–7, where 1 indicates 'most free', and 7 'least free'

liberal space, a process so subtle that it is hardly noticeable, and yet has powerful implications for freedom of expression in the longer run.

Regarding Poland, the year 2015 marked a watershed in Polish post-1989 politics. First, the May 2015 presidential elections revealed that things should not be taken for granted on Polish social and political scenes. The victory of Andrzej Duda, a figure previously largely unknown to the broader audience, signalled that a turn on the Polish political scene was on the cards. Elections to the parliament, with the landslide victory of the Law and Justice Party (PiS), cemented change on the political scene thus paving the way towards a dramatic institutional backsliding in Poland. Since then, Poland's civil liberties rating declined from one down to two and it received a downward trend arrow (Freedom House 2017c). This is due to sustained attempts to increase government influence over the country's media, judiciary, civil service, and education system.

The case of the Czech Republic suggests slightly different dynamics of developments. Illiberal rhetoric is on the rise in the public discourse in the Czech Republic. Corruption remains the key problem:

> A hint of the issue's scale was revealed during the Panama Papers scandal that emerged in April 2016, when a trove of documents was leaked from a Panama-based law firm and unveiled by media organizations. Of the 11 million documents released, over 250,000 had a connection to the Czech Republic, with nearly 300 Czech business figures appearing in the files. Many of the cases involved alleged tax evasion or money laundering..
> (Freedom House 2017a)

Similarly, Slovakia seems to be looking for a new identity, even if the freedom indicators remain unchanged (Freedom House 2017d).

Conclusion

The objective of this chapter was to place developments in Central-Eastern Europe, a part of Europe traditionally misunderstood and frequently underappreciated, in a broader context of developments taking place either in the EU itself or in the wider region. For the sake of restoring objectivity and unbiased perspective to the debate on the region of Central-Eastern Europe, the economic performance and freedom indicators were showcased. The picture that emerges is puzzling, i.e. on the one hand, macroeconomic performance indicators suggest a robust growth and growth potential, even if competitiveness would have to be boosted in these countries. On the other hand, freedom seems to be shrinking in Hungary and Poland, while it remains uncertain what is to happen next in the Czech Republic and Slovakia.

It would be easy to jump to quick conclusions and thereby suggest that there is a connection between failed/unfinished transition and transformation and the developments on the political scene taking place in Hungary and Poland and possibly looming on the horizon elsewhere. However, rather than contributing to the debate on how bad things have become, the imperative today is to dwell on the determinants of these developments.

In times of crisis, perhaps because of the crisis, the role and image of the Visegrád Group has become more pronounced; although not always in a positive context. The V4, otherwise a grouping of a symbolic nature, acquired a certain status in the context of the annexation of Crimea as well as in the context of the migration and refugee crises. What is important about the re-emergence of this informal, non-institutionalized grouping is that the external attention it received, both on the account of the uneasy process of consensus building over the issue of the annexation of Crimea, and of the relocation quota, triggered a rethink on the part of the V4 group members regarding what the group is about. Even if some critics might argue that the debate on V4 and the diverse V4 specific fora at which issues pertinent to its impact, ways of collaboration, image etc. could be strengthened lacked essence, the V4 has established itself as a club on the EU scene.

Over the past 25 years the V4 countries have undergone a remarkable economic, political and social transformation. As a result, a reconstitution of the foundational principles that initially defined the nature of transition, transformation and institutionalization of external relations has taken place. This includes the notion of democracy, national identity, and the role of the state in the economy, as well as the meaning of the transatlantic space. Arguably, in the shadow of the perpetual crises, the emergence of this state of a new normalcy in Central Europe has been largely ignored elsewhere in the EU. As a result, today, the CEEs are at a turning point. Given the unfinished business of the EU economic governance reform and the return of geopolitics in the EU, this chapter sought to shed light on this issue.

In the centre of this chapter was an apparent juxtaposition, i.e. the four countries forming the core of Central-Eastern Europe, including Poland, Hungary, the Czech Republic and Slovakia, served as a success story of European integration a few years ago; now, they do not. Even if each country-specific story is different and many ways of telling these stories are possible, the fundamental question today is what this change is an instance of. In as much as today's developments in Hungary and Poland are worrying, it is equally plausible that similar consideration should be given to very specific mechanisms at play at the EU level and beyond as they may have had an impact on where the V4 countries are today. These and other issues are the subject of our forthcoming research.

References

Bohle, D. and Greskovits, B. (2012) *Capitalist Diversity on Europe's Periphery*. Ithaka and London: Cornell University Press.

Csaba, L. (2007) *The New Political Economy of Emerging Europe*. Budapest: Akadémiai Kiadó.

EnergyMarketPrice (2016) Poland: PGNiG Anticipates Norway Gas Pipeline Connection by, Energy Market Price, 1 February. [ONLINE] Available from: http://www.energymarketprice.com/energy-news/poland-pgnig-anticipates-norway-gas-pipeline-connection-by-2022?act=ps&pid=81&prid=4 (accessed 7 October 2017).

European Commission (2017a) *Country Report Hungary. Commission Staff Working Document (Accompanying the document Communication from the Commission to the European Parliament, the Council, the European Central Bank and the Eurogroup)*, Brussels, 28 February, SWD (2017) 82 final/2.

European Commission (2017b) *Country Report Poland, Commission Staff Working Document (Accompanying the document Communication from the Commission to the European Parliament, the Council, the European Central Bank and the Eurogroup)*, Brussels, 22 February, SWD (2017) 86 final.

European Commission (2017c) *Country Report Slovakia.* Commission Staff Working Document (Accompanying the document Communication from the Commission to the European Parliament, the Council, the European Central Bank and the Eurogroup), Brussels, 27 February, SWD (2017) 90 final/2.

European Commission (2017d) *Country Report the Czech Republic., Commission Staff Working Document* (Accompanying the document Communication from the Commission to the European Parliament, the Council, the European Central Bank and the Eurogroup), Brussels, 22 February, SWD (2017) 69 final.

Farkas, B. (2016) *Models of Capitalism in the European Union – Post-crisis Perspectives.* London: Palgrave Macmillan.

Freedom House (2017a) *Country Profile: Czech Republic.* Freedom in the World. 18 August. [ONLINE] Available from: https://freedomhouse.org/report/freedom-world/2017/czech-republic (accessed 8 October 2017).

Freedom House (2017b) *Country Profile: Hungary.* Freedom in the World. 18 August. [ONLINE] Available from: https://freedomhouse.org/report/freedom-world/2017/hungary (accessed 7 October 2017).

Freedom House (2017c) *Country Profile: Poland.* Freedom in the World. 8 August. [ONLINE] Available from: https://freedomhouse.org/report/freedom-world/2017/poland (accessed 7 October 2017).

Freedom House (2017d) *Country Profile: Slovakia.* Freedom in the World. 18 August. [ONLINE] Available from: https://freedomhouse.org/report/freedom-world/2017/slovakia (accessed 8 October 2017).

Gill, I., Raiser, M. (2012) *Golden Growth: Restoring the Lustre of the European Economic Model.* Washington, D.C.: World Bank.

Goettig, M. (2017) *UPDATE 1-Poland Suspends Russian Gas Supplies via Yamal Pipeline Due to Poor Quality.* Reuters 21 June. [ONLINE] Available from: https://www.reuters.com/article/pgnig-gazprom-yamal/update-1-poland-suspends-russian-gas-supplies-via-yamal-pipeline-due-to-poor-quality-idUSL8N1JI4TC (accessed 2 October 2017).

Hanley, S. and Dawson, J. (2017) *Poland Isn't a Democracy and It Never Was.* Foreign Policy 3 January. [ONLINE] Available from http://foreignpolicy.com/2017/01/03/poland- was-never-as-democratic-as-it-looked-law-and-justice-hungary-orban/ (accessed 2 October 2017).

Hornik, R. (2014) *The Other June 4, 1989. The Globalist.* 4 June. [ONLINE] Available from: https://www.theglobalist.com/the-other-june-4-1989/ (accessed 7 October 2017).

Magone, J., Laffan, B. and Schweiger, C. (eds) (2016) *Core-Periphery Relations in the European Union: The Politics of Differentiated Integration in the European Political Economy.* London and New York: Routledge.

Merkel, W. (2008) Plausible Theory, Unexpected Results: The Rapid Democratic Consolidation in Central and Eastern Europe. *Internationale Politik und Gesellschaft Online/International Politics and Society*, 2008(2).

Offe, C. (1991), Das Dilemma der Gleichzeitigkeit. Demokratisierung und Marktwirtschaftin Osteuropa (The Dilemma of Simultaneity. Democratisation and Market Economy in East Europe). *Merkur* 45(4), pp. 279–292.

Pachocka, M. (2016) Understanding the Visegrád Group States' Response to the Migrant and Refugee Crises 2014+ in the European Union. *Yearbook of Polish European Studies (YPES)*, 2016(19), pp. 101–132.

Pap, A.L. (2018) *Democratic Decline in Hungary: Law and Society in an Illiberal Democracy*. London and New York: Routledge.

Piketty, T. (2014) *Capital in the Twenty-First Century*, trans. A. Goldhammer, Cambridge: Harvard University Press.

Riedel, R. (2017) In der Falle? Polens Suche nach einem neuen Wachstumsmodell. [Poland's search for a new growth model]. *OSTEUROPA* 67(3/4), pp. 77–86.

Serdült, V. (2016) Brain Drain Damaging Hungarian Economy. *The Budapest Beacon*. 26 July [ONLINE] Available from: https://budapestbeacon.com/official-brain-drain-damaging-hungarian-economy/ (accessed 2 October 2017).

Visvizi, A. (2010) A Country is Never on its Own, Others Can be Helpful. External Linkages: Institutionalization and Support of Individual States. In: Żukrowska, K. (ed.) *Transformation in Poland and in the Southern Mediterranean. Sharing experiences*. Warsaw: Poltext, pp. 60–80.

Visvizi, A. (2012) The Eurozone Crisis in Perspective: Causes and Implications. *Yearbook of the Institute of East-Central Europe* 10(5), pp. 13–32.

Visvizi, A. (2016) Book Review: Models of Capitalism in the European Union – Post-crisis Perspectives by Beáta Farkas. *Yearbook of the Institute of Central-Eastern Europe* 14(4), pp. 241–247.

Visvizi, A. (2017) *Querying the Migration-Populism Nexus: Poland and Greece in Focus*. IED Discussion Paper. July. Brussels: Institute of European Democrats (IED).

Visvizi, A., Lytras M. and Daniela, L. (2018) (Re)defining Smart Education: Toward Dynamic Education and Information Systems for Innovation Networks. In: Lytras, M., Daniela, L. and Visvizi, A. (eds) *Enhancing Knowledge Discovery and Innovation in the Digital Era*. Hershey, PA: IGI Global, pp. 1–12

World Bank (2016) *Bilateral Remittance Matrix, Brief: Migration Remittances Diaspora Issues*. [ONLINE] Available from: https://www.worldbank.org/en/topic/migrationremittancesdiasporaissues/brief/migration-remittances-data (accessed 7 October 2017).

World Bank (2017) *Ease of Doing Business Rankings*. Washington, D.C.: World Bank.

World Economic Forum (2017) *The Global Competitiveness Index 2017–2018 Edition*. Geneva: World Economic Forum.

Żukrowska, K. (2012) The Global Financial Crisis, the Eurozone Crises and Their Consequences for the Polish Economy. *Yearbook of the Institute of East-Central Europe (YIESW)* 10(5), pp. 45–62.

Żukrowska, K. (ed.) (2010) *Transformacja Systemowa w Polsce [Systemic transformation in Poland]*. Warsaw: Warsaw School of Economics Press.

5 Central European relations in turbulent times

Beáta Farkas

Introduction

Although the assessment of economic transition in the Central and Eastern European (CEE) post-communist EU member states varies in the literature[1], there is a common point which is generally accepted. There is an agreement that foreign direct investment (FDI) plays a unique role in the modernization of the economies of this region. The most successful example of this development model is the German–Central European supply chain.

Since their EU membership, Visegrád countries (V4: the Czech Republic, Hungary, Poland, and Slovakia) have been supporters of German economic policy in the EU. Poland, the Czech Republic and Slovakia followed disciplined fiscal policies. Hungary was placed under excessive deficit procedure between 2004 and 2013 but Hungarian governments were not theoretical opponents of strict fiscal policy even in this period. The support of V4 (and of the CEE countries) took on significance during the 2008 global crisis, more precisely during the euro zone crisis when a deep split between 'the North' and 'the South' appeared. Visegrád countries were interested in the stabilization of the euro zone and accepted German leadership. The strength of bilateral political relations was different, some tensions emerged. Examples were the relations with Russia, energy policy, cautious German criticism of the Hungarian (Orbán) government since 2010. Nevertheless, relations between Germany and the Visegrád group basically remained harmonious (Handl and Paterson 2013).

The migration crisis in Europe has broken these harmonious relations since 2015. Germany and Visegrád countries have followed completely different migration policy approaches. While Germany opened its border to migrants, the V4 aimed at keeping migrants outside of the EU, which has caused severe political tensions between them. Detailed analyses of migration issues are available in chapters 6 and 11 of this book. The Visegrád group, which has very mixed past experiences (Fawn 2013; Kiss 2015; Strážay 2014), has been strengthened and a common position has been formed on migration issues. Although the conflicts over migration policy and the relocation of migrants emerged at the level of European institutions, the Commission's proposals coincided with the German position and these conflicts implied political tensions between Germany and the V4. This situation raises the question whether the political tensions impair the economic relations.

In the Single Market, the possibility of state intervention is very limited. However, there are channels through which political relations influence economic cooperation. Companies assess the business environment before investment decisions and political stability is one of the most important criteria. If they are informed about political conflicts via the media, formal or informal political and public meetings, they can consider the business environment risky which deters them from investment.

Connection between political and economic relations is a significant issue because the idea that the V4 group could move from policy-taking to policy-shaping in the EU is now emerging outside of the literature (Schweiger 2016). In recent years both the Polish and the Hungarian prime ministers have definitely claimed a policy shaping role for V4.[2] The population size of V4 is substantial in European terms (approximately 64 million people) but their economic performance is lagging far behind that of Germany or France. Tensions about migration policy can be seen as a test to study whether economic dependency on German FDI constrains the policy shaping of V4. However, it is a difficult methodological task to grasp the connection between political and economic relations. The possible impacts of political debates on migration cannot be observed in the last available hard statistical data on trade relations and so I investigate the soft data of investors' climate surveys, which are available on the four countries. Furthermore, I focus on the Hungarian case because the policy followed by the Orbán government has provoked international conflicts since 2010 and the economic consequences of which can already be scrutinized. Besides using statistical data, I undertook interviews with officials from both the Hungarian Ministry of Foreign Affairs and Trade and the German-Hungarian Chamber of Industry and Commerce (DUIHK). Hungarian experiences highlight the mechanism of the interaction between political and economic relations, which may be instructive for the Visegrád group if it is aiming at a policy-shaping role.

In this chapter first the economic relations between Germany and Visegrád countries are analysed in order to assess the economic dependency/interdependency between them. This is followed by an assessment of the V4 position in the German external economic relations, which have recently moved from Europe to Asia. Special attention is paid to the Central European manufacturing core and German FDI inflows into the V4 after the 2008 global crisis. In the next section the Hungarian case is investigated. Finally, I draw conclusions about the outlook of Central European economic relations and the possible role of V4.

Trade relations

After a difficult decade of economic unification, Germany has become the engine for the European economic integration again during the 2008 global crisis (Foders and Vogelsang 2014). With the exception of Hungary, the Visegrád countries had not accumulated notable disequilibria prior to the crisis and they suffered from the smallest decline of growth rate among the CEE countries during the crisis (Farkas 2012). These processes resulted in raising interest in the research of the Central European region.

Germany has been a large trading partner for East Central Europe since the late nineteenth century. The origins of the current economic relationship with Visegrád countries date to the German *Ostpolitik* of the 1970s. Using the *détente* and the end of Cold War, Chancellor Willy Brandt normalized political relations with Germany's Eastern neighbours. The Ostpolitik paved the way for West German companies to move to the Eastern bloc. The 1970s were the period of economic stagnation after the extensive growth of socialist industrialization that induced the Soviet bloc to cooperate with Western partners. From 1968 to 1978 German trade with Poland, Hungary and Czechoslovakia nearly quadrupled. After the collapse of communist systems, the relationships changed qualitatively and in the 1990s German direct investment surged into the region. This FDI enabled German companies to incorporate East Central European subsidiaries into their production chain by the early 2000s (Gross 2013).

Germany has become the first export and import partners in each Visegrád country and Germany has accounted for 25 to 30 per cent of their exports and imports (German trade represents the largest share in the Czech Republic and the smallest one in Slovakia.). It is not surprising that the smaller and less developed countries are dependent on German economy but this dependency is mutual. Selecting the top three and some traditionally important trading partners, the outstanding role of V4 is remarkable (Figure 5.1).

Since the 2008 global crisis, the share of V4 in Germany's exports and imports has slightly increased measured in both volume and EUR (Figure 5.2).

The strong trade linkages reflect the integration of Visegrád countries into the German–Central European supply chain, which is indicated by the high

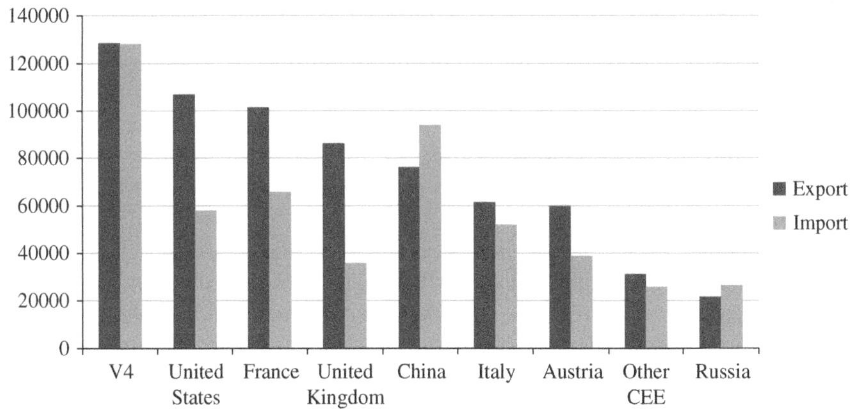

Figure 5.1 Germany's exports and imports with selected trading partners in 2016 (EUR million)

Source: Statistisches Bundesamt: Genesis-Online, own calculation.

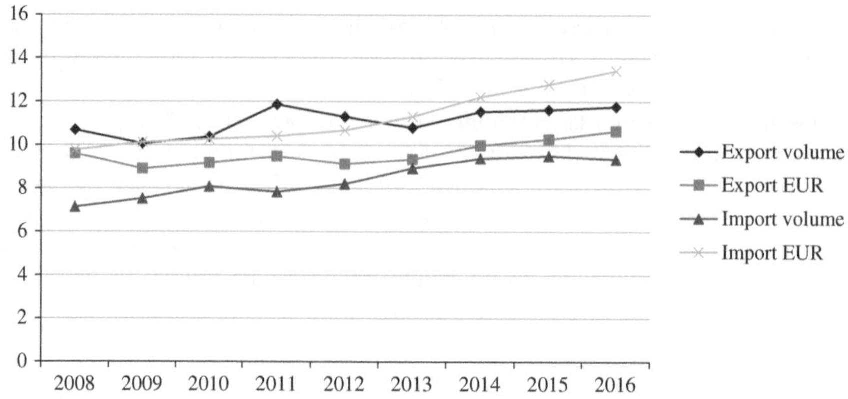

Figure 5.2 The share of V4 in Germany's exports and imports, 2008–2016
Source: Statistisches Bundesamt: Genesis-Online, own calculation.

prevalence of trade in intermediate goods (Elekdag and Muir 2013: 9). The embeddedness in this supply chain explains that since their EU accession in 2004 mutual trade of the V4 has expanded much faster than these countries' trade with the old EU members (Hunya and Richter 2011). In addition, one of the V4 countries has overtaken Austria and Italy among the most important export partners in each V4 country (Kopint-Tárki 2013).

The Central European manufacturing core

German FDI has played a crucial role in the modernization of manufacturing bases in V4 countries. In the early 2000s one quarter of German FDI went into manufacturing in which automotive industry has special importance. As a result, this region, next to China, has become the world's fastest growing automotive production location (Kőrösi 2014; Gross 2013).

The relative importance of their manufacturing is salient in the EU. Among the first eight countries, which have the largest share of value added in manufacturing, there are the V4 and Germany. Only two, Ireland and Italy, definitely do not belong to the Central European manufacturing core. The fourth country, Slovenia has also strong relations with German manufacturing.[3]

The manufacturing sector is a source of technological progress and an expected advantage of FDI inflows is that they promote technological transfer. The change of export structures and revealed comparative advantages (RCA) in manufacturing show that transformation in V4 countries complies with the expectation based on literature. Between 1995 and 2009 the RCA increased most substantially in the knowledge-intensive sector (Table 5.1). In the EU the share of advanced manufacturing value added to the Central European manufacturing core (including Austria) increased from 39.2 per cent to 47.2 per cent between 1995 and 2011 (Stehrer and Stöllinger 2015: 9).

Table 5.1 Revealed comparative advantage in manufacturing

	1995			*2009*		
	Labour-intensive	*Capital-intensive*	*Knowledge-intensive*	*Labour-intensive*	*Capital-intensive*	*Knowledge-intensive*
Germany	0.64	1.07	1.48	0.64	1.20	1.49
Czech Rep.	1.29	1.30	0.56	1.01	1.16	1.18
Hungary	0.68	1.06	0.50	0.37	0.77	1.18
Poland	1.95	1.39	0.59	1.52	1.39	0.93
Slovakia	1.05	1.61	0.60	1.16	1.41	1.11

Source: IMF 2013: 9.

Recently two research reports, an IMF Staff Report (IMF 2013) and the study of the Austrian Research Centre FIW (Forschungsschwerpunkt Internationale Wirtschaft) (Stehrer and Stöllinger 2015) thoroughly analysed the Central European supply chain. Both of them provide a very favourable picture on economic cooperation in the region.

The econometric model of IMF researchers suggests that – with the exemption of Hungary – V4 countries have grown more rapidly than can be explained by initial income. Presumably, the participation in the supply chain accelerated income convergence. As a significant part of the countries' exports are intermediate goods that are processed and re-exported by a third economy; V4 countries are not so vulnerable to domestic demand shocks in Germany as the data of traditional trade statistics indicate. Greater trade openness has increased the vulnerability of both Germany and V4 countries to global shocks (IMF 2013).

To assess the economic relations between Germany and V4 countries, the crucial point is the analysis of production sharing in the supply chain. The IMF Report does not highlight the different roles and positions in the supply chain and important aspects remain unrevealed. The in-depth analysis of the FIW study provides a more complex investigation. The participation in the global value chain (GVC) is defined as the sum of the foreign value added in a country's exports and the country's value-added contributions to other countries' exports, expressed as a percentage of gross exports. The V4 countries have very high rankings in GVC participation rate (Slovakia 2nd, the Czech Republic 3rd, Hungary 5th and Poland 9th). The low ranking of Germany (23rd in the EU-27) is due to the size of economy. The important difference is that the foreign value-added content in domestic exports contributes to a larger extent to the GVC participation in V4 countries not only in Germany but in Austria, which is also a member of the Central European manufacturing core (Figure 5.3). Their econometric model strengthens the well-known fact that relatively lower wages and geographic proximity to Germany foster production integration. The Central European supply chain is driven by the activities of leading German companies. However, the country size does not determine the

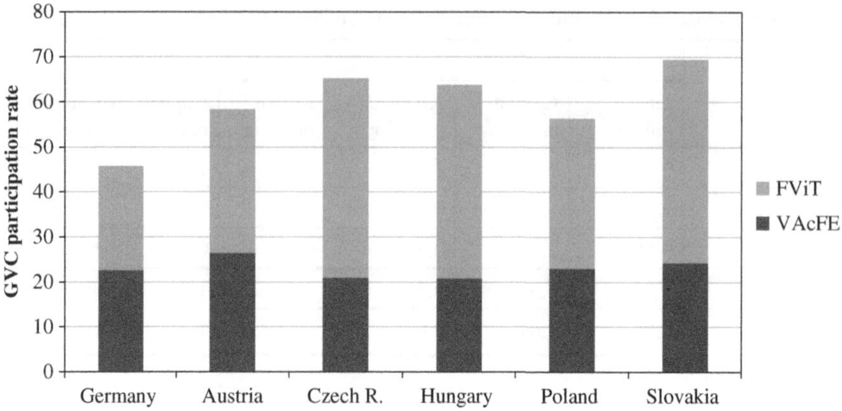

Figure 5.3 Manufacturing exports value added supplied by manufacturing industries in the Central European manufacturing core, 2011

Note: FVAiT = foreign value added in trade; VAcFE = value added contributions to foreign exports; GVC participation rate = the sum of the foreign value added in a country's exports and the country's value added contributions to other countries' exports, expressed as a percentage of gross exports.

Source: own construction based on Stehrer and Stöllinger 2015: 19.

role in the production integration. Austria does not have a leading role. Nevertheless it is not an offshoring destination like V4 countries but a supplier of specialised inputs, a technology provider, like Germany (Stehrer and Stöllinger 2015).[4]

German FDI inflows into V4 after the 2008 global crisis

Since the global crisis new features of FDI have emerged in CEE. FDI inflows fluctuation has become extremely volatile and there is no close connection with economic growth or changes in business environment. Capital reserves, profits and losses are moving within multinational companies in various forms of FDI. Tax optimisation seems to be more important in the choice of a host country than it was prior to the crisis. FDI inflows have become much smaller than they were before the crisis and they did not increase even in the global FDI upturn in 2015 (Hunya and Schwarzhappel 2016).

In these turbulent years, Germany remained an important investor in CEE. Contrary to the Eurozone, the German outward stock has increased in absolute terms in both the CEE-11 countries and the V4. In relative terms, the share of European countries has decreased in every grouping with the exemption of some individual countries (e.g. Poland, Romania). From 2012–2015 the share of V4 in the total German outward stock accounted for approximately 7.5 per cent (Table 5.2).

Germany is one of the major partners among the home countries of FDI in the V4: the third in Czech Republic, the first in Hungary, the second in Poland and

Table 5.2 German FDI outward stock in Europe, 2010, 2012–2015 (consolidated data)

	EUR million				*% of total*			
	2012	2013	2014	2015	2012	2013	2014	2015
All countries	925.912	916.820	984.192	1.034.082	100	100	100	100
Europa	491.804	495.273	483.126	507.112	53.12	54.02	49.09	49.04
EU Members	410.048	416.016	408.609	429.842	44.29	45.38	41.52	41.57
Eurozone	200.799	199.312	179.638	193.897	21.69	21.74	18.25	18.75
CEE-11	84.344	82.732	89.169	93.624	9.11	9.02	9.06	9.05
Estonia	268	242	245	198	0.03	0.03	0.02	0.02
Latvia	472	518	519	534	0.05	0.06	0.05	0.05
Lithuania	967	1.098	918	1.056	0.10	0.12	0.09	0.10
Bulgaria	2.709	2.748	2.610	2.678	0.29	0.3	0.27	0.26
Croatia	2.520	2.449	2.552	2.631	0.27	0.27	0.26	0.25
Romania	6.773	6.871	7.465	7.925	0.73	0.75	0.76	0.77
Slovenia	1.159	1.243	1.576	1.753	0.13	0.14	0.16	0.17
Poland	23.636	24.353	25.782	28.069	2.55	2.66	2.62	2.71
Hungary	14.769	14.794	14.760	14.942	1.60	1.61	1.50	1.44
Slovakia	7.781	7.637	7.762	7.468	0.84	0.83	0.79	0.72
Czech Republic	23.290	20.779	24.980	26.370	2.52	2.27	2.54	2.55
V4	69.476	67.563	73.284	76.849	7.5	7.37	7.45	7.43
Non-EU European countries	81.756	79.257	74.517	77.270	8.83	8.64	7.57	7.47

Source: Deutsche Bundesbank 2017, own calculation.Note: EU members including Croatia since 2013, Eurozone: including Latvia since 2014.

the fifth in Slovakia. German FDI stock in these countries amounted to between 6.7 and 23 per cent of their total FDI inward stock in 2014 (Table 5.3). The substantial data differences between Table 5.2 and 5.3 indicate the difficulties of research in this field. Beyond methodological issues the reason for differences may be that, while Bundesbank relies on the reports of German companies and persons, Hunya and Schwarzhappel (2016) collect data from national banks.

The latest statistical data are available from 2015 and they testify to the relative stable position of V4 in German FDI outward stock since the global crisis as well. The possible consequences of political tensions triggered by the migration in 2015 cannot be reflected in them. However, the German Chamber of Commerce Abroad has conducted a survey among their members in EU and non-EU Central and Eastern European countries since 2006. The managers and investors assess 20 CEE countries from one to six by their attractiveness for

Table 5.3 Inward FDI stock in Visegrád countries from Germany in EUR (million) and the share of Germany in their total inward FDI stock

	2011	*2012*	*2013*	*2014*	*2011*	*2012*	*2013*	*2014*
	EUR million				*% of total*			
Poland	21.482	26.898	28.115	27.979	13.7	15.1	16.7	16.3
Hungary	19.371	19.500	19.076	18.710	29.3	24.7	24.2	23.0
Czech Rep.	13.906	14.533	10.978	12.600	14.9	14.0	11.3	12.6
Slovakia	4.459	4.511	3.284	2.877	11.1	10.8	7.8	6.7

Source: Hunya and Schwarzhappel 2016: 81, 89, 101, 109.

investment. The assessment of their own country is not taken into consideration and the countries are ranked by the assessment. Apart from the volatile ranking of Hungary, the other three Visegrád countries have retained the first three places and the position of Hungary has also been stable in recent years (Figure 5.4).

From the V4 viewpoint, the development perspectives of the current production sharing depend on the opportunity of upgrading in the GVC. Based on a very thorough literature review, Sass and Szalavetz (2014: 65) summarize the 2008 global crisis related changes in GVCs:

> The consequence for advanced countries is greater specialization in the activities requiring higher skills at the two ends of the GVC, while reliance on less-advanced countries with lower wages in the 'middle' of the GVCs has grown more robust.

Although there are successful examples of upgrading (Szalavetz 2016), the literature suggests that the opportunity of upgrading in GVC is a difficult,

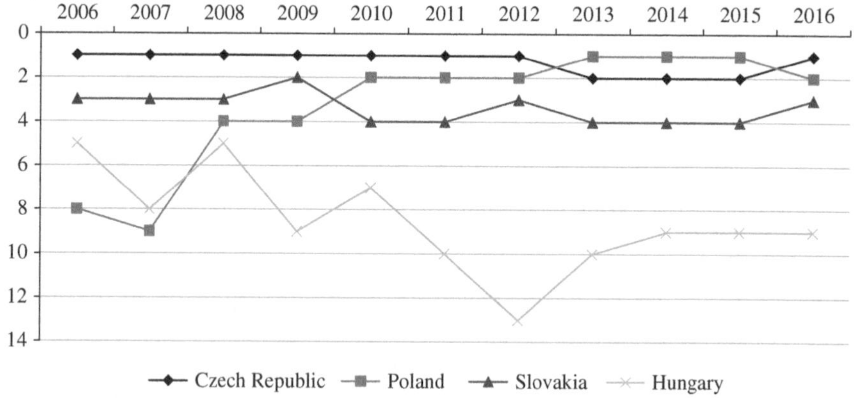

Figure 5.4 Investment attractiveness: ranking of the V4 countries in Central and Eastern Europe

Source: own construction based on DUIHK 2017: 53.

complex task in V4 countries (e.g. Capik and Drahokoupil 2011; Filippov 2014; Rugraff and Hansen 2011).[5] In relations with Germany, the trade structure in V4 concentrates on transport equipment and machinery. The share of transport equipment in German export is between 10 and 17 per cent; and 12 and 34 per cent in German import in V4 countries. Together with machinery, the data range from 38 to 70 per cent and trade structure between Poland and Germany is the most diversified.[6] This concentration poses a risk of instability in V4 economic development. However, the coming technological changes (electric cars, digitalization and robotic technology) may bring even more severe challenges. The attractiveness of low wages will depreciate. For example, the Hungarian government must potentially manage with the loss of between 300,000 and 400,000 jobs due to digitalization. At the same time these changes mean new opportunities for the desired upgrading in GVC. The shortage of engineers and IT specialists in Germany strengthens the companies' willingness to relocate jobs with higher technological skills.

However, the V4 countries also experience a shortage in skilled employees. The latest PISA report, which measures 15-year-old students' knowledge and skills, projects better chances for Poland than for Hungary and Slovakia in technological adaptation (Figure 5.5).

The Hungarian case

In 2010 the Hungarian economy was at the beginning of consolidation when the right-wing party, Fidesz was elected by a two-thirds majority. The Orbán government continued its crisis management but used an 'unorthodox' economic policy toolkit. Several measures were harmful for foreign investors. For example, the government imposed special taxes on those sectors of the

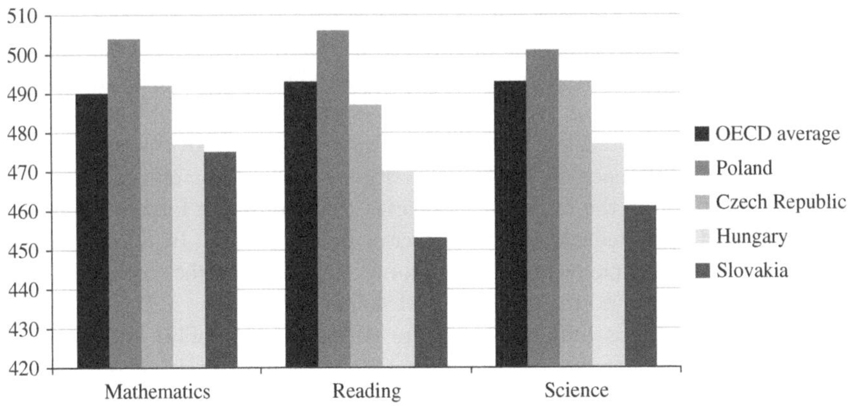

Figure 5.5 Students' average scholastic performance in V4 countries based on the 2015 PISA report

Source: own construction based on OECD 2016: 5.

economy that were mainly in foreign ownership. It intends to increase state ownership in those fields considered to be of strategic importance (primarily the energy sector, public utilities and the banking sector). In order to achieve this aim, the government would go to any lengths, and it does not hesitate to make financial sacrifices or to come into conflict with foreign owners. Furthermore, the government handles FDI in a selective manner and concludes strategic agreements with those industrial companies that it considers economically desirable.[7]

Despite the hectic years, bilateral trade with Germany has increased.[8] Although German FDI stock has decreased somewhat, it is very difficult to identify a trend due to data uncertainty (cf. Tables 5.2 and 5.3). In addition, firstly in 2016, the Hungarian National Bank published data on FDI by non-residents in Hungary broken down not only by the country of the direct investor, but also that of the ultimate investor. It highlights that more than 40 per cent of FDI arrived in Hungary via transit countries. While the FDI stock of the Netherlands and Luxembourg dramatically diminished in this breakdown, German FDI stock grew from €18.721 million to €21.446 million in 2014.[9]

Hungary's investment attractiveness reflects much better the changing circumstances in economic policy. The political instability following the unexpected austerity measures in 2006, the deep financial crisis in 2008 and the crisis management after 2010 provoked a large decline in attractiveness for investors (Figure 5.4). Both the Hungarian officials and the representatives of the German-Hungarian Chamber of Industry and Commerce agree that the subsidiaries of multinational companies, which are already incumbent in Hungary, make their decisions by their own experiences and their company's performance. A disadvantageous image of Hungary in international media deters new entries, mainly among small and medium sized enterprises. If the economic outlook is appropriate, personal motivation can outweigh the unfavourable political appraisal, e.g. if ancestors lived in Hungary as a member of a German minority, or a family member spent years at a Hungarian university. This personal network at grassroots level is not negligible.

The dominant role of economic interests is underpinned by the fact that the largest regional German partners for Hungary like the regions of Bavaria, Baden-Württemberg and North Rhine-Westphalia are ruled by centre-right (CDU and CSU) and left (social democratic and green) governments, which have no special influence on economic relations. It must be emphasized because there is an illusion in the circles of Hungarian opposition that foreign capital will 'punish' the Orbán regime and will force a policy change. In the opinion of businessmen, the attractiveness of economy depends on the competitiveness ranking of Hungary and the availability of skilled staff.

The government is fully aware of the dependence on FDI and strives to improve the relations with selected multinationals, especially in manufacturing. In his policies, the prime minister keeps a cautious balance between economic rationale and populist rhetoric and measures. There is no significant domestic pressure on the Orbán government to change its policy in migration issues[10] and the positions of pro-immigration politicians have been weakening in many

European countries. The call for solidarity issued by Western partners has no wider social echo. The support of EU Funds is not regarded as a gesture of solidarity, which would oblige for adapting proposals on either migration or any other policy fields. The EU support is considered as compensation for the extra high profits which were earned by the multinational companies prior to the global crisis.[11]

The Orbán government used one-off opportunities (e.g. surtaxes on special sectors, nationalization of compulsory private pension funds, high level of EU Funds and improving terms of trade due to low commodity prices) to consolidate the economy without direct and general austerity measures. Macroeconomic stability enables Hungary to maintain a separate path in the European political arena. The government is fully aware that growth driven by one-off factors should turn into growth driven by improving competitiveness and technological progress. Here is the Achilles heel of Orbán's system. The extremely centralized, power-centred management in every sphere of the society promotes rent-seeking rather than innovation, creativity and fair competition. The recent political conflicts concerning the 'Stop Brussels!' campaign, the laws on Central European University and NGOs generated very wide international and European protest[12] and frightened away even the right-wing Hungarian intelligentsia from the ruling party. However, the government assesses that these conflicts strengthen its position among the voters and will help them to win the election in 2018.

In Poland a new government, which follows similar economic and social policies, was elected in 2015 and the role of the state has strengthened. For example, in January 2017 a reform was carried out on state-owned enterprises (SOE) governance to increase the role of SOEs. Share of government-controlled banks in bank assets grew from around 16 per cent in 2010 to 36 per cent in 2016 (European Commission 2017b). It is still an open question, whether the Law and Justice party will be able to maintain political power in the next election and to achieve deep political and economic changes, such as Fidesz in Hungary could.

Although there are populist phenomena in both Czech and Slovak political life, there are no signs of a similar economic policy turn as has occurred in Hungary and Poland (European Commission 2017a, 2017c). Both the Czech and Slovak governments seem to be more cautious about getting into conflicts with the European Commission than Hungary and Poland. In the ongoing debate on the future of the EU, Slovak prime minister, Fico declared: 'The eurozone should be even more united internally and Slovakia wants to be part of its core.'[13] According to the chief editor of Lidové noviny (a right-wing daily) the Czechs consider themselves as a member of the core countries and they consider Hungary, Slovakia and Poland as peripheral EU countries (G. Fehér 2017b). Neither their economic performance, nor their institutional arrangement supports that these two countries belong to core EU countries (Farkas 2016). Both are in asymmetric interdependency with North Western core countries especially with Germany as the above mentioned analysis of global value chain indicates. However, their self-perception may hinder their readiness for V4 cooperation. In addition, the political isolation of Hungary and Poland in the EU may be discouraging.

Conclusion

Although economies in the EU were severely hit by the 2008 global crisis, the development of the Central European manufacturing core has not come to a halt. The V4 countries have remained important trade partners for Germany, partly due to their participation in the Central European supply chain driven by German companies. It is obvious that V4 countries are dependent on German FDI, even if the degree of dependence is different according to the size of their economy. However, the share of V4 in German external economic relations has reached the level that dependency of V4 countries has turned into an asymmetric but mutual dependency. This interdependency is the reason that economic relations seem to be quite resistant to political turbulences. The sign of stability is that the Council of Economic Experts, which is an academic economic advisory body of the highest level in Germany, pays no attention to V4 economies in its Annual Economic Report 2016–17. They map the crucial issues, problems at both domestic and international level and the V4 Group is not on the list. Poland is the only country which is mentioned in a potentially new role. While Schweiger (2014) has already forecast the increasing role of Poland prior to the Brexit referendum, the Council of Economic Experts now proposes that Poland could be a substitute for the United Kingdom in forming the blocking minority of countries which follow liberal economic policy (Sachverständigenrat 2016).

The Hungarian case indicates that using favourable opportunities, a small country can create room for maneuverers. This experience may be promising for the V4 but apart from migration policy, the V4 (and the CEE) countries have limited negotiating influence in the EU (Copeland 2014). However, European integration will definitely be transformed and many challenges affect the V4 countries similarly: e.g. the issues of budget after Brexit, the idea of multispeed integration, the above mentioned technological changes (digitalization, robotic technologies) and sharpening competition for qualified, skilled labour etc. If the V4 is able to move beyond the migration agenda and develop common positions in other decisive topics, there is a chance it can play a more active role in EU policy making. However, due to sharpening conflicts, the isolation of Hungary and Poland on the EU political scene may reach a degree which undermines the willingness of the Czech Republic and Slovakia to widen V4 cooperation.

Acknowledgement

I am very grateful to Martin A. Dale (President & CEO of Siemens Zrt., President of DUIHK German-Hungarian Chamber of Industry and Commerce), Dirk

Wölfer (Head of Communication German-Hungarian Chamber of Industry and Commerce) and Zsolt Bóta (Head of Department, Hungarian Ministry of Foreign Affairs and Trade) for their assistance.

Notes

1 See the literature review: Farkas 2016.
2 http://www.portfolio.hu/gazdasag/orban_engedelyt_kaptunk_a_legmagasabb_vilagi_helyrol.242903.html and G. Fehér (2017a).
3 Eurostat online database.
4 On the political aspects of core-periphery relations see Ágh (2016).
5 On the broader context of Polish economic policy see Visvizi and Tokarski (2014) and on recent developments see Tokarski and Visvizi (2015).
6 Statistisches Bundesamt https://www-genesis.destatis.de/genesis/online.
7 More details on economic background see Farkas (2016).
8 Statistisches Bundesamt https://www-genesis.destatis.de/genesis/online.
9 http://www.mnb.hu/statisztika/statisztikai-adatok-informaciok/adatok-idosorok/viii-fizetesi-merleg-kozvetlen-tokebefektetesek-kulfolddel-szembeni-allomanyok/kozvetlentoke-befektetesek/bpm6-modszertan-szerinti-adatok.
10 The Orbán government will not give up its stance not only because of its popularity in the majority of voters. There is a real fear that the integration of refugees/migrants would fail such as the efforts of Roma integration essentially have failed since the systemic change so far.
11 Kőrösi (2014) estimates the net profit rate of foreign companies at 7 to 8 per cent in Hungary prior to the crisis, contrary to the 2 to 2.5 per cent in the manufacturing firms of EU-15.
12 http://www.euronews.com/2017/04/27/council-of-europe-urges-hungary-to-suspend-laws-on-ngos-universities
13 https://newsnow.tasr.sk/foreign/fico-eurozone-should-be-closer-knit-slovakia-aims-to-be-in-its-core/

References

Ágh, A. (2016) The Core-Periphery Divide in the EU Transformation Crisis: Challenge of the Visegrád Forum. *Yearbook of The Institute of East-Central Europe* 14(2), pp. 113–130.

Capik, P. and Drahokoupil, J. (2011) Foreign Direct Investments in Business Services: Transforming the Visegrád Four Region into a Knowledge-based Economy? *European Planning Studies* 19(9), pp. 1611–1631.

Copeland, P. (2014) Central and Eastern Europe: Negotiating Influence in an Enlarged European Union. *Europe-Asia Studies* 66(3), pp. 467–487.

Deutsche Bundesbank (2017) *Bestandserhebung über Direktinvestitionen*. Frankfurt am Main.

DUIHK (2017) Konjunktúrajelentés 2017. Budapest: Német-Magyar Ipari és Kereskedelmi Kamara. [Online] Available from: https://www.ahkungarn.hu/fileadmin/AHK_Ungarn/Dokumente/Publikationen/Konjunkturbericht/KB_2016_hu_FINAL_low.pdf (accessed 21 July 2017).

Elekdag, S. and D. Muir (2013) Trade Linkages, Balance Sheets, and Spillovers: The Germany-Central European Supply Chain. IMF Working Paper, WP/13(210). [Online] Available at: https://www.imf.org/en/Publications/WP/Issues/2016/12/31/Trade-Linkages-Balance-Sheets-and-Spillovers-The-Germany-Central-European-Supply-Chain-40987 (accessed 21 July 2017).

European Commission (2017a) *Country Report Czech Republic 2017*. Brussels, SWD69 final.

European Commission (2017b) *Country Report Poland 2017*. Brussels, SWD 86 final.

European Commission (2017c) *Country Report Slovakia 2017*. Brussels, SWD 90 final/2.

Farkas, B. (2012) The Impact of the Global Economic Crisis in the Old and New Cohesion Member States of the European Union. *Public Finance Quarterly* 57(1), pp. 53–70.

Farkas, B. (2016) *Models of Capitalism in the European Union – Post-crisis Perspectives*. Basingstoke, New York: Palgrave Macmillan.

Fawn, R. (2013) Visegrád: Fit for purpose? *Communist and Post-Communist Studies* 46(3), pp. 339–349.

Filippov, S. (2014) Knowledge-Sharing Subsidiaries in Central and Eastern Europe. *Europe-Asia Studies* 66(9), pp. 1553–1571.

Foders, F. and Vogelsang, M.M. (2014) *Why is Germany's Manufacturing Industry so Competitive?* Kiel Policy Brief No. 69. [Online]. Available at: https://www.files.ethz.ch/ isn/176658/KPB_69.pdf (accessed 21 July 2017).

G. Fehér, P. (2017a) Ellensúlyt Brüsszelnek! Jarosław Kaczyński exluzív interjúja. *Heti Válasz* 17(1–2), pp. 20–23.

G. Fehér, P. (2017b) Távolodóban Magyarországtól. *Heti Válasz* 17(23), pp. 26–28.

Gross, S. (2013) The German Economy and East-Central Europe. The Development of Intra-Industry Trade from Ostpolitik to the Present. *German Politics and Society* 31(3), pp. 83–105.

Handl, V. and Paterson, W.E. (2013) The Continuing Relevance of Germany's Engine for CEE and the EU. *Communist and Post-Communist Studies* 46(3), pp. 327–337.

Hunya, G. and M. Schwarzhappel (2016) *FDI in Central, East and Southeast Europe: Slump Despite Global Upturn. WIIW FDI Report 2016*. Wien: The Vienna Institute for International Economic Studies.

Hunya, G. and S. Richter (2011) Mutual Trade and Investment of the Visegrád Countries before and after their EU Accession. *Eastern Journal of European Studies* 2(2), p. 77–91.

IMF (2013) German-Central European Supply Chain – Cluster Report. IMF Country Report No. 13/263. [Online]. Available at: https://www.imf.org/en/Publications/CR/Issues/2016/12/31/German-Central-European-Supply-Chain-Cluster-Report-Staff-Report-First-Background-Note-40881 (accessed 21 July 2017).

Kiss, J. (2015) Prospects of the Visegrád Cooperation in Changing Economic, Political and Social Conditions: Identifying Converging and Diverging Factors. In: G. Túry (ed.) *Prospects of the Visegrád Cooperation: Identifying Converging and Diverging Factors*. Budapest: Institute of World Economics, Centre for Economic and Regional Studies, Hungarian Academy of Sciences, pp. 329–367.

Kopint-Tárki (2013) *A német gazdaság szerepe a magyar gazdaság teljesítményében: A németgazdaság helyzete, jellemzői és kilátásai, és a magyar gazdaság növekedésére való hatásai*. Budapest: Költségvetési Tanács Titkársága.

Kőrösi, I. (2014) Wächst Mitteleuropa zusammen? Das wiedervereinigte Deutschland und Ostmitteleuropa als Wirtschaftspartner. Kritische Zeiten. *Zeitschrift für Humanwissenschaften* 5(1–2), pp. 62–74.

OECD (2016) *PISA 2015 Results in Focus*. Paris: OECD.

Rugraff, E. and M.W. Hansen (eds) (2011) *Multinational Corporations and Local Firms in Emerging Economies*. Amsterdam: Amsterdam University Press.

Sachverständigenrat (2016) *Zeit für Reformen. Jahresgutachten 2016–17*. Wiesbaden: Statistisches Bundesamt.

Sass, M. and A. Szalavetz (2014) Crisis-related Changes in the Specialization of Advanced Economies in Global Value Chains. *Competition and Change* 18(1), pp. 54–69.

Schweiger, C. (2014) Poland, Variable Geometry and the Enlarged European Union. *Europe-Asia Studies* 66(3), pp. 394–420.

Schweiger, C. (2016) The CEE Countries' First Decade of EU Membership: From Policy-takers Towards Agenda-setters? *Problemy polityki społecznej – Problems of Social Policy* 31(4), pp. 99–118.

Statistisches Bundesamt (2015) *Statistisches Jahrbuch 2015*. Wiesbaden.

Stehrer, R. and R. Stöllinger (2015) *The Central European Manufacturing Core: What is Driving Regional Production Sharing?* FIW-Research Reports 2014/15 No. 2. [Online] Available at: http://www.fiw.ac.at/fileadmin/Documents/Publikationen/Studien_2014/02_Stoellinger_FIW%20Research%20Report_The%20Central%20European%20Manufacturing%20Core%20What%20is%20Driving%20Regional%20Production%20Sharing.pdf (accessed 21 July 2017).

Strážay, T. (2014) Neither Beautiful nor Ugly, but Functional: A Pragmatic View on the Visegrád Group. *Contemporary European Studies* 9(2), pp. 37–47.

Szalavetz, A. (2016) Global Crisis and Upgrading of MNCs' Manufacturing Subsidiaries: A Case Study of Hungary. *Central European Business Review* 5(1), pp. 37–44.

Tokarski, P. and A. Visvizi (2015) Poland's Winding Road to the Eurozone: From a Cost-Benefit Stance to Risk Aversion. *The Polish Quarterly of International Affairs* 24(3), pp. 65–84.

Visvizi, A. and P. Tokarski (2014) Poland and the Euro: Between Lock-in and Unfinished Transition. *Society and Economy* 36(4), pp. 445–468.

Part II

National perspectives: between *good citizenship* and *backsliding*

6 European Union at the crossroads

Which route will Poland take?

Maciej Duszczyk

Introduction

The year 2015 brought about fundamental changes on the Polish political stage. The coalition of a liberal-democratic party (the Civic Platform) and a peasant party (the Polish People's Party), ruling uninterruptedly for eight years, was replaced by a Christian-conservative party (Law and Justice,[1] PiS). A few months earlier Andrzej Duda, a candidate supported by the Law and Justice party, had been elected to the office of the President of the Republic of Poland. Consequently, since November 2015, and for the first time since 1989, Poland has had a single-party government, additionally enjoying the support of the President. The forthcoming 2018 local level administration elections will presumably be an easy win for PiS, allowing the ruling party to make any changes it desires and put forward the positions of its choice in the debates taking place in the European Union (EU). It seems that the sole purpose of many actions, e.g. those under social policy or changes in electoral law, is to win local elections and consequently to gain full power, allowing the ruling party to disregard the opposition.

Simultaneously, 2015 and 2016 were the years of turbulence in the functioning of the EU. The inflow of refugees and migrants from states torn with armed conflicts, who were joined by economic migrants, caused a crisis related to decision-making and the implementation process, and a significant decline of trust amongst member states. Moreover, in contrast to prior forecasts, UK citizens voted against staying in the EU, aggravating even more the already difficult situation of the Union. On top of those developments, one can add the uncertainty of relations between Turkey and the EU, as well as uncertainty with regard to foreign policies of Donald Trump – the new US President. The uncertainty concerns in particular the place of the EU in those policies. There still seems to be a danger that Donald Trump will be more interested in weakening rather than strengthening of the EU. Therefore, the assertion that the EU is at a crossroads can be very easily defended.

As a gross oversimplification, the ways in question can be defined as follows. One of them leads to the loosening of the European integration process and the restriction of the subsidiarity principle, i.e. a return to making many decisions at the national level and a greater competition between the member states. Hence, under such a model the EU functions as a community of powerful nation states with a reduced role for its institutions. The second road translates into continuation of the integration of the member states by extending integration onto successive areas of actions and increased significance of the European Parliament and the European Council accompanied by leaving the decision-making powers at the level of the Council of the European Union. Consequently, the European Commission (EC) would remain the major executive body of the Community. Therefore, that model might be termed as a community of enhanced cooperation with powerful EU institutions. As a generalisation those two contradicting models define for us the two-speed EU, i.e. one divided into two camps. One camp represents the co-existence of states interested in transferring sovereignty to the EU level and comprising the so-called hard core. The other camp represents those that limit their membership only to selected integration areas. It is certainly justifiable to ponder on whether there is some other option being the third route for European integration. Unfortunately, it has not been defined yet, and the source literature is based largely on analyses of the two integration models described above. The main question this paper tries to answer is which of them Poland is going to opt for in the coming years and how relevant this will be for the EU. Will this be a route towards loosening of integration or rather a search for opportunities to become part of the hard core, where central decisions will be made; or perhaps Poland will try to propose some third route offering exit from the apparently unavoidable conflict. To answer this question, an analysis will be performed of the positions of the previous and present Polish government related to major challenges Europe has been facing in recent years in the field of European integration. We will also invoke statistical data and selected results of public opinion surveys. The analysis made in this paper is largely based on statements by government officials, which have been published and approved by both the websites of government institutions and the media.

Poland's membership in the EU: a balance of challenges and benefits

When acceding to the European Union with seven other Central and Eastern European countries (CEEs) in 2004, Poland expected both economic and political benefits. Thirteen years after the accession one can assert that both have been accomplished. As an example, in the end of 2016 the level of unemployment was less than 6 per cent compared to over 20 per cent in 2004 (GUS 2016) and it was much lower than EU average. Despite economic crisis, Poland has also recorded a constant year-on-year economic growth and has largely narrowed the gap separating it from the best-developed MS of the Community. What also matters a lot, for the first time since 2004 at the end of 2015 the risk of poverty or social exclusion indicator in Poland was below the

EU average. As concerns political position, transition of Poland into the group of states deciding about the functioning of the EU is evidenced among others by the election of Jerzy Buzek to the position of the President of the European Parliament[2] and of Donald Tusk to the position of the President of the European Council[3]. This has allowed for formulation of a thesis that Poland moved from the periphery to the core of decision-making process in the European Union (Duszczyk 2016; Schweiger 2015). Such a thesis is upheld by the sustained high social support for Poland's membership of the EU, one of the highest in the community. As an example, in April 2016 support for Poland's presence in the EU was declared by 85 per cent of the respondents. Opponents of membership corresponded to nine per cent of Polish society (CBOS 2016). Based on objective indicators, one can unambiguously state that Poland has derived undisputable benefits from membership in the EU, becoming one of its biggest beneficiaries in history.

Since accession to the EU, Poland has pursued a very consistent European policy. It can be summarized in a single statement – the more European integration there is, the better it is for Poland. Certainly, this was not tantamount to consent for all ideas of Brussels. As an example, all governments opposed imposition of too stringent norms related to carbon dioxide emission reduction or restriction of single market principles. This does not change the fact, however, that until 2015 Poland had pursued an unambigously pro-European policy. Two arguments can be highlighted in this context: the belief that on the one hand this is the only option for Poland to have a real share in the decision-making process, and to secure itself against threats coming from renewed imperialistic tendencies of 'Putin's Russia' on the other. The European policy of the previous government was probably most clearly summarised by the minister of foreign affairs, Radosław Sikorski, in his famous and widely commented speech in Berlin (Sikorski 2011). He contrasted two visions of the future of the EU, i.e. an integrational and disintegrational one and asserted that the latter would be the biggest threat for Poland. Moreover, he called on Germany as the biggest member state to assume greater responsibility for the future of the continent and declared that Poland would do anything to support Germany in drafting a new treaty aimed to deepen the integration. Therefore one can state with some generalisation that in his speech, the Polish minister of foreign affairs defined one key issue. He supported further European integration, including rescuing the euro and Schengen zone, and named Germany as the core ally in this ambition. This position had not changed fundamentally until the presidential and parliamentary elections that took place in 2015, resulting in a change of president and government. The new government, which took office in November 2015, was forced virtually at once to present its position related to the refugee crisis and the British referendum. A shift in the emphasis of the Polish European policy was already visible in the opening statement of PM Beata Szydło and of particular government members. As an example, Beata Szydło in her first speech delivered in the Parliament stated that:

> We value everything afforded to us by membership in the European Union. Therefore, we will strive to improve the effectiveness of the activities of the Union. To achieve full compliance with European law and the rules underlying the process of Europe's unification. We are convinced that departure from them brings harm to the EU as a whole and each state belonging to the Union individually. Regardless of its present-day situation.
> (Szydło 2015)

In his opening statement Witold Waszczykowski, the minister of foreign affairs, spoke much more emphatically about the necessity of EU reforms towards restoring the significance of nation states. It is true that in his speech there was a sentence that could be endorsed by members of the previous government. He stated that

> Poland is a beneficiary of European unity. The cracks that emerged in the design successfully built for several dozen years, are an undesirable and dangerous phenomenon. We want to create a Union of free nations and equal states, solidary and competitive in economic terms, enjoying authority in the world. However, we think that the road towards this goal does not lead through two-speed Europe, tightening of economic and political cooperation by Eurozone states.
> (Waszczykowski 2016)

At the same time in another place he stated that:

> The European Union should return to its roots, to four fundamental freedoms, governing movement of people, services, goods and capital. Supporters of close integration of the Eurozone want coordination of economic governance and – in fact – of political one. One can be sometimes under an impression that the idea of ever closer union is treated as a method of forward escape. As if someone wanted to conceal mistakes made in connection with the single currency, and recently also with the migration crisis
> (Waszczykowski 2016)

In such context it can be reiterated that the above example demonstrates the willingness to reverse the existing direction of the European integration process, consistent with a search for increasingly newer areas of enhanced cooperation aimed at restoring the significance of nation states and restricting the subsidiarity rules within the EU.

The refugee crisis as a catalyst of the changes of Poland's European policy

Virtually since the onset of the functioning of the new Polish government, there has been an escalation of tension with European institutions. The climax took place during attempts to establish a joint European system of responding to inflow of refugees and other migrants. However, it is difficult to blame conflict escalation only on the government of Poland, which clearly opposed the ideas put forward by the EU. Proposals related to mandatory relocation of foreigners or imposition of financial penalties on the states refusing to receive refugees in their territories did not help to achieve a compromise and were rather purely political. The reactions of the governments of Poland and other CEE countries to such proposals were easily predictable. At the same time, the conflict between Poland and European institutions started earlier and was related to changes being introduced in judicature. Actions aimed against the Constitutional Tribunal led to Poland being called upon to explain its position before the European Parliament (EP). This took place on 19 January 2016 during a debate on observance of the democratic foundations in Poland.[4] During the debate prime minister Beata Szydło categorically denied accusations of violating democratic rights and declared her willingness to cooperate towards strengthening the EU, but on the basis of the principle of a community of nation states. This was the first signal expressed in the European arena that the vision of the previous government was not shared and that Poland would change its position in that respect. However, a decisive polarization of views took place in connection with the refugee crisis. It seems that the debate about ways to resolve the EU crisis caused by inflow of refugees was used by the new Polish government to demonstrate the weakness of the Community and to reveal the mistakes made by the EU institutions. One has to be aware that many of those accusations were very justified. At the same time, however, the decision-making chaos that affected the EU in the end of 2015 and 2016 was unambiguously used by the government to force its own vision of further European integration.

Despite many objections related to the soundness and effectiveness of the solution regarding relocation of refugees between member states, the previous Polish government agreed to receive 2,000 and then another 5,082 refugees from camps in Greece, Italy and Lebanon. The decision was criticised by the then opposition, mainly by the President of Law and Justice party, Jarosław Kaczyński.[5] Even before the new government had taken over power, the scepticism towards the proposal of the EC related to the resolution of the refugee crisis was expressed by Prime Minister Beata Szydło stating:

> We are ready to provide humanitarian aid, to allocate funds for assistance to those who need such humanitarian aid, but we are critical about receiving immigrants in Poland.
>
> (Szydło 2015a).

At the same time during the aforementioned debate in the EP, to the amazement of the observers, she confirmed that Poland would nevertheless deliver on the commitment of the previous government related to receiving seven thousand refugees. However, this position swiftly changed, with terrorist attacks in Paris and Brussels used as a pretext. On 23 March 2016 prime minister Beata Szydło stated in an interview for a television station that:

> in view of the present terrorist threat related to people of Islamic denomination I do not see the possibility to receive migrants in Poland at the moment.
>
> (Szydło 2016)

Since that time Poland's position has not changed and all preparations to receive refugees were put on hold.

The data presenting the scale of immigrants' inflow into the EU show that Poland remains on the margins of the main migration routes. The number of applications for granting of refugee status in Poland has been very small in the past decade (Table 6.1). Even 2015 and 2016 did not bring any significant change in this respect, although the number of applications increased by over 4,000.

The most frequent applicants for refugee status in Poland are Russian citizens of Chechen nationality, Georgians and Syrians. In 2015 the number of Ukrainian nationals applying for international protection increased. At the same time a decisive majority of their applications are rejected. Poland considers Ukraine a safe country, with a broad capacity to cope with its migration problems by moving so-called internally displaced people who are in danger in one region to another one, where such a risk is absent. For many years, Poland was a definite leader in terms of the number of accepted applications. In 2014, 2015 and 2016 Poland lost the top position to Hungary, which received the first wave of refugees (in 2015 Hungary registered over 177,000 applications for refugee status). Poland was also exceeded by Bulgaria. However, one has to assume that the past three years were exceptional. After the closing of its external borders by Hungary and the declaration of Bulgaria that it would do the same, Poland is likely to return to first place again in 2019-2020. The statistics show that Poland should not fear receiving a few thousand refugees. Poland seems to have adequate experience and resources in this respect, which would allow it to provide shelter to a limited number of foreigners. However, it seems that the position of the current government is founded on ideological rather than economic arguments.

Unfortunately, such a position was influenced also by an incomprehensible policy approach of the EU. In the first months of the inflow, when it was already clear that its scale would exceed prior expectations, EU institutions

Table 6.1 Number of applications for granting of refugee status in Poland in the period 2008–2016

Year	*2008*	*2009*	*2010*	*2011*	*2012*	*2013*	*2014*	*2015*	*2016*
Poland number of applications	8.515	10.595	6.540	6.890	10.750	15.240	8.020	12.190	12.305

Source: Eurostat.

focused mainly on pushing forward a solution aimed at relocating migrants amongst member states, something countered with a resolved opposition from the V4 states and scepticism from many others, including France and Belgium. Pushing forward the idea of relocation at all costs has to be considered as a mistake.

In the case of Poland, it is feasible that refugees may be granted leave to stay there, but their real desired destination would be Germany or Sweden. Refugees would be aware of Poland's situation and of how easy it would be to get to the states being their real destination. We are not assuming a situation whereby member states would be put under an obligation to stop migrants physically from leaving. The latter would be equivalent to placing migrants in guarded centres, which would be an extremely inhumane action. In practice the relocation would lead to further uncontrolled movements within the EU, providing another argument for the introduction of border checks, i.e. the suspension of the functioning of the Schengen zone. Some actions of the EC caused irritation among Polish politicians, both of the ruling and of the opposition parties. The proposal to enforce a penalty of € 250,000 per person on the member states which are refusing to receive refugees (European Commission 2016) encountered the same reaction. This proposal should be viewed from the perspective of an earlier proposal assuming coverage of the costs of receiving a refugee amounting to € 6,000. Unfortunately, nobody explained this discrepancy. In practice, if such a solution were applied, then Poland would have to pay more than €1.75 billion if it refused to receive 7,000 refugees. Therefore, the steady opposition of the Polish government shall come as no surprise. The lack of understanding and emotional reactions from both sides resulted in the immediate decline of mutual trust, and consequently in conflict escalation. Governments of several member states (e.g. Italy or Greece) supported by the EU accused the Polish government of violation of the principles of European solidarity. In reaction to that charge, a proposal was put forward to review the rules under which financing from structural funds and cohesion policy would be allocated to Poland. At the same time, Poland accused the EC of transgressing beyond European law and interfering with its internal affairs, which is incompatible with the principles enshrined in the treaties. What is extremely interesting, in the same period the government – although it did not admit so officially – supported the position of the President of the European Council, Donald Tusk, who questioned the soundness of the application of forced relocation. The following ideas for coping with the refugee crisis could be identified in the statements by members of Beata Szydło's goverment:

- tighten border checks,
- fight human trafficking more effectively,
- establish hotspots within the EU migrants' centres,
- improve living conditions in refugee camps outside EU borders and – what is of utmost importance
- cooperate with Turkey with a view to reducing the volume of unlawful border trespassing.

In reality such proposals appeared in the conclusions of the European Council held on 17 December 2015 in Brussels. They were put forward by Donald Tusk with objection from Angela Merkel, among others. What is extremely important, in the second half of 2016, the position of V4 states was officially supported both by Jean-Claude Juncker, who claimed the reception of refugees must not be imposed upon anyone (Juncker 2016) and by the President of the EP, Martin Schulz, who supported a greater financial involvement in exchange for not receiving refugees (Schulz 2016). Unfortunately, this did not lead to warming up of mutual relations, because the Polish government made no gesture towards the EC in the context of resolving the refugee problem.

Summing up, the position of the EC and of some member states related to the resolution of the refugee crisis caused the deepening of the mistrust of the new Polish government towards EU institutions. As we have already mentioned, one can assert that bad proposals and pushing them forward without any discussions were used by the Polish government as an argument in favour of weakening EU institutions and returning the decision-making process in many areas to national level. At the same time, the Polish government was unable to propose a real alternative to the EU approach and the presented position was of a rather general nature and it was not followed by specific decisions. A sceptical position towards the continuation of integration processes was detailed during discussions about effects of the British referendum on further membership in the EU. Therefore, referring to the question asked in the introduction, one can state that migration crisis and the conflict between Poland and European institutions built on that crisis became a catalyst for redefinition of Poland's position on European integration. The government of the Law and Justice party definitely used the bad EU proposals to justify the position that integration deepening would be disadvantageous for Poland and that the government should make efforts to stop such tendencies.

Brexit: will the UK remain the most important ally for the Polish government in the EU?

The UK is perceived by politicians of the currently ruling PiS party as the closest ally within the EU. Already in his first speech before the Parliament, Minister of Foreign Affairs, Witold Waszczykowski stated that Poland would

> hold the dialogue and regular consultations at various levels with major European partners – first with the UK, which we share with not only understanding of many important elements of the European agenda but also a similar approach to the problems of the European security.
>
> (Waszczykowski 2016).

This was a clear breach from the approach taken by the previous government which had focused on coalition building within the Weimar Triangle, i.e. with

Germany and France. At that time this was a concept aimed to take Poland into the core group of states who decide about the future of the EU. In his speech Minister Waszczykowski referred in a clearly confrontational way both to relations with Germany and within the Weimar Triangle. In the former case he stated that:

> Polish–German contacts will be even better if accompanied by honesty and openness instead of sometimes pretended superficial agreeableness.
> (Waszczykowski 2016)

In the case of the Weimar Triangle he stated that:

> The 25th anniversary of the establishment of the Weimar Triangle celebrated in 2016 will be the basis for recapitulation of the cooperation with France and Germany so far and for setting out its new directions.
> (Waszczykowski 2016)

Unfortunately, he failed to point out which directions these would be and what such recapitulation of the effects of cooperation would consist of. With these omissions he showed that the government of the Law and Justice party was not interested in high levels of activity in the Weimar Triangle, instead promoting relations with the UK and within the framework of the V4.

In the discussion before the British referendum the Polish government resolvedly supported the UK staying in the European Union in consideration of the fact that Brexit would cause a loss of a very important ally and the necessity for consolidation within the V4. However, government representatives were aware that many ideas would be unfeasible without support of the UK as an EU member. In an interview for the Polish Press Agency, the Minister of Foreign Affairs, Witold Waszczykowski stated just before the referendum that 'a negative referendum result followed by UK's exit from the EU, which could take a few years, would be highly detrimental for Poland'. In another fragment of the interview he said: 'for us Brexit would signify a loss of an important partner in the discussion about the future of the EU, because we have a lot in common here' (Waszczykowski 2016a).

However, despite such emphatic rhetoric it is difficult to find any specific actions encouraging the British to remain in the EU. When attacking the Union's institutions and the EU as such, representatives of the Polish government in a way confirmed the arguments of Brexit supporters. Based on the performed analysis, one is under an impression that the Polish government was fully convinced that Brexit would not happen but wanted to use the debate before the referendum to show the weaknesses of the Community. One may presume that in the case of a different referendum result, arguments would immediately emerge that this was the last moment to reform the EU and to base its future shape on powerful nation states.

The decision of the British nation to exit the EU was received by the Polish government with disbelief and sadness. PM Beata Szydło said in the Polish Parliament that:

> This is a critical moment for the entire EU. For the first time in the history of EU integration we are dealing with a situation where a member state decides to make such a step.
>
> (Szydło 2016a)

At the same time in her opinion this development resulted from the position at which the EU has arrived. It cannot be repaired without changes to the treaties targeted at restoration of power to national parliaments. In addition, the President of the Republic of Poland, Andrzej Duda, spoke about Brexit. In an interview for Onet.pl portal he stated among others that:

> The EU needs the UK as an economic partner, but also the UK itself needs the Union. Brexit is bad news for Poland.

At the same time, he named those responsible for the decision on the UK's exit from the EU. In his opinion the 'Brussels bureaucracy' was too extensive and incomprehensible for EU citizens and was therefore to blame. Simultaneously he said that the decision of the British would not cause the end of the strategic partnership between Poland and the UK within the EU. The interview also gave the president an opportunity to express his opinion about the direction the EU should take. Among other things he said that he was:

> the supporter of a Europe of motherlands, or as some say a Europe of nation-states, and not of the EU as an entity in which states will melt and cease to exist.

At the same time, he spoke in favour of strengthening of the role of the EP, which in his opinion is:

> democratically elected. It is elected by societies; this is where the real will of the representatives elected by European nations is expressed.
>
> (Duda 2016)

This statement was surprising because the PiS government rather criticised the European Parliament for accusing Poland of restricting the democratic rights of citizens and initiating a conflict with the Constitutional Tribunal.

After the British referendum, the Polish government faced a dilemma related to its position towards the conditions governing the exit of the UK from the EU. On the one hand, it became a top priority issue to guarantee the rights of Poles living in Britain. This would favour a very tight position in negotiations related to Single Market principles. One has to bear in mind that the issue of migration within the EU after its enlargements in 2004 and 2007 profoundly affected the referendum outcome. Therefore, British negotiators cannot afford maintaining the right of free movement of workers as if the UK remained a full EU member. This means that e.g. the option of gaining membership in the European Economic Area (EEA) is out of the question. However, on the other hand the declared friendship with the United Kingdom should result in a pressure on the EU to keep as flexible as possible and try to meet the expectations of the British negotiators. This would unavoidably translate into the deterioration of the status of Poles on the British Isles. According to statements of the representatives of the Polish government, this won general support.

Involvement of the Polish government for the benefit of the UK during negotiations related to the conditions of its exit from the EU is confirmed in an interview given by PM Beata Szydło to *The Daily Telegraph*. She said among others that Poland would be the UK's ally during talks with the European Commission. Simultaneously she stated again that:

> Poland was saddened, probably more than any other country, with the result of the British referendum. This result means that the camp of reforms and economic pragmatism in the EU will be soon deprived of invaluable British support.
>
> (Szydło 2016b)

This shows how great the expectations of the Polish government towards the UK were in connection with planned reforms of the EU. The decision on exit from the Community greatly hampered those plans. Since the British referendum, there has been a visible decline in the involvement of the Polish government representatives on EU reform. They are aware that without the UK and support virtually only from V4 states those plans are bound to fail. Poland's decision to support the UK during the negotiations with the EU necessarily influenced its position towards the rights of Poles residing on the Isles. During the visit of PM Theresa May to Poland it was agreed that, until the UK's exit from the EU, the rights of Poles would not change but at the same time Poland accepted the fact that after Brexit those rights would be restricted. Such a conclusion can be drawn from the statement by PM Beata Szydło after the visit of the British government delegation in Warsaw. She stated that:

> in the time after exit from the EU this will be governed by mutuality principle, i.e. the situation of EU citizens in the Great Britain will be the same as the situation of British citizens in the EU.
>
> (Szydło 2016c)

The absence of any reference to free movement of people and workers clearly demonstrates lack of consent for the renegotiation of the rules, which in practice translates into restricting the access for Poles to the British labour market and guarantees of equality related to labour law or social benefits. Paradoxically, this does not have to be disadvantageous for Poland because it is likely to reduce the scale of labour migration from Poland, something all Polish governments have made efforts to achieve. However, one has to be aware of the consequences of this type of choice in relations between the EU and the UK. Supporting the UK in the negotiations is bound to have an adverse impact on relations with the EC. The main question in this context is whether Poland will inform the UK about interstate bargaining agreements. One has to remember that already representatives of the UK do not participate in meetings of European groups discussing Brexit conditions.

In summary one can state that the Polish government, surprised by the decision of the British on exit from the EU, reacted in a typical manner. It blamed Brexit on the current style of the Community's functioning and its striving at all costs at imposition on member states of the will of EU institutions, particularly of the EC. Therefore, a remedy could be to reform the EU, which would result in a new treaty defining relations: both interstate relations and relations between member states and EU institutions. From the point of view of the Polish government such cooperation should be much looser than it is now. At the same time the decision of the UK did not translate into changing Polish priorities related to alliances in the EU. Those alliances are still the same as ever, i.e. the UK and the V4. Therefore, once again referring to the questions asked in the introduction, one can state that Brexit only strengthened the position of the present Polish government aimed at loosening European integration and returning to a community of nation states.

Conclusions

The period since accession of Poland to the EU has allowed Poland to gain significant influence on the decision-making process in the Community and greatly improve its economic situation. The political changes that took place in 2015 questioned the pro-European direction Poland used to head towards and translated into taking Poland a step back into the group of states which play a marginal role in shaping up the future of the EU. Statements from government politicians clearly show that they reject the direction the Community has taken so far. The events of 2015 and 2016, including Brexit and the crisis of support for the EU amongst a large number of the societies of member states, who show their dissatisfaction in elections, demonstrate that the conclusions drawn by the Polish government are not totally senseless. It seems that the Law and Justice party, and first and foremost its president Jarosław Kaczyński, correctly defined the main problem of the EU as one of divergent interests between the citizens and political decision-makers. Brexit, declining support for German chancellor Angela Merkel, permanently high support for Victor Orban, Marie Le Pen or Geert Wilders are no longer coincidences but a trend that has to be taken into account. The failure of the right-wing and anti-European candidate for the president of Austria and the election of Emanuel Macron as French president gives no reassurance. The EU is definitely at a crossroads and it has to make a rational decision. Keeping at any cost the direction towards deepening integration currently seems to make no sense as it is likely to be met with resolute opposition from a majority of the societies in the member states, which – as I have already mentioned before – will be reflected in elections both for national parliaments and for the EP. Is the only alternative therefore comprised by the concept proposed by Poland and V4 states, i.e. departure from supporting further integration and strengthening the nation states? This would translate into selection of the second scenario outlined in the introduction. However, the answer has to be negative, because the correct diagnosis is followed by inadequate policy proposals. Challenging a majority of EU initiatives, reluctance to support Donald Tusk for his second term in office as the President of the European Council and first of all failure to react to positions of EU institutions and the Venice Commission related to the issue of restriction of democratic rights in Poland greatly weaken the position of the Polish government in the discussion on the future of the Union. A country that questions everything and makes little contribution to the discussion on how to resolve the current crisis of the EU lacks credibility. The well-founded opposition to the EU's proposals to resolve the refugee problem was not followed on with proposals that would help to cope with the crisis. The same concerns Brexit. The Polish support for the UK, a country which has caused the EU's most profound crisis since its foundation, cannot be recognised as a responsible act. Poland consequently fails to take advantage of a real opportunity to remain in the group of decision-makers who determine the future of the EU, putting itself in the group of states which have very little to offer. The statements by prominent politicians of the Polish government and of the president of Poland presented in this chapter suggest that they unanimously support the second route which wants to loosen the European integration process through weakening EU institutions and strengthening national ones. However, this concept can be hardly expected to win a wide political support in the coming years. It can only lead to the worst possible scenario for Poland, i.e. a two-speed EU. Meanwhile there is a real chance to put forward a third route for the EU. However, such a proposal has to take into account the trust for Union institutions and in particular for the states that determined the course of integration, i.e. Germany and France. Hanging on to the UK and cooperation within the V4 marginalizes Poland in the discussion about the future of the EU and hence pushes it to the peripheries of the decision-making process. The UK is preoccupied with the Brexit negotiations and Hungary's prime concerns are upholding cooperation with Russia and trying at any cost to rebound from economic downturn. Neither can be expected to propose sensible EU reforms. On the other hand, Poland could embark on this task – it only has to start talking about the real conditions of the changes that are necessary in the EU to secure its survival. This should be an absolutely key priority for the Polish government. Poland has a very good economic situation, its uses the financing from structural funds and cohesion policy coherently and still has a highly pro-European society.

Therefore, it has to assume some responsibility for the future of the EU and try to support the good diagnosis with responsible proposals.

There is therefore only limited cause for optimism. It seems that it will be much easier for representatives of the Polish government to question EU initiatives and promote chimeras about a well-functioning and safe Community of nation states, which would be supposedly beneficial for Poland. Proposing a third route would require admitting that European integration brings many benefits to Poland and that its future depends on cooperation with Germany and France. It would also mean recognition of the fact that European solidarity has to operate in both directions. This would also require the swiftest possible termination of the counterproductive conflict with the EU around the Constitutional Tribunal and withdrawal from several projects that restrict democratic rights in Poland. However, we should not assume that this will actually happen. Consequently, the Polish government will support the weakening of Union institutions and enhanced competition between member states, even if this will lead to the end of the best period for Poland since the late seventeenth century.[6]

Notes

1 In reality Law and Justice incorporates additionally two small right-wing parties.
2 Elected for two-and-a half-year term in the office on 14 July 2009. He fulfilled this function until 17 January 2012.
3 He was elected on 31 August and he assumed the function on 1 December 2014.
4 Owing to lack of progress related to the constitutional crisis in Poland, on 27 July 2016 the EU decided to proceed onto the second stage of the procedure governing the protection of the rule of law.
5 The position of the President of the Law and Justice party is specific. Without fulfilling any government function he largely decides about policy-making directions of the government. Poland has a well-rooted tradition of such behaviours. In the late 1990s this function was fulfilled by the president of the 'Solidarity' trade union, Marian Krzaklewski. Before WWII Marshal Józef Piłsudzki was an undisputable political leader without fulfilling any government function.
6 The chapter was prepared within the project 'IMINTEG: In Search of Models of Relations Between Immigration and Integration Policies' (No. 2014/14/E/HS5/00397), funded by the Polish National Science Centre under the Sonata Bis program.

References

CBOS (2016) Poparcie dla członkostwa Polski w Unii Europejskiej [Support for Poland's membership in the European Union], *CBOS newsletter* 18.

Duda, A. (2016) An Interview with the President of the Republic of Poland for Onet.pl portal on 29 of July 2016.

Duszczyk, M. (2016) Periphery, or Perhaps Already the Centre? In: J.M. Magone, Laffan B., Schweiger, C. (eds) *Core-Periphery Relations in the European Union: The Politics of Differentiated Integration in the European Political Economy*. Routledge, pp. 251–265.

European Commission (2016) *Towards a Sustainable and Fair Common European Asylum System*, Brussels, 4 May 2016.

GUS (2016) *Kwartalna informacja o rynku pracy w trzecim kwartale 2016 roku [Quarterly information about the labour market in Q3 2016]*, Warsaw.
Juncker, J.C. (2016) *State of the European Union*, Brussels, 14 September.
Schulz, M. (2016) *A Statement for Frankfurter Allgemeine Zeitung*, 24 September.
Schweiger, C. (2015) The CEE Countries' First Decade of EU Membership: From Policy-takers Towards Agenda-setters? *Problemy Polityki Społecznej* 31(4), pp. 99–118.
Sikorski, R. (2011) *Poland and the Future of the European Union*, Berlin 28 November.
Szydło, B. (2015) *The Opening Statement by Prime Minister Beata Szydło, the Sejm of the Republic of Poland*, Warsaw, 18 November.
Szydło, B. (2015a) *A Statement Before the EU-Turkey Brussels Summit*. 27 November.
Szydło, B. (2016) *An Interview for Superstacja*. 23 March.
Szydło, B. (2016a) *A Statement During the Debate on Brexit, the Sejm of the Republic of Poland*. 21 July.
Szydło, B. (2016b) *Poland Stands Ready to Help its Old Friend Britain Reach the Best Possible Brexit Deal. The Daily Telegraph*, 27 November.
Szydło, B. (2016c) *A Statement for the Press of Prime Minister Beata Szydło after the Visit of Prime Minister Theresa May*. Warsaw, 28 July.
Waszczykowski, W. (2016) *The Opening Statement by Minister Witold Waszczykowski, the Sejm of the Republic of Poland*. Warsaw 28 January.
Waszczykowski, W. (2016a) *An Interview for the Polish Press Agency*. 29 May.

7 Hungary in the Visegrád group

Introducing a three-level game approach

Krisztina Arató and Boglárka Koller

Introduction

The Visegrád co-operation can be considered as a Hungarian invention. The establishment of the group was inspired by the symbolic, historical event of the 1335 Visegrád summit when the Polish, Czech and Hungarian kings agreed to cooperate in the fields of commerce and politics. There is no consensus, however, on the circumstances of the birth of the cooperation in 1991. Hungarians claim that prime minister József Antall initiated the cooperation, while the Czechs think that it was Vaclav Havel's idea (Cabada and Waisova 2011: 75). In the 1991 declaration the countries confirmed their same objectives derived from the communist past, such as: restoration of state independence, democracy and freedom, elimination of social, economic and spiritual remedies of totalitarianism and construction of market economy. They also declared their common desire to be integrated in the European political and economic system. They further confirmed that they would like to achieve these goals together by taking the same routes (Visegrád Declaration 1991). Despite the declared similarities, it shortly turned out, however, that the three, and later four countries (Czechoslovakia was dissolved in 1993) would have different paths to take.

What proved to be the same was the desire to get 'back to Europe'. The number one foreign policy objective of each country in the nineties was to get into the EU as fast as possible. Although the EU did not have a clear enlargement strategy (Ágh 2006), its institutions, foremost the European Commission, set the conditions and determined the timing as well. Throughout the nineties, the European Commission was communicating that the best prepared countries would be involved in the first wave of enlargement, which resulted in a heated competition among the candidates. The so called 'myth of differentiation' was withdrawn only by deciding on 'Big Bang enlargement' in 2002. Hungary, for example, one of the best prepared countries in the 1990s, expecting to be in the first wave, was clearly disappointed when the number of the countries to be taken in was extended to ten. The myth of differentiation had negative consequences on the relationship of the East Central European countries, including the Visegrád group members and proved to be peculiarly unfortunate because the candidates could have developed a stronger negotiating position in EU accession as well. The Visegrád co-operation proved to be a rather weak and less successful initiative in the nineties (Arató-Koller 2009: 209).

The Visegrád cooperation was re-launched in 1999, due to the progress in Eastern enlargement, but also the accomplishment of the objectives set in 1991. The V4 prime ministers in 1999 agreed to maintain the regional profile of the group and set policy objectives in the fields of education, culture, science, technology, infrastructure, environment, science and cross-border cooperation. They also agreed to maintain the non-institutional, but intergovernmental character of the group with a rotating presidency of one country in-between the yearly presidential meetings. Up until now, Hungary has presided the V4 group four times.

Although the Visegrád group aims to represent a unique regional club, and a close cooperation of Central Europeans, the accession to and later membership of the European Union determined the frames of its existence. By becoming full members of the European Union in 2004, the V4 countries, including Hungary agreed to cooperate closer in achieving EU policy goals as well, such as contributing to the development of Common Foreign and Security Policy or achieving the eurozone membership (Guidelines on the Future Areas of Visegrád Cooperation 2004), although the latter dropped out of the Hungarian EU objectives.

At the beginning of the post-enlargement period, the V4 countries were still in the adaptation phase and tried to learn the rules of European integration and adjust their legal, economic and institutional systems to the Union. However, as they took their places at the table of common Europe, the V4 countries, including Hungary, started to elevate the accession-related constraints, and express their national interest more intensively. As examples, we can mention Václav Klaus's euroscepticism in prolonging the ratification of the Lisbon Treaty or the Kaczyński brothers, who became symbols of fighting for Polish national interests (Koller 2011). Hungary also provided numerous examples of 'emancipation': the Hungarian prime minister Orbán, in introducing the official programme of the Hungarian EU Presidency in January 2011 in the European Parliament steadily emphasised that he was firmly resolved to defend the 'Hungarian national interest' at all times. The phase of 'emancipation' of East Central European countries gained new impetus when the migration crisis reached its peak in 2015. The Visegrád countries, in campaigning for better protection of the EU's external borders, went against the open door policy of Germany and other Western European states. 'They are convinced the German and European Commission-led response to the migration crisis is wrong and contrary to European interests' (Hokovsky 2016).

Parallel to the changing political rhetoric of East Central European countries, the importance of the V4 group has gradually increased within the Union, although the four countries are not of the same opinion on several issues. Poland and Hungary for example have opposing positions on EU-Russian relations. The eurozone member Slovakia has stronger interest in developing a genuine economic and monetary union than the other V4 countries. They started to use the V4 group as a platform to express their arguments in the hope of finding supporting partners in the region in order to gain stronger representation in the wider EU arena as well.

The aim of this chapter is to examine Hungary in this unique, regional group. The underlying assumption of our chapter is that the V4 group has just recently become an essential actor in the EU sphere. Therefore, we will mainly concentrate on recent developments.

By conducting a political science analysis, we examine Hungarian V4 participation in the three dimensions of politics: first, we introduce the polity dimensions, second we interpret the policy aspects of the group and third we discover the political dimension of the V4 co-operation. By applying the *triangular model* of politics referring to *polity, policy* and *politics*, we are convinced that we can understand better the Hungarian role in the Visegrád group. Although the polity, policy and political aspects are going to be covered in three sub-chapters, it will be demonstrated that they are strongly connected and can only be interpreted together. For example, by examining the Hungarian and V4 positions in the migration crisis that could be considered as the policy angle of the V4 group, it will be demonstrated that the issue appears in high politics at domestic, V4 and EU levels too, and significantly influences agenda setting at EU level as well.

In our chapter, we intend to find answers to the following questions: What does the non-institutional, intergovernmental set-up look like in the Hungarian case? What are the new developments? What are the priority policy areas for Hungary in the V4 group? How does V4 co-operation appear in the Hungarian foreign policy discourse? To what extent did Hungary lead V4 in forming a common position in the migration crisis? Is there a common position on the Brexit issue? What was the Hungarian and the V4 position in relation to the Ukraine crisis and Russian sanctions (Eastern Partnership)? What were the main Hungarian inventions in EU agenda-setting? Is there a V4 identity? If yes, to what extent does Hungary share this?

In order to answer these questions, we have carried out a document analysis including the Hungarian foreign policy strategies, politicians' speeches, V4 declarations and presidency programs. Additionally, we have carried out a semi-structured interview with the Hungarian V4 coordinator in order to gain practical insights.

Theoretical background

Visegrád cooperation was born at the beginning of the EU enlargement process of Hungary, re-launched in 1999, but only became an essential framework of regional cooperation in the post-enlargement period. Therefore, the analysis of the V4 cooperation cannot be detached from the understanding of the effects of EU membership on the politics of newly accessed states. The political science literature defines this phenomenon under the term of *Europeanisation* by referring to the processes and outcomes by which the institutional logic, norms, political discourse and actions become 'European alike' in the new member states (Ladrech 1994, 2010; Börzel 1999, 2002; Radaelli 2003; Risse et al 2001; Graziano and Vink 2008; Simmelfennig and Sedelmeier 2008; Olsen 2002 etc.). These theories mostly emphasized the top-down character of the phenomenon, but as the newly joined member states started to provide bottom-up examples of it, meaning the provision of their own approaches, ideas for EU policy-making and political interaction, the top-down character of Europeanisation was supplemented with the bottom-up logic as well. This led the scholars to the conclusion that Europeanisation has to be understood in a much broader sense than providing only unidirectional interpretations of it (Olsen, 2002: 944). Translating it into the Hungarian case, this means that as Hungary became more emancipated as an EU member state, it has begun to represent its own interest more intensively, question the EU agendas more often, and initiate its own EU-policy proposals. The size limitations of this chapter do not allow a deeper analysis of Europeanisation, it should be, however, emphasized that: when the importance of V4 was increased in the second decade of the twenty-first century, it was the same time as when Poland, Slovakia, Czech Republic and Hungary were in the multi-directional process of Europeanisation. Agreeing with Radaelli and Pasquier we interpret Europeanisation as an 'EU-level system of interaction' (Radaelli and Pasquier 2008: 12) emphasizing the complexity and interconnectivity of domestic and European political spaces. For us it is hence a phenomenon with multidirectional effects on political actors, institutions and individuals of the society.

Visegrád cooperation can be interpreted a newly invented political arena within the European Union that is able to have a direct effect on both the EU integration and domestic political developments. Robert Putnam in his widely quoted work argued that EU politics and the notions of participant actors, for example member states and their politicians can merely be understood if we consider it as two-level-game 'where each political leader appears at both game board' (Putnam 1988: 434) They act according to the pressure coming from domestic groups in order to maximize their power and also at the international level they act in order to be able to 'satisfy domestic pressures and minimize the adverse consequences of foreign developments' (Putnam 1988: 434). Due to the recent resurrection of the V4, the two-level political game could be extended to three levels in the case of the Visegrád group, where the first level indicates the member state – i.e. the domestic politics, the second the V4 interaction and the third EU politics. In line with Putnam's approach, it means that each Visegrád member state has three tables to sit at. First of all, they play their domestic game in order to satisfy the main actors, such as the parties, interest groups, opinion leaders but foremost the voters. Secondly, they play the EU level game in a quasi-supranational community, and try to deliver home outputs that will satisfy the domestic political objectives. If there is an unwanted policy or political outcome at EU level, however, tensions at domestic level will appear too. For example, the opposition parties will immediately question the ability of the government to represent the national interest. In this case, the leading political actors will be searching for coalition partners at EU level to minimize the domestic effects of a non-desired EU initiative. In playing this game, the Visegrád group could be interpreted as a little smaller, but important table within the European Union, where support can be gained and partners can be gathered for playing the bigger EU game. Nevertheless, it shall be emphasized that at the Visegrád table, common positions can only be formed if they fit the aspirations of the leading political forces of the members. If it is not the case, the members can go away from the table and turn back to their two-level game with the EU. The intentionally maintained non-institutional character of the V4 group makes this option available at any time.

In this chapter, we provide a political science analysis on the Hungarian V4 participation. In order to be able to examine the various aspects of politics, we apply the triangular model of politics and analyse Hungary along *polity, policy, politics aspects* (the three Ps) (Pennings et al 1999: 23–28). The three junctures of the triangular model where Hungarian V4 participation can be examined are the following: (i) the *polity* including the institutional set-up, (ii) the *policy* concerning all policy initiatives and decisions that result in specific policy outcomes and (iii) the *politics* including conflicting interest and political leadership. In the triangular model, the three Ps are interconnected and they constantly influence and affect each other at all three levels of the political game. The non-institutional, intergovernmental character of the V4 determines the nature of interaction among V4 countries and the policy-outcomes. Further, the EU level politics and V4 interaction affect domestic politics, but domestic policy decisions also affect V4 and EU politics too. In the same vein, the European institutions are in a central role of agenda-setting, but the domestic and V4 policy initiatives could also be uploaded to the EU political system (Börzel 2002) as well. Moreover, if the EU agenda and the V4 plans in policy-making are in opposition, as they are in the case of managing the migration crisis, it can even generate a conflict in high politics at EU level.

The polity of Visegrád and Hungary

Already the categories used to characterize the Visegrád group – e.g. subregional partnership (Törő et al 2014), subregional cooperation (Dangerfield 2008), interstate formation (Fawn 2013), regional alliance (Dangerfield 2014), 'initiative' or 'platform'[1] – indicate that the group lacks clear-cut institutional setup. Analyses dealing with the historical development of the V4 are mostly satisfied with this quasi non-institutional structure, arguing that this way of cooperation is fit for purpose (Fawn 2013) or that it provides a flexible platform (Dangerfield 2014) for the common activities.

However, after the 1999 re-launch of the Visegrád cooperation, certain structures were set – two regular meetings per year of prime ministers; two regular meetings per year of foreign ministers, meetings of other ministers as needed, meetings of V4 presidents, meetings of V4 parliamentary representatives, appointment of national V4 coordinators meeting at least twice a year, ministerial cooperation at the expert level. The rotating presidency (lasting for one year from July to the following June) provides a certain kind of leadership for the group (workplan, reporting, regular meetings of V4 coordinators and also ambassadors, etc.) (Contents of Visegrád Cooperation, Visegrád group 1999; Dangerfield 2008 and 2014). Hungarian V4 presidency programmes (2005/2006, 2009/2010, 2013/2014) indicate how a presidency country influences common priorities: all of them include cooperation with the West Balkans and key policy areas (e.g transport and energy) important for Hungary.

Connected to the 1999 reforms, the International Visegrád Fund (the only institution with permanent staff and budget), was established which extended the cooperation from the world of politics to academia, research and technology and civil society.[2]

Hungary, especially during V4 presidencies, contributed to the strengthening of this quasi-institutional stability of V4. Especially after the 2013 Polish and the 2014 Hungarian presidencies, key policy cooperation areas (energy and transport) were supported by high level working groups that have rules of procedure and roadmaps that set deadlines for common activities. These have been essential in keeping policy cooperation on track when acute political crises took attention (interview, Arató 2016).

Further flexibility is provided for the group with the V4 plus formula – this enables V4 to cooperate with third parties, and it was enhanced by the 2007/2008 Czech presidency.[3] Hungary has given high priority to V4+ meetings with countries of the West Balkans before the refugee crisis started, and initiated negotiations with the newest EU member (Croatia) in 2013 (Visegrád group 2013a).

The fact that cooperation within the European Union is the highest priority for the V4 is expressed in institutional terms. V4 meetings are regularly held prior to European Council meetings – one of the first examples of this was in 2012 when the V4 prime ministers sent a letter to Herman van Rompuy (President of the European Council) about their joint position concerning issues on the agenda[4] – and joint declarations are adopted by the V4 prior to the European Council meetings. Common positions may be formed with the help of non-papers as well (Törő et al 2014: 373).

V4 Policies and Hungary

Policy areas covered by the V4 cooperation have been wide in all periods of the history of the Visegrád group (1991–1999, 1999–2004 and post-EU-accession). However, the depth of cooperation shows significant differences in the time of EU accession and in later periods – this is shown by the mere length of V4 presidency reports. Whereas for example the report of the Polish presidency in 2001/2002 was only three pages long, the 2013/14 report of the 2015/16 Hungarian presidency comprises 92 pages, covering as many as 16 areas of cooperation (*Report of the Hungarian presidency of V4*, Visegrád group

2014). The scope of this paper only allows us to focus on policies highly important for Hungary, such as energy, transport, defence, Eastern partnership and new initiatives like the EU digital agenda and R&D (Interview 2016).

Energy cooperation is one of the key priorities within the V4 cooperation for Hungary – in the 2013/14 presidency report it is the first and longest chapter. Stress is put on the EU member states' right to define their own energy mix, with special attention to the non-discrimination of the use of nuclear energy. Obviously, this should be understood in the context of Hungarian plans to build Paks II, a new nuclear power station – the one which is planned to be built in cooperation with Russia. Energy cooperation of the V4 also included third partners, such as the Ukraine, Bulgaria, Greece and Romania and special attention was given to the issue of the use of LNG (*Report of the Hungarian presidency of V4*, Visegrád group 2014: 8–9).

Cooperation in the area of transport highlighted the importance of the development of North–South transport networks, with special attention to the development of railway connections. V4 partners in March 2014 set up a High Level Working Group on Transport, and adopted a roadmap for the coordination of transport network development in the V4 countries – that is an important institutional innovation for the V4 as indicated above. The Visegrád countries intend to cooperate in financing their transport development plans during the finalization of their operational programmes in the 2014–20 budgetary period but they plan to start their cooperation in time for the preparation of the 2021–27 Multiannual Financial Framework (*Report of the Hungarian presidency of V4*, Visegrád group 2014: 10).

Defence cooperation is also of high importance for Hungary. Preparations for the V4 Battlegroup (see chapter 14, Cooperation or integration?) were started in 2011 but reinforced in the times of Russian military intervention in the Ukraine in 2014. During the Hungarian V4 presidency, V4 prime ministers adopted the Budapest Declaration on the New Opening in V4 Defence Cooperation, including the task for the defence ministers to prepare an action plan. Cooperation does not only include the tasks about the Battlegroup but also the elaboration of a V4 Training and Exercise Strategy. (Weiss 2012; interview, Arató 2016).

Presence in the Eastern Partnership (EaP) programme of the European Union appeared strongly in the 2013/14 Hungarian V4 presidency that reflects the commitment of the country to the EaP countries. Whereas the activities of Hungary supported the region and the V4 presidency programme included a widescale informal foreign ministerial meeting with the participation of Visegrád and Eastern Partnership countries, as well as the representatives of the EU Presidency, the Commission, the European External Action Service and the Nordic-Baltic countries (*Report of the Hungarian presidency of V4*, 2014: 18), we can identify certain inconsistencies in the Hungarian position. First, the presidency report identifies very politely the Ukrainian crisis and Russia's role in it (calling it a 'change in the geopolitical context', *Report of the Hungarian presidency of V4*, 2014: 18) that caused political conflict within the group that we discuss in the following section. Second, the Hungarian international development policy – the part of which is strongly related to the donations to the Eastern Partnership countries – is considered to be strategically and institutionally the least developed of the V4 countries (Végh 2016).

Hungary strongly supports the V4 cooperation in new areas of EU policies, such as the Digital Agenda for Europe that is one of the priorities of the EU's broader Europe 2020 strategy. Visegrád activities include in this area innovative start-ups, increasing digital literacy and e-skills, improving the regulatory environment for cross-border electronic sales, simplifying the conditions for setting up new businesses, supporting research and the development of digital technologies, etc. (*Report of the Czech presidency of V4* 2016).

However, the intensification of V4 cooperation during the post-accession period as indicated in the Kroměříž Declaration of 2004 (Visegrád Declaration, Visegrád group 2004) could be identified in the field of the above policy areas and that did not reach the understanding of the public until the mid-2010s. Developments in the different fields of politics however led to the re-positioning of V4 within the EU. In the next chapter we look at this development and Hungary's role in it.

Hungary and politics in the V4 cooperation

Foreign policy is a policy area where – as indicated in 'Theoretical background' above, based on Putnam's two-level game-theory, internal political strategies are expressed visibly in comparison with other policies. If we have a look at the most recent Hungarian foreign policy documents (the 2008 strategy by the Gyurcsány-government and the 2011 strategy of the Orbán government) we find the V4 cooperation identified as a major tool for Hungarian foreign policy in both, having a special role in Hungary's relation to the European Union (Molnár 2011, 2013). The 2008 strategy of the Gyurcsány government states that 'Hungary as a full member of the EU will become a policy-maker, leaving behind the former adaptive, passive, reactive behaviour and thinking, if we can provide necessary financial and human resources.'[5] The role of V4 was stressed in chapter XX, on the priorities of Hungarian foreign policy as well as in the part on the relations with neighbouring countries. In the political practice, however, V4 did not receive a high profile. Cooperation was operational on the policy level, in the political arena it was underused. The prime example of this was an event in 2008 when the prime minister introduced an unprepared initiative at the December European Council meeting – financial assistance requested for the East Central European member states, with the major aim to ask for help for the troubled Hungarian budget (Kerényi 2011) from the EU that was immediately turned down by the Czech and Slovak governments (Ballai 2009).

The second Orbán government published its foreign policy strategy in 2011 after the Hungarian presidency of the European Union. It gives a detailed picture about the V4 group as the most important framework for cooperation in the country's immediate neighbourhood and it notes its special role after EU accession. The document identifies the priorities of the V4 cooperation for Hungary in the fields of economic development, energy policy and transport infrastructure, within the EU it highlights the importance of V4 cooperation in the area of cohesion policy, the common agricultural policy, energy policy, multiannual financial framework, neighbourhood policy and enlargement.[6] Visegrád became increasingly important for the Hungarian government since it triggered several conflicts with the European Union after 2010. Whereas the 2011 foreign policy strategy states that Hungary's aim is to contribute to a strong and united Europe – successful crisis management and the dominance of the community method in decision-making – the practice of foreign policy was dominated by the strengthening of national and economic sovereignty (Gazdag 2014: 214). The EU policy of the second Orbán government is closely related to its unorthodox economic policy, the new Basic Law replacing the Constitution, new media law and the decrease of powers of the Constitutional Court (Arató and Koller 2015). The institutions of the European Union applied several legal and political instruments to resolve the alleged democracy problems: Hungarian issues were dealt with in infringement proceedings, sessions and reports in the European Parliament (European Parliament 2013). The conflict has been crosscutting legal, political and ideological layers.

The political crises starting in 2013 in the Ukraine found Hungary in an altogether conflictual situation within the European Union with a strong need to rely on V4 partners. If we only read V4 documents in relation to the Ukrainian conflict, we see rather unequivocal common statements, the majority of which were issued during the Hungarian presidency. The 2014 March Statement of the V4 prime ministers emphasises that

> The Prime Ministers of the Visegrád countries are deeply concerned about the recent violation of Ukraine's territorial integrity and the fact that the Russian parliament has authorized military action on Ukrainian soil against the wishes of the Ukrainian government. (…) We condemn all action threatening the sovereignty and territorial integrity of Ukraine and call on to decrease the tensions immediately through dialogue, in full respect of Ukrainian and international law (…) The Visegrád countries believe that the recent military actions by Russia are not only in violation of international law, but also create a dangerous new reality in Europe. The Czech Republic, Hungary, Poland and Slovakia are appalled to witness a military intervention in 21st century Europe akin to their own experiences in 1956, 1968 and 1981.
>
> (*V4 Prime Ministers Declaration*, Visegrád group 2014)

There were three other statements of the V4 that show the gravity of the conflict and the language of the quoted one (violation of territorial integrity, being appalled by the situation and bringing V4 examples from the Soviet past) show a strong common position. However, behind the scenes there were several tensions among the Visegrád countries. The Hungarian position was rather controversial: while the country signed up for direct criticism of Russia's actions, Hungary made steps in several areas that showed tight connections to Putin's Russia (Sadecki 2014). We offer just two examples here: first, according to the agreement of the Hungarian government and Rosatom signed in January 2014, the Russian company will expand the Paks nuclear power station, financed 80 per cent by a 10 billion euro credit line from Russia (Rácz 2014). Second, the Hungarian government, since their introduction in 2014, has been emphasising that EU sanctions against Russia cause harm to the Hungarian economy. In spring 2016 Hungary – as well as Italy – announced that there will be no automatic extension of EU sanctions towards Russia – whereas the Baltic states and Poland strongly disagree with this position (Emmott and Baczynska 2016). These developments show that while common positions are possible in V4, Hungary represents its own interest in the same area irrespective of the direction of V4 declarations. In fact, the opposing foreign policy attitude to Russia creates an apparent fragmentation line among the V4 members.

The migration crisis[7] is another policy that has been highly political and that showed controversies among the V4. There has been consensus about the need to act together in times of crisis. Even in June 2015, when mass inflow of migrants did not reach V4 borders, the joint statement of Visegrád heads of government included (on Hungarian request) a paragraph that indicates that the European Agenda on Migration fails to address and find adequate solutions to the migration problem and that the V4 prefers voluntary options in terms of resettlement and relocation (Visegrád group 2013b). V4 countries supported the firm Hungarian refugee policy when at EU meetings the representatives of the Hungarian government expressed the importance of border control, raised the issue of the security element of the crisis and supported consequent use of an alternative terminology – migration instead of the term refugee crisis used commonly by the EU. Apart from diplomacy and political support, V4 countries sent police and military support to Hungary, V4+ meetings were organised with the participation of e.g. Serbia and Macedonia and joint technical V4 support was sent to the West Balkans (Interview 2016). The four countries submitted a proposal called 'flexible solidarity' in September 2016 during the Slovak presidency of the EU that means that countries that do not want to take migrants/refugees should be able to contribute to the EU's migration policy with other means, either financially with equipment or manpower (Zalán 2016). However, beside common positions, the V4 made several non-common steps during the crisis. In September 2015 when EU interior ministers approved the plan to relocate 120,000 migrants across the EU over the following two years, Romania, the Czech Republic, Slovakia and Hungary voted against accepting mandatory quotas, whereas Poland voted for it (BBC 2015). Early 2016 after the European Commission submitted a proposal for amending the (EU) No 604/2013 Regulation on application for international protection lodged in one of the member states by a third country national or a stateless person,[8] the parliaments of Hungary, Slovakia and the Czech Republic initiated a yellow card procedure against the proposal while Poland refrained from doing so. There was no consensus among the V4 in the question of relocation. While Hungary listed zero persons to be relocated, all other V4 countries took on some (Interview 2016). The Hungarian government chose a special political strategy to deal with the migration crisis: it held a referendum in October 2016 asking citizens: 'Do you want to allow the European Union to mandate the resettlement of non-Hungarian citizens to Hungary without the approval of the National Assembly?' With the referendum being on the internal political agenda for six months in 2016, Hungary was the only V4 country that gave a high internal political profile to the crisis (Rácz 2015; Győri 2016). However, despite internal divisions the refugee crisis meant the V4 was perceived as a newly emerging bloc within the EU. The perception of this new development is also controversial: whereas some authors want to explain why this happened and how it works (Hokovsky 2016), others stress the destructive nature of the V4 policy arguing that Visegrád nowadays sounds like a bad word (Economist 2016). The latter argument is supported by the democratic backsliding (Bermeo2016) in key V4 countries like Hungary and Poland – the democracy problems that have been identified by EU institutions (European Commission, European Parliament) and documents (e.g. the Tavares report of the EP on Hungary) add to the evaluation of the Visegrád cooperation (Arató 2016; Markowski 2016).

For the Visegrad countries Germany is not only the – however 'reluctant' (Paterson 2011) – hegemon within the European Union, but also a centre of gravity in economic (trade, investments) and political terms. Whereas the multiple crisis in the European Union after 2008 seemed to call for a more active German leadership – as Radek Sikorski, Polish foreign minister said in 2011 'I fear German power less than I am beginning to fear German inactivity' (Sikorski 2011) – more recently the enthusiasm is combined with distrust in key crisis areas. The refugee crisis triggered an atmosphere of mutual dissatisfaction – Germany did not find V4 (especially Hungarian and Polish) reactions to the migration crisis appropriate and showing enough European solidarity, whereas V4 felt betrayed because Germany did not consult its migration policies with them. The situation is full of misunderstandings and is frequently called 'a crisis of mutual expectations' (Cieslar and Pojar 2016).

The ongoing political challenge for the European Union and the V4 in it is the process of Brexit. While V4 and East Central European EU member states unequivocally supported the agreement between the EU 27 and David Cameron, the outcome of the referendum of 23 June 2016 in the UK brought about an unprecedented situation. The strategy of Theresa May, PM of post-referendum UK seems to be to conduct bilateral talks outside the EU and within. Among the V4, she met Viktor Orbán, Prime Minister of Hungary 9 November 2016 and Beata Szydlo Polish PM 28 November 2016, and there were talks with Robert Fico, being the PM of the EU presidency country. Whereas Hungary would agree with a 'fair deal' with the UK, Slovakia would urge a 'hard Brexit' (Interview 2016). While the Brexit strategies of all parties are yet to be defined, it seems that apart from individual talks, there is a common position among the V4 – no compromise on the rights of EU citizens working in the UK. The Slovak Prime Minister stated in September 2016 that V4 would veto any Brexit deal that would limit their citizens' rights to work in Britain (Politico, 18/9/2016). This statement sounds especially strong since it was made during the Slovakian EU presidency – when politicians usually seek compromise rather than express controversies. Apart from Brexit issues, there is the open question of how the EU 27 will work in the post-Brexit period. Nevertheless, Brexit could also open up new perspectives for V4 states. In a re-defined, more continental geopolitical order in Europe, V4 is going to be closer to the new centre of European integration. The only question is whether V4 countries are going to cooperate closer with Germany.

While Hungary would agree with treaty amendments if deemed necessary, Slovakia and the Czech Republic seem to oppose an IGC (Interview 2016). Both in the question of Brexit and post-Brexit EU the Hungarian position is clear – while in the case of Slovakia and the Czech Republic there are internal political divisions (between the president and the prime minister) in these issues.

Conclusion

Hungary and the Visegrád cooperation are both examples of the bottom-up type of Europeanisation. Whereas post-accession Hungarian foreign policy reflected on becoming a policy-maker as an EU member, especially after 2010, the Visegrád group seemed to follow the same path. Within Putnam's framework, understanding foreign policy – in our case especially Hungarian EU policy – as a two-level game, we saw that Visegrád became a special extra layer, a kind of third level in between the two. For Hungary, Visegrád is a useful tool that can be used to support Hungary's interests if common positions can be reached without hindering independent Hungarian strategies not shared by other V4 states.

With our 3P analysis we proved that the (although limited) development of common V4 institutions and the significantly stronger policy coordination would not have shown V4 to be a substantial subregional cooperation within the EU without the emerging political coordination especially visible in the migration/refugee crisis. We shall see whether Christian Schweiger's assessment continues to be right:

> The Visegrád countries are a microcosm of Europe's divisions. Slovakia is in the euro and staunchly pro-German, Poland has also stuck close to Berlin but is more sceptical than Slovakia about euro membership, the Czechs have at times sounded downright British about their opposition to integration but may be changing views (and governments), while Hungary sits outside – and its government sometimes seems to thrive on bashing EU policies.
>
> (Schweiger 2013)

Notes

1 To be found on the website of the Visegrád Group: Visegrád Group – Aims and Structure. Available from http://www.visegradgroup.eu/about/aims-and-structure. [ONLINE] (accessed 5 January 2017).
2 International Visegrád Fund. Available at: http://visegradfund.org/home/ [ONLINE] (accessed 5 January 2017).
3 See the 2007/2008 Czech V4 Presidency Programme. [ONLINE] Available from http://www.visegradgroup.eu/documents/presidency-programs/2007–2008-czech-110412 (accessed 6 January 2017).
4 Letter of the Prime Ministers of the Visegrád Group Countries to President Barrosso, President van Rompuy and President Schultz of 22 June 2012. [ONLINE] Available at: http://www.visegradgroup.eu/calendar/2012 (accessed 7 January 2017).
5 1012/2008. (III. 4.) Korm. határozat Magyarország külkapcsolati stratégiájáról. (Hungarian foreign policy strategy of 2008).
6 Magyar külpolitika az uniós elnökség után. Külügyminisztérium, Budapest, 2011. (Hungarian foreign policy after EU presidency). [ONLINE] Available at: http://eu.kormany.hu/download/4/c6/20000/ kulpolitikai_strategia_20111219.pdf
7 In the use of terminology concerning the migration/refugee crisis we agree with the BBC: the term migrant refers to all people on the move who have yet to complete the legal process of claiming asylum. This group includes people fleeing war-torn countries such as Syria, who are likely to be granted refugee status, as well as people who are seeking jobs and better lives, who governments are likely to rule are economic migrants. [ONLINE] Available at: http://www.bbc.com/news/world-europe-34329825.
8 See http://www.ipex.eu/IPEXL-WEB/dossier/document/COM20150450.do

References

Ágh A. (2006) *Magyarország az Európai Unióban. Az aktív Európa-politika kezdetei. Századvég*, 11. Budapest: BKF Tankönyvek.

Arató K. (2016) *Democracy Control in the European Union*. Paper presented at the ECPR General Conference, Prague, 7–10 September 2016. [ONLINE] Available from: https://ecpr.eu/Filestore/ PaperProposal/d40e7294–7398d-4f6d-80d1-bf5efec7eb41.pdf (accessed 15 January 2017).

Arató, K. (2016) Interview with the Hungarian National Visegrád and CEU Coordinator. 19 December.

Arató K. and Koller B. (2009) *Európa utazása. Integrációtörténet*. Budapest: Gondolat Kiadó.

Arató K. and Koller, B. (2015) *Magyarország és az Európai Unió. Körösényi András (szerk.) A magyar politikai rendszer – negyedszázad után*. Budapest: Osiris Kiadó, pp. 377–400.

Ballai, V. (2009) *Feltámadhat Gyurcsány hamvába holt ötlete Brüsszelben*. Origo, 19 March. Available at: http://www.origo.hu/itthon/20090318-gyurcsany-valsagkezelesi-javaslatai-es-az-europa-tanacs-soros-ulese.html (accessed 5 January 2017).

Bermeo, N. (2016) On Democratic Backsliding. *Journal of Democracy* 27(1), pp. 5–19.

BBC (2015) Migrant Crisis: EU Ministers Approve Disputed Quota Plan 22 September. [ONLINE] Available from: http://www.bbc.com/news/world-europe-34329825 (accessed 5 January 2017).

Börzel, T. (1999) Towards Convergence in Europe? Institutional Adaptation to Europeanization in Germany and Spain. *Journal of Common Market Studies* 39(4), pp. 573–596.

Börzel, T. (2002) Member State Responses to Europeanization. *Journal of Common Market Studies* 40(2), pp. 193–214.

Cabada, L. and Waisova, S. (2011) *Czechoslovakia and Czech Republic in the World Politics*. Lanham, Boulder, New York, Toronto, Plymouth: Lexington Books

Cieslar, J.S. and Pojar, T. (2016) V4 Between Germany and Russia. Cevro Institut. http://www.cevroinstitut.cz/data/v4-germany-russia-final.pdf (downloaded 6 October 2017).

Dangerfield, M. (2008) The Visegrád Group in the Expanded European Union: From Preaccession to Postaccession Cooperation. *East European Politics and Societies* 22(3), pp. 630–667.

Dangerfield, M. (2014) V4: A New Brand for Europe? Ten Years of Post-accession Regional Cooperation in Central Europe. *Poznań University of Economics Review* 14(4), pp. 71–90.

Economist (2016) *Big, Bad Visegrád. The Migration Crisis has given an Unsettling New Direction to an Old Alliance*. [ONLINE] Available from http://www.economist.com/news/europe/21689629-migration-crisis-has-given-unsettling-new-direction-old-alliance-big-bad-visegrad (accessed 5 January 2017).

Emmott, R. and G. Baczynska (2016) Italy, Hungary say No Automatic Renewal of Russia Sanctions. Reuters, 14 March 2016. Available from: http://www.reuters.com/article/us-ukraine-crisis-eu-idUSKCN0WG1AU (accessed 5 January 2017).

European Parliament (2013) *Report on the Situation of Fundamental Rights: Standards and Practices in Hungary (Pursuant to the European Parliament Resolution of 16 February)* (2012/2130(INI)) 25 June.

Fawn, R. (2013) Visegrád: Fit for Purpose? *Communist and Post-Communist Studies* 46(3), pp. 339–349.

Gazdag, F. (2014) *A magyar külpolitika 1989–2014*. Budapest: Nemzeti Közszolgálati Egyetem, Nemzetközi Intézet.

Graziano, P. and Vink, M. P. (2008) *Europeanization: New Research Agendas*. Basingstoke: Palgrave Macmillan.

Győri G. (2016) The Political Communication of the Refugee Crisis in Central and Eastern Europe. Available at: http://www.feps-europe.eu/assets/3f672c37-1e17-4332-976b-ac395bc30ddd/political-communication-of-the-refugee-crisis-in-ceepdf.pdf (accessed 17 January 2016).

Hokovsky R. (2016) How Migrants Brought Central Europe Together. Visegrád Countries Might Decide They're Better Off Alone if the EU Sticks to its Guns on Migration, *Politico*. 2 September. [ONLINE] Available from: http://www.politico.eu/article/how-migrants-brought-central-europe-together-visegrad-group-orban-poland/ (accessed 5 January 2017).

Kerényi, Á. (2011) Financial Assistance for Hungarian Crisis Management – A Case Study. In: Farkas, B. (ed.) *Studies in International Economics and Finance*. Szeged: JATEPress, pp. 35–61.

Koller, B. (2011) *Trajectories of Identity Formation in the Post-Enlargement Era. The Hungarian Example. Krakow Jagiellońskie Forum Europejskie* [Jagiellonian European Forum], 20, pp. 7–29.

Ladrech, R. (1994) Europeanization of Domestic Politics and Institutions: The Case of France. *Journal of Common Market Studies* 32(1), pp. 69–88.

Ladrech, R. (2010) *Europeanization and National Politics*. Basingstoke: Palgrave Macmillan.

Markowski, R. (2016) The Polish Parliamentary Election of 2015: A Free and Fair Election That Results in Unfair Political Consequences. *West European Politics* 39(6), pp. 1311–1322.

Molnár, A. (2011) Idea of Europe in Hungarian Political Discourse. In: Ramos, C.T. (ed.) *Ideas of Europe in National Political Discourse*. Bologna: Il Mulino, pp. 229–263.

Molnár, A. (2013) EU Membership and the Question of Hungary's Sovereignty: Ideas of the European Union Before and Following the Crisis. In: Rye, L. (ed.) *Distant Voices: Ideas on Democracy and the Eurozone Crisis*. Trondheim: Akademika Forlag, pp. 75–105.

Olsen, J. P. (2002) The Many Faces of Europeanization, *Journal of Common Market Studies* 40(5): 921–952.

Paterson, William E. (2011) The Reluctant Hegemon? Germany Moves Centre Stage in the European Union, *Journal of Common Market Studies* 49 (annual review), pp. 57–75.

Pennings, P., H. Keman and J. Kleinnijenhuis (1999) *Doing Research in Political Science*. London: Sage Publications.

Fico, R. (2016) Visegrád Countries Could Veto Brexit Deal. Politico 18 September. [ONLINE] Available from: www.politico.eu/article/robert-fico-visegrad-countries-could-veto-brexit-deal-hungary-poland-czech-republic-slovakia-right-to-work/ (accessed 17 January 2017).

Putnam, R. (1988) Diplomacy and Domestic Politics: The Logic of Two-Level Games, *International Organization* 42(3), pp. 427–460.

Radaelli, C. (2003) The Europeanization of Public Policy. In: Featherstone, K. and Radaelli, C. (eds) *The Politics of Europeanization*. Oxford: Oxford University Press, pp. 27–56.

Radaelli. C. and R. Pasquier (2008) Conceptual Issues. In: Graziano, P. and Vink, M.P. (eds) *Europeanization: New Research Agendas*. Basingstoke: Palgrave Macmillan, pp. 35–46.

Rácz G. (2014) It's Official: Rosatom Backs Plans to Double Paks Capacity, *Budapest Business Journal* January 14. [ONLINE] Available from http://bbj.hu/business/its-official-rosatom-backs-plans-to-double-paks-capacity_74439 (accessed 5 January 2017).

Rácz A. (2015) *A Calculated Non-action Miscalculated: Hungary's Migration Crisis. Visegrád Revue 20*. October 2015. [ONLINE] Available from http://visegradrevue.eu/a-calculated-non-action-miscalculated-hungarys-migration-crisis/ (accessed 17 January 2017).

Risse, T., Cowles, M.G. and Caporaso, J. (2001) Europeanization and Domestic Change: Introduction. In: Cowles, M.G., Caporaso, J. and Risse, T. (eds) *Transforming Europe: Europeanization and Domestic Change*. Ithaca, NY: Cornell University Press, pp. 1–20.

Sadecki, A. (2014) Hungary's Stance on the Ukrainian-Russian conflict. Centre for Eastern Studies (OSW) 21 May. [ONLINE] Available from https://www.osw.waw.pl/en/publikacje/analyses/ 2014-05-21/hungarys-stance-ukrainian-russian-conflict (accessed 5 January 2017).

Schweiger, C. (2013) *Insiders vs Outsiders: The V4 in a Changing EU*. [ONLINE] Available from: http://www.cepolicy.org/publications/insiders-vs-outsiders-v4-changing-eu (accessed 5 January 2017).

Sikorski, Radek (2011) Poland and the Future of the European Union, Speech given in Berlin, 28 November 2011. Available from: http://www.mfa.gov.pl/resource/33ce6061-ec12-4da1-a145-01e2995c6302:JCR (downloaded 6 October 2017).

Simmelfennig, F. and Sedelmeier, U. (2008) *The Europeanization of Central and Eastern Europe* (first published 2005). Cornell University Press.

Törő, C., Butler, E. and Grúber, K. (2014) Visegrád: The Evolving Pattern of Coordination and Partnership After EU Enlargement, *Europe-Asia Studies* 66(3), pp. 364–393.

Végh Z. (2014) *Visegrád Development Aid in the Eastern Partnership Region*. Warsaw: Centre for Eastern Studies.

Visegrád group (1991) *Visegrád Declaration*. Available at: http://www.visegradgroup.eu/documents/visegrad-declarations/visegrad-declaration-110412-2 (accessed 5 January 2017).

Visegrád group (1999) *Contents of Visegrád Cooperation approved by the Prime Ministers' Summit Bratislava.* 14th May. [ONLINE] Available from www.visegradgroup.eu/cooperation/contents-of-visegrad-110412 (accessed 5 January 2017).

Visegrád group (2004) Declaration of Prime Ministers of the Czech Republic, the Republic of Hungary, the Republic of Poland and the Slovak Republic on cooperation of the Visegrád Group countries after their accession to the European Union (12 May 2004). [ONLINE] Available from http://www.visegradgroup.eu/documents/visegrad-declarations/visegrad-declaration-110412-1 (accessed 5 January 2017).

Visegrád group (2004) *Guidelines on the Future Areas of Visegrád Cooperation,* 12 May 2004. [ONLINE] Available from http://www.visegradgroup.eu/2004/guidelines-on-the-future (accessed 17 January 2017).

Visegrád group (2013a) *Joint Declaration of the Foreign Ministers of the Visegrád Countries and Croatia on the Occasion of the Croatian Accession to the EU* [ONLINE] Available from: http://www.visegradgroup.eu/calendar/ 2013/joint-declaration-of-the (accessed 5 January 2017).

Visegrád group (2013b) *Joint Statement of the Visegrád Group Prime Ministers,* 19 June. Available at: http://www.visegradgroup.eu/calendar/2015/joint-statement-of-the (accessed 5 January 2017).

Visegrád group (2014) *Statement of the V4 Prime Ministers on Ukraine,* March 4. [ONLINE] Available from: www.visegradgroup.eu/calendar/2014/statement-of-the-prime (accessed 5 January 2017).

Visegrád group (2014) *Report of the Hungarian Presidency of the Visegrád Group July 2013-June 2014.* [ONLINE] Available from: www.visegradgroup.eu/documents/annual-reports (accessed 5 January 2017).

Visegrád group (2016) *Report of the Czech Presidency of the Visegrád Group July 2015-June 2016.* [ONLINE] Available from: http://www.visegradgroup.eu/documents/presidency-programs/20152016-czech (accessed 5 January 2017).

Weiss, T. (2012) Visegrád Battlegroup: A Flagship that Should not Substitute for Real Defence Cooperation. *Visegrád Revue.* 4 June. [ONLINE] Available from: http://visegradrevue.eu/visegrad-battlegroup-a-flagship-that-should-not-substitute-for-real-defence-cooperation/ (accessed 5 January 2017).

Zalán, E. (2016) EU Migrant Quota Idea is Finished, Fico says. EUobserver 27 September. [ONLINE] Available from: https://euobserver.com/migration/135245 (accessed 5 January 2017).

8 Slovakia

Farewell to a passive policy-taker role?

Zsolt Gál and Darina Malová

Introduction: welcome to the country of the 'in between'

The[1] EU's multiple crises have had a major impact on Slovak economy and politics. Since the EU accession (and even more prior to it) Slovakia traditionally has been rather a passive policy-taker country, a kind of responsible and silent good student, going along with the crowd, fulfilling its obligations, trying to achieve the largest possible degree of integration by getting to the EU core and staying there (Malová et al 2005, Nič et al 2014). However, this time something unusual has happened. Slovakia openly and loudly revolted against the EU mainstream on two major issues: it refused to take part in the first Greek bailout (2010) and refused to accept the reallocation mechanism ('refugee quotas') proposed by the European Commission (2015). These two EU-related issues – as never before – became hot and widely discussed topics in domestic politics and influenced the outcome of parliamentary elections in 2010 and 2016. However, regarding the durable effects of the revolts, similarities end here. The reluctance to help the Greeks, who were regarded as irresponsible and lazy, turned out to be an exceptional episode with its impact gradually fading away. Slovakia subsequently participated in the bailouts by joining EU rescue funds (EFSF, ESM), supported and implemented all new EU-legislation enhancing fiscal responsibility (like the Fiscal Compact). It also adopted – with an overwhelming majority in the parliament – a constitutional debt-break and established an independent fiscal council (Council for Budget Responsibility – CBR) in 2011. Overall Slovakia consolidated its public finances and returned to the unofficial elite club of fiscally prudent Eurozone members. However, the legacy of the refugee crisis is here to stay since it contributed to the rise of populism and extremism and riding these waves several non-standard, nationalist and anti-establishment extremist parties made it to the parliament in 2016.

This is a large paradox since it has been the economic and sovereign debt crisis, which had a real adverse impact on Slovakia while the refugee crisis has been virtual due to its distance, almost without any real refugees coming to the country. Parallel to this we can observe contradictory policies of the mainstream political elites: despite its negative impact they mostly resisted the temptation to use the EU's economic problems in a populist anti-EU manner, blaming Brussels for domestic problems (like recession, unemployment or the necessary austerity measures). On migration the opposite is true, only with a minor difference: this time the German government personalized by chancellor Angela Merkel turned out to be an even bigger scapegoat than all the eurocrats in Brussels.[2] On the other hand, in both cases the majority of leaders remained responsive to their voters: the general support for EU and euro membership is still relatively high, the refusal to accept any immigrants even higher.

Taking into account all the paradoxes and contradictions, it is hard to answer the question where Slovakia actually belongs. Is it definitively anchored at the EU core or it is still part of the periphery? Is it an example of successful transition towards liberal democracy or just the next in line heading for an illiberal turn? Has it finally arrived in the West or has it never really left the East in its mindset? Usually there are a number of good arguments to underpin different answers. In this chapter we argue that Slovakia is somewhere in between – we might call it the *semi-periphery*. Although Europeanization has been successful economically it has been so mostly on the level of integrating into the single market and technically implementing EU rules. Social norms, informal rules and cultural values of the EU mainstream have not been fully internalized by local political elites, let alone society. Mostly following strictly economic purposes elites accepted EU norms and rules via the mechanism of strategic calculation but this did not ensure durable behavioural changes (Checkel 2005). What has emerged in Slovakia is rather an unbalanced political system, with elitist and personalised parties that have failed to establish strong and stable ties with (civil) society, high levels of corruption, low levels of popular trust in national political institutions, and a weakly institutionalised party system (Malová and Dolný 2016). Additionally, many symptoms of state capture are present and politicians usually do not hesitate to turn towards populist rhetoric and policies if these look profitable in electoral terms.

On the following pages, using examples of EU crises with the largest impact on Slovak economy and politics, we will try to explain the moving forces behind contradictory political decisions often resulting in paradoxical outcomes. The fiscal consolidation (a consequence of economic crisis) is a good illustration of the Europeanization of Slovak politics. It demonstrated the prevailing and durable willingness of political elites to comply with EU rules and norms even at the expense of sacrifices but at the same time its context and two-sided nature shows the limits of this Europeanization as well. The refugee crisis on the other hand fully revealed these limits showing the weak embeddedness of crucial values and norms among the political elite and society.

Before turning to the main analyses it is important to underline some general characteristics of the country and its economy because they intertwined with the impacts of the crises influencing economic, social and political development.

First, and most important, Slovakia is one of the most open economies in the World, very much dependent on export demand and very vulnerable to external shocks. Export to GDP ratio has been over 90 per cent during the last few years (Table 8.1). The main driver of the recession in 2009 as well as the

Table 8.1 Some major economic indicators in Slovakia (2006–2016)

Indicator/year	*2006*	*2007*	*2008*	*2009*	*2010*	*2011*	*2012*	*2013*	*2014*	*2015*	*2016*
Real GDP growth rate (%)	8.5	10.8	5.6	-5.4	5.0	2.8	1.7	1.5	2.6	3.8	3.6
GDP per capita in PPS, Index (EU28 = 100)	63	67	71	71	74	75	76	77	77	77	77
Export (% of GDP)	81.0	83.3	80.0	67.6	76.3	85.0	91.4	93.8	91.8	93.5	-
Export (annual % growth)	22.9	14.6	3.0	-16.8	15.7	12.0	9.3	6.7	3.7	7.0	5.5
FDI inflow (% of GDP)	10.0	6.5	4.9	1.9	2.3	5.6	1.9	1.0	-0.4	1.3	-
Budget deficit (% of GDP)	-3.6	-1.9	-2.4	-7.8	-7.5	-4.3	-4.3	-2.7	-2.7	-2.7	-2.0
Public debt (% of GDP)	31.0	30.1	28.5	36.3	41.2	43.7	52.2	54.7	53.6	52.5	53.5
Private debt (% of GDP)	51.8	60.4	64.9	69.2	67.4	70.2	70.6	74.0	77.6	81.4	-
Public revenue (% of GDP)	35.2	34.4	34.5	36.3	34.7	36.5	36.3	38.7	39.3	42.9	39.8
Public expenditure (% of GDP)	38.8	36.3	36.9	44.1	42.1	40.8	40.6	41.4	42.0	45.6	41.8
Unemployment rate (%)	13.5	11.2	9.6	12.1	14.5	13.7	14.0	14.2	13.2	11.5	9.8

Source: Eurostat, World Bank (for annual export growth) and Ministerstvo financií SR 2016: 5, 10, 15 (for 2016 forecasts). Notes: PPS – purchasing power standards; export – exports of goods and services; FDI – foreign direct investments; budget deficit – general government deficit according to the European System of Accounts (ESA 2010); public debt, revenue and expenditure – general government gross debt/revenue/expenditure according to the European System of Accounts (ESA 2010); private debt – private sector debt is the stock of liabilities held by the sectors non-financial corporations and households and non-profit institutions serving households; unemployment – unemployed persons as a percentage of the labour force based on the Labour Force Survey. Data for 2016 are forecasts by the Slovak Ministry of Finance from the 2017–2019 budget proposal.

recovery since then has been the shrinking and rising export demand. Naturally, in such a country, economic policies at national level, (mainly fiscal policy) have very limited effects on growth – at least in the short and medium-term. The massive fiscal stimulus of 2009 did not save the economy from shrinking but fiscal consolidations did not kill off the recovery in 2011 or 2013 either (Table 8.1).

Obviously the policies at national level have a crucial role in influencing long-term growth. This should be the second point: Slovakia was in very good economic condition when the crisis hit. Mainly thanks to the in-depth structural reforms of two consecutive governments led by prime minister Mikuláš Dzurinda, especially the centre-right second Dzurinda administration's (2002–2006) comprehensive reform package.[3] A successful, neoliberal growth model had been created. Slovakia became the fastest growing EU economy, often nicknamed 'Tatra tiger', with one of the lowest public debts and most stable financial sectors. Not a single bank bailout was needed during the crisis.

Successful consolidation and the death of the 'Tatra tiger'

Between 2010 and 2014, two different Slovak governments managed to reduce the budget deficit from almost eight per cent of GDP to less than three per cent. This enabled the country to quit the EU's excessive deficit procedure and succeed in stabilizing the public debt at around 53 per cent of GDP. Considering the current plans to reach – for the first time in history – a balanced budget till 2019[4] – there is a good chance of achieving it; and the fiscal consolidation process is a definite success. Slovak governments demonstrated several times that – in order to get to the euro core and remain there – they are willing to sacrifice quite a lot (i.e. conduct deep, sometimes unpopular structural reforms and austerity measures). The strategic goal of governments to achieve the maximum degree of integration shared by most mainstream political elites has been present at least since 2006 when the first Fico government – after a short hesitation – opted to continue on the track towards Eurozone membership, which resulted in the adoption of the single currency from 2009.

In spite of this impressive record, there are still some serious question marks about the embeddedness of prudent fiscal policies among main political actors. Yes, Slovakia technically has fulfilled its obligations or (in the case of the balanced budget) is on the way to do it. But would political leaders stick to EU-conformist sober budgetary policies even if it seems to be politically too costly? There are good reasons for some scepticism.

One reason is a mixed history of fiscal policies, the other the nature and character of consolidation. The Smer-SD party with its leader and prime minister, Robert Fico has been running the county, leading different multi-party coalitions or alone, for almost a decade from 2006 to 2017 (with a short interruption of less than two years between 2010–2012).

The first Fico government (2006–2010) left office with public finances out of control. In 2009–2010, they failed to adjust the fiscal policy to the economic crisis and it resulted in huge budget deficits of around €5 billion or almost eight per cent of the GDP in 2009 and 2010. Naturally Slovakia entered the excessive deficit procedure imposed by the European Commission in 2009. There is no rational explanation for this behaviour other than pure political calculations.[5]

A closer look at the consolidation record of the second Fico government shows a much less impressive picture. The consolidation was short and occurred basically in one single year – 2013. It was also shallow and helped by a very favourable external environment (see below). More than 40 per cent of it has been achieved by cutting social security contributions to the fully funded second pillar of the pension system and simply channelling them back to the public social security funds (Table 8.2) – a short-term gain at the expense of long-term sustainability of public finances. Further consolidation targets, like achieving the balanced budget, have been postponed several times. Ľudovít Ódor, one of the board members of the Council for Budget Responsibility (and one of the CBR's founding fathers) reminded us in his blog that the first plans to achieve a balanced budget had a target date of 2010 and as time has passed

> it seems to be it is a constant priority: doesn't matter in which year we are, what we promised, how fast we grow against the plans, how much additional money we have from taxes, we always want to achieve a balanced budget in three or four years from now.
>
> (Ódor 2016)

Additionally, the adoption of the debt-break law and the creation of CBR from the viewpoint of the Smer party could be interpreted also as necessary costs in a bigger political pact that opened the way for the early elections in March 2012, when they achieved a triumphant historic victory. Its risks were considered low at that time and once effects started to bite (limiting the government in its fiscal policy) rumours appeared on how to circumvent and plans for how to soften it. The aim for some kind of a 'strategic public investment' exception in the constitutional law is part of the third Fico government's official manifesto.[6]

There were two major consolidations in Slovakia after the crisis, one in 2011 – mostly on the expenditure side, the other in 2013 – mostly on the revenues side, both in the first (full) year after the parliamentary elections.[7] The centre-right Radičová government (2010–2012) was mostly made up from the former 2002–2006 reformers and their supporters. It was therefore no surprise that it tried to consolidate while maintaining and repairing the neoliberal growth model that it had previously created. The consolidation therefore had been occurring mostly on the expenditure side and revenues were raised to harm employment minimally, thus not targeting workers and businesses but rather consumption (for example the value-added tax increased from 19 to 20 per cent). The government managed to cut deficit significantly in 2011 but during the autumn of that year it collapsed. Its fate had been influenced by the EU's sovereign debt crisis. After just weeks in office, concerned because of a possible moral hazard and reasoning that 'the more responsible, poorer [countries] should not be raising money for the less responsible, richer ones' (PM Radičová), most coalition MPs refused the first Greek bailout in the Slovak parliament. But shortly after – all parties together – approved guarantees of €4.4 billion (6.7 per cent of GDP) as part of the European Financial Stability Facility – EFSF.[8] However, with the ongoing crisis an EU request arrived to expand ESFS. PM Radičová joined this vote with the vote of confidence in her government but still failed to persuade the liberal party Freedom and Solidarity (SaS – one of the four coalition members) which declined to vote for the proposal. The expansion of EFSF was adopted in a second vote just two days later – opposition Smer MPs joined the rest of the former coalition in exchange for the promise of preliminary elections. These were held in March 2012.

The clean-up of the fiscal mess left behind by the first Fico government landed on the shoulders of the second Fico government (2012–2016) – fair and square at the end. Contrary to the first Fico cabinet (2006–2010) when the framework of previous neoliberal reforms enacted by the centre-right Dzurinda government remained untouched (which came as a surprise),[9] this time the consolidation tasks had been accomplished at the expense of dismantling the previous growth model. Nevertheless, this is not the only reason why we question the real embeddedness of prudent fiscal policies. The arguments and criticism could be summarized as follows:

First, the consolidation sacrificed the previous neoliberal growth model which was very successful but did not replace it with an equivalent which could be classified as social democratic. The most important symbol of the previous reforms, the flat income tax was abolished and the second-pillar of the pension system seriously weakened (See Table 8.2 for a more detailed description of the 2013 consolidation package).

Second, the consolidation mix raises some questions. Contrary to the previous centre-right government, tax increases were targeting mostly the labour force and businesses, thus being much more distortive. This might explain to a large degree why development at the labour market was lagging so much behind economic growth. GDP reached its pre-crisis level already in 2011, labour market conditions just at the end of 2016. Economic convergence and FDI inflow also slowed down significantly. In addition, it is hard to understand why a party which identifies itself as social democratic failed to use many instruments widely regarded as leftist. For example, immovable property taxes are very low in Slovakia, there was some discussion about increasing them but no legislative action followed.[10] The same is true for universal welfare benefits, which could be limited for households with higher income (like childcare allowances): some discussion but no action. In the case of personal capital income taxes or environmental taxes even serious discussion was absent.

Third, consolidation could have been much more ambitious for economic reasons. It happened in very favourable external environment: the demand on the main export markets had been growing (Table 8.1), Slovakia had been a

Table 8.2 The consolidation package that killed the 'Tatra tiger' (most important measures of the second Fico government's consolidation package and their estimated fiscal effects)

Description of the most important measures	*Estimated positive impact on public budget (ESA 95 methodology, millions of €)*	
	2012	2013
Pension system: the contribution rate to the second pillar reduced from 9 to 4% of gross wage, possibility to return from the combination of two pillars to just the first PAY-GO one (up to the end of January 2013).	185	701
Abolishing the 19% flat income tax: the corporate income tax increased from 19 to 23%; in the case of personal income tax a second rate of 25% introduced for a monthly income above EUR 3 311.	0	351
Social security and health-care contributions to be paid from earnings from temporary work agreements (previously only 19% income tax and a minor 1% insurance was deducted).	0	125
Maximum assessment base for social security and health-care contributions increased and unified at five times the average wage.	0	130
Increasing the bank levy: the tax base of the bank levy (0.4% of the liabilities) introduced in 2012 broadened to the deposits guaranteed by the state (basically household deposits), plus an extraordinary single levy for 2012.	62	89
Temporary extra taxes levied on profits **in regulated sectors** (like energy, telecommunication, insurance, postal services).	31	81
Higher social security and health-care contributions paid by the self-employed.	0	52
Fees for public (TV and radio) broadcasting reintroduced.	0	74
Total	279	1,628

Source: Ministerstvo financií SR (2013) pp. 15–16. Note: Numbers were rounded up, several measures with smaller (positive or negative) effect on the public budget were left out, therefore the sum of the listed measures does not equal the total fiscal impact in the last row.

great beneficiary of the net transfers from the common EU budget. Due to the low interest-rate environment it had been very cheap and easy to refinance public debt and even the change in EU accounting rules was helpful to (statistically) improve fiscal indicators.[11]

Fourth, consolidation could have been much more ambitious for political reasons as well. The unprecedented unique opportunity to use a single-party government with disciplined and stable parliamentary majority to proceed faster with deficit reduction had been missed. At the end, the feeble, multi-party

Radičová government with a narrow majority consolidated more in one single year (2011) than the one-party second Fico government during its whole four-year term.

Fifth and finally, the sustainability of the public finances is still a major concern, slow consolidation was not able to create fiscal buffers for any future crisis. To make it worse, this time the problems might come from the previously remarkably stable banking sector as well. Although the public debt has been stabilised, private debt is just the opposite mainly due to the sharply rising indebtedness of the households. As the Slovak National Bank warned (in May 2016) the rate of housing loan growth in Slovakia has been by far the highest in the whole EU for five consecutive years. The same is true for household debt generally within the Central and Eastern European new member states of the EU – as a result Slovaks probably became the most indebted nation in the region (regarding household debt to GDP ratio).[12]

The refugee crisis paradox: a virtual problem with real and enduring consequences

The number of foreigners residing in Slovakia reached almost 90 thousand (1.6 per cent of total population) and the number of asylum applications in 2015 had been 330, asylum was granted to eight people; in both cases Slovakia has one of the lowest numbers as a share of its population within the EU (Mesežnikov 2016).[13] It's not an exaggeration to state that the 2015–2016 refugee crisis has been virtual for the vast majority of Slovaks. They could watch it on TV and the internet but they have barely met any refugee, or in most cases even an immigrant, in their neighbourhood.

To show dramatic pictures of refugees and use them in a heated pre-election contest, which was dominated by the question of who is going to defend Slovakia more from the migrants, PM Robert Fico with his interior minister had to visit the Macedonian-Greek border. Officially they visited Slovak policemen helping to guard the border but since it happened three days before the parliamentary elections the real intention was quite obvious. So here we have a big paradox: Slovakia was almost untouched by the refugee crisis but the issue still resonated in the pre-election contest with shocking intensity.

In 2015, the Slovak parliament adopted two resolutions refusing to accept the relocation mechanism's quotas proposed by the European Commission. In a fast-track regime it changed the constitution and several laws, as part of the so-called anti-terrorist package. The government, after failing to block the quotas in the EU's Justice and Home Affairs Council (only Slovakia, the Czech Republic, Hungary, and Romania voted against), filed a lawsuit against the Council decision at the European Court of Justice (Mesežnikov, 2016: 118–119; Baboš et al 2016: 26). The Slovak rebellion turned not just against the refugee quotas and Brussels proposing them but against the very idea of accepting refugees or any migrants, especially Muslims.

The revolt had been led by the governing Smer-SD party and its leader, PM Robert Fico. They even adjusted their main campaign slogan to the events, changing it from 'We work for the people' to 'We protect Slovakia'. The campaign and its aftermath revealed many things, among others the marketing of Smer as a catch-all party character, the twofold strategy of prime minister Fico, the dangers of playing with the extremist card and the weak embeddedness of European values and norms among elites and the electorate.

At first look, it might seem stunning that a party which is nominally centre-left, a member of the Party of European Socialists bloc in the EU and includes the term social democracy even in its name (Smer-SD means Direction-SD where SD refers to social democracy) uses nationalism, xenophobia and islamophobia to attract voters. However, Smer-SD always has been a catch-all party with lot of marketing and little, if any, ideological substance pursuing changeable policies responsive to the feelings of its voters and potential voters (Malová 2013). It has been its modus operandi for a long time to make public opinion polls for internal use, map the concerns of the people and shape policies – quite often pseudo policies – accordingly. Considering the astonishing resistance to accepting any migrants in Slovakia, no surprise Smer-SD and Fico followed the never-failing recipe again. According to various public opinion polls in 2015–16 70 per cent of respondents refused to accept any refugees who might be sent to Slovakia on the basis of the relocation mechanism; 70 per cent had fears over the influx of refugees to Europe; 63 per cent shared the concern that these refugees represent a threat for Slovakia and its citizens; 86 per cent agreed with the government's decisions to refuse the quotas and to strengthen controls and 70 per cent supported its lawsuit against the quotas (Baboš et al 2016: 26; Mesežnikov, 2016). A substantial majority of citizens even refuses to accept the need for legal labour migrants in certain sectors of the economy[14] in spite of the fact that employer associations are in favour of their entry.

No wonder Fico entered the election campaign with statements like 'There is No Room for Islam in Slovakia'. He also talked about 'immensely high' security threat for Slovaks and reassured them that his government monitors 'every single Muslim' in the country. Fico promised that 'Slovak citizens and their security is of higher priority than the rights of migrants' adding that 'the only way to eliminate risks like Paris and Germany is to prevent the creation of a compact Muslim community in Slovakia' (quoted by Cunningham 2016). However, this has been the local political folklore for domestic-use only, he and his government also displayed a constructive European attitude externally (especially during the Slovak presidency of the EU Council in the second half of 2016). Janus-faced politics is also a permanent characteristic of Fico and Smer-SD.[15] This time the human face of the Slovak government and Smer-SD party has been represented by Fico himself, especially during various meetings of the EU presidency but also by his Foreign Minister Miroslav Lajčák, who happened to be the candidate of Slovakia for the post of the UN Secretary General. While Fico was giving his tough speeches on Muslims and migrants at home, Lajčák gave a speech at the UN headquarters in New York in which he was calling for humane treatment, safety and dignity for all refugees and migrants. He condemned Islamophobia as something unacceptable since it would be discrimination on the basis of religious beliefs, which is prohibited under the UN Charter.

Despite all efforts the populist/extremist card turned out to be a two-edged sword this time. Fico had to realise that although his tough speeches and the hysteria around migrants were a successful mobilization tool, they roused the nationalist, extremist and non-standard protest parties who then made it to the parliament; while Smer-SD suffered heavy losses.[16] There are a number of probable reasons: the alternative parties perhaps had been much more authentic in their resistance against migration than an incumbent governing party, which had been in power for almost a decade with eroding legitimacy due to a large number of corruption scandals. The record of Smer-SD in other areas, such as health-care, education and the fight against corruption was relatively poor. These issues had been also important campaign topics and the timing and intensity was problematic. Smer-SD came with the migrant topic too early and overshot. The challenging new parties were much more active on the internet, especially on Facebook, and attracted many young people. Whatever the reason, the genie is already out of the bottle, public discourse has radicalised, the extremists are sitting in the parliament and there are no signs of improvement.

Finally, from our viewpoint the most important thing revealed by the refugee crisis has been the weak embeddedness of European norms and values – the vast majority of the political elite broke with humanitarian EU norms when it faced high domestic costs. They followed public opinion and even incited the refusal of and hatred against migrants. There were very few dissenting voices, notably the small Hungarian-Slovak mixed party Most-Híd ('Bridge') and president Andrej Kiska, who is not directly involved in party politics.

Conclusion

With flourishing populism and extremism, the question remains if Slovakia may be the next country which turns towards the illiberal way? We argue that this scenario is still unlikely. Certainly, there are some signs of an illiberal turn: notably the political control over large parts of the justice system (especially police and prosecutors) and the neutralization of many institutions, which should serve as checks and balances but fall short of their mission. This often includes the public media which has a tradition of frequent political interference and includes a number of private printed and electronic media bought by local oligarchs and financial groups with political ties. Yet there are still more barriers. First, the proportional electoral system makes it hard to form a single-party government (the only exception was the 2012–16 period), let alone one with a constitutional majority. Second, directly elected president Kiska who defeated PM Fico with a great margin in the second round of the 2014 presidential elections is still popular and committed to democratic values.

Third, there are still a number of independent institutions which could work as barriers such as fiscal rules (the debt-brake law) and institutions (CBR) or the Slovak National Bank (member of the Euro system). Fourth, EU membership is still popular amongst the population, even more across the business elites. In the end even the Slovak state showing strong symptoms of 'state capture' is pro-European in its nature and its oligarchs have a rational economic interest to stay in the EU to have access to the Single Market and EU funds. Finally, the Slovak civic sector and media is still relatively experienced in fighting governments with authoritative tendencies.

The most important party, Smer-SD is currently in decline, so the main threat to democracy is not a scenario that it will take over the state and master an illiberal turn but rather the consequences of the captured state itself. The endemic, systemic and unpunished corruption machine run by the untouchable governing elite and their crony oligarchs is fuelling frustration among the electorate. This might further increase support for populist and extremist ideas and parties and undermine trust in democratic institutions creating a serious threat to the unconsolidated and feeble democracy.

To conclude, we see Slovakia inhabiting a semi-periphery in between, standing with one leg in the EU-core Western club of liberal democracies and with the other still in the EU-periphery Eastern club of unconsolidated democracies. Naturally, regarding different areas, the country is more on one than on the other side. For example, considering economic integration, it is much closer to the EU-core but looking at the embeddedness of democratic norms and cultural values it is situated closer to the (Eastern) periphery. It is currently not possible to identify a clear direction for Slovakia. The future hence remains uncertain. While it seems to be rather unlikely that Slovakia will take the illiberal turn the quality and stability of Slovak democracy nevertheless faces serious challenges.

Notes

1 This research was supported by the Slovak Grant Agency for Science (VEGA) under grant number 1/0599/17 and by the Slovak Research and Development Agency (grant number APVV145–0732).

2 Slovak PM Robert Fico responded to German criticism of his government's stance in the refugee crisis in February 2016 with the following words: 'They [the Germans] mind that we do not want to listen. The idea is simple: I invited to my house a million guests, currently I am unable to cope with them, so I am knocking on the doors of my neighbors, take care about my guests… Germany made a mistake, when unfolding and saying, come here. I do not need here unified ghettos with different religion. Nobody will force us to bring here migrants, never.' (Cited by Mesežnikov 2016: 126) The leader of the main opposition party (SAS) and member of the EU Parliament, Richard Sulík presented very similar ideas even directly to the German public as he quite frequently appeared in German TV debates (notably at public broadcaster ARD) criticizing the Merkel-government, the EU Commission and other European players for mishandling the refugee crisis. For the detailed

picture on the views of relevant Slovak political parties on the refugee crisis see Mesežnikov 2016.

3 The most important reforms included tax, pension, health-care, labour market and welfare reforms and fiscal decentralisation. See Mikloš 2008 for a more detailed overview of the reforms.

4 For the general government budget proposal for the 3-year period of 2017–2019, see Ministerstvo financií SR 2016.

5 There were five different elections in row (presidential elections followed by elections to the European Parliament and regional elections in 2009 and parliamentary elections followed by municipal elections in 2010), so it is quite clear why the incumbent government was reluctant to cut the deficits. A good illustration for the conflict of political and economic cycles.

6 'In order to secure constitutional majority, the Government will initiate a wide discussion of experts and the public, as well as political discussion... on achieving the neutrality of the so-called debt brake in the management of public debt by linking the sanction brackets to net public debt rather than gross public debt, while taking into account strategic public investments in the application of sanctions and setting the parameters of sanction brackets in a manner that will facilitate Slovakia's economic development.' Úrad vlády SR (2016).

7 See Goliaš (2015) for the analysis and overview of fiscal consolidations in Slovakia 2010–2015.

8 See the paper of Goliaš and Jurzyca (2013) on the solutions to the EU's debt crisis from the Slovak perspective.

9 See Gould (2009) for a comprehensive analysis of this period and the explanations for the surprising development of Fico's policies.

10 See Remeta, J. et al 2015, for the evolution of the tax mix in Slovakia and its possible reforms.

11 The change in the European System of National and Regional Accounts (ESA), the EU's accounting framework (from ESA 95 to ESA 2010) led to a revision and nominal increase of the Slovak GDP and this decreased the debt to GDP ratio in 2013 by 1.1 percentage points. See RRZ 2014.

12 See Národná banka Slovenska (2016: 5). According to the Slovak National Bank's data at the end of 2015 with 33.2 per cent of household debt to GDP ratio Slovakia has been 'only' third in the region following Poland (35 per cent) and Croatia (37.3 per cent). However, considering the trend of 2015 (strong annual growth in Slovakia by 12.6 per cent, only modest growth in Poland by 3.4 per cent, and slow decline in Croatia) and assuming a similar development for 2016 it is very likely that Slovakia has gained the first position since.

13 See Mesežnikov 2016 for a comprehensive overview of the migration crisis in Slovakia.

14 Only 19 per cent of Slovak respondents agreed with the statement '(OUR COUNTRY) needs legal migrants to work in certain sectors of the economy' – putting Slovakia in last place within the EU (the average for EU-28 was 51%). See: European Parliament (2015: 33).

15 See Szomolányi and Gál (2016) for a more detailed view on Fico's double speak and Janus-faced politics.

16 In the 2016 parliamentary elections Smer-SD lost more than a third of its voters compared to 2012 and gained 'just' 28.3 per cent. The extreme right-wing People's Party – Our Slovakia (ĽSNS) with neo-Nazi roots gained 8 per cent of the vote, another newcomer was a populist protest party 'We Are Family–Boris Kollár', which achieved 6.6 per cent and the traditional nationalist force in Slovak politics SNS (Slovak National Party) also returned to the parliament (after 4 years) with 8.6 per cent support. During the campaign all used tough anti-immigrant rhetoric.

References

Baboš, P., Világi, A. and Oravcová, V. (2016) *Spoločenské Problémy, Politické Riešenia*. Bratislava: Stimul.

Checkel, J.T. (2005) International Institutions and Socialization in Europe: Introduction and Framework, *International Organization* 59(4), pp. 801–826.

Cunningham, B. (2016) 'We Protect Slovakia'. Voters Worry About Jobs and Health care – but the PM is Obsessed with Non-existent Migrants, Politico, 17 February. [ONLINE] Available from: http://www.politico.eu/article/slovakia-fico-migrants-refugees-asylum-crisis-smer-election/ (accessed 10 December 2016).

European Parliament (2015) *European Parliament Eurobarometer (EB/EP 84.1) – Parlemeter 2015*. [ONLINE] Available from: http://www.europarl.europa.eu/atyourservice/en/20150630PVL00108/2015-parlemeter (accessed 10 December 2016).

Eurostat (2016) *Database*. [ONLINE] Available from: http://ec.europa.eu/eurostat/data/database (accessed 10 December 2016).

Goliaš, P. (2015) Public Finance Consolidation in Slovakia. In: Goliaš, P. (ed.) *Public Finance Consolidation in V4 Plus Ukraine*. Bratislava: INEKO – Institute for Economic and Social Reforms, pp. 4–12.

Goliaš, P. and Jurzyca, E. (2013) *Solutions to the Debt Crisis in the EU from the Slovak Perspective*. Bratislava: INEKO – Institute for Economic and Social Reforms.

Gould, J. (2009) Slovakia's Neoliberal Churn: The Political Economy of the Fico Government, 2006–2008. Institute of European Studies and International Relations, Working Paper Series 1, Bratislava.

Malová, D. (2013) Slovakia. In: J.-M. De Weale, F. Escalona, M. Vieira (eds) *The Palgrave Handbook of Social Democracy in the European Union*. Basingstoke: Palgrave Macmillan, pp. 550–574.

Malová, D., Láštic, E. and Rybář, M. (2005) *Slovensko ako nový členský štát Európskej únie: Výzva z periférie? Slovakia as a New European Union Member State: A Challenge from Periphery*. Bratislava: Friedrich Ebert Stiftung.

Malová, D. and Dolný, B. (2016) Economy and Democracy in Slovakia during the Crisis: From a Laggard to the EU Core, *Problems of Post-Communism* 63(5–6), pp. 300–312.

Mesežnikov, G. (2016) Problematika migrácie a utečencov na Slovensku v rokoch 2015–2016: spoločenská atmosféra, verejná mienka, politickí aktéri. In: Hlinčíková, M. and Mesežnikov, G. (eds) *Otvorená krajina alebo nedobytná pevnosť? Slovensko, migranti a utečenci*. Bratislava: Inštitút pre verejné otázky, Heinrich-Böll-Stiftung.

Mikloš, I. (2008) Slovakia: A story of Reforms. In: Bienkowski, W., Brada, J.C. and Radlo M.J. (eds) *Growth versus Security*. London, NY: Palgrave Macmillan, pp. 54–88.

Ministerstvo financií SR (2013) *Rozpočet verejnej správy na roky 2013 až 2015 – schválený NR SR*. [ONLINE] Available from: http://www.finance.gov.sk/Default.aspx?CatID=8842 (accessed 10 December 2016).

Ministerstvo financií SR (2016) *Návrh rozpočtu verejnej správy na roky 2017 až 2019*. [ONLINE] Available from: http://www.finance.gov.sk/Default.aspx?CatID=11224 (accessed 10 December 2016).

Národná banka Slovenska (2016) *Financial Stability Report*. May 2016. [ONLINE] Available from: http://www.nbs.sk/en/publications-issued-by-the-nbs/financial-stability-report (accessed 5 December 2016).

Nič, M., Slobodník, M. and Šimečka, M. (2014) Slovakia in the EU: An Unexpected Success Story? DGAPanalyse 6.

Ódor, L. (2016) Prázdne reči? Blog, Rada pre rozpočtovú zodpovednosť. [ONLINE] Available from: http://www.rozpoctovarada.sk/svk/rozpocet/315/prazdne-reci (accessed 10 December 2016).

RRZ – Rada pre rozpočtovú zodpovednosť (2014) *Vplyv metodiky ESA 2010.* [ONLINE] Available from: http://www.rozpoctovarada.sk/svk/rozpocet/250/vplyv-metodiky-esa2010 (accessed 10 December 2016).

Remeta, J. et al (2015) *Moving Beyond the Flat Tax: Tax Policy Reform in the Slovak Republic.* OECD Taxation Working Paper, 22, Paris.

Szomolányi S. and Z. Gál (2016) Slovakia's Elite: Between Populism and Compliance with EU Policies. In: J. Pakulski (ed.) *The Visegrád Countries in Crisis*, pp. 67–86. [ONLINE] Available at: https://depot.ceon.pl/bitstream/handle/123456789/12433/The-Visegrad-Countries-in-Crisis-%20-ed.-J.-Pakulski-2016.pdf?sequence=1 (accessed 4 September 2017).

Úrad vlády SR (2016) *Manifesto of the Government of the Slovak Republic 2016–2020.* Bratislava: Government Office of the Slovak Republic. [ONLINE] Available from: http://www.vlada.gov.sk/manifesto-of-the-government/ (accessed 10 December 2016).

World Bank (2016) *Exports of goods and services (annual % growth), Slovak Republic.* World Development Indicators. [ONLINE] Available from: http://data.worldbank.org/indicator/NE.EXP.GNFS.KD.ZG?end=2015&locations=SK&name_desc=false&start=1993&view=chart (accessed 10 December 2016).

9 The politics of internal and external migration in the enlarged EU

Bulgaria and Romania from policy-takers to policy-makers?

Nicole Lindstrom and Mihnea Căuţi

Introduction

Few EU states can be more aptly described as passive 'policy-takers' within the EU than Bulgaria and Romania. The two member states entered the EU in 2007, three years after the 'big bang' enlargement to eight other Central and East European (CEE) states like Hungary, Poland, the Czech Republic or the Baltic states. Not only were they subjected to a uniquely strict regime of pre-accession conditionality; the European Commission placed additional conditions on Bulgaria and Romania after they joined the EU. Through the so-called Cooperation and Verification Mechanism (CVM) the European Commission has monitored the progress of each state since 2007 in judicial reform, the fight against corruption and, in the case of Bulgaria, the fight against organised crime. Sanctions, including the withholding of aid, can be imposed if progress is not met. Similar to the case of other CEE states, many EU members introduced special transitional restrictions on Romanian and Bulgarian citizens' rights to free movement. However, the restrictions were both more widely imposed and lasted for a longer duration than was the case for other CEE citizens. In addition, as of 2016 neither Bulgaria nor Romania had been accepted into Schengen. Therefore, the relationship that Bulgaria and Romania have with the EU can be characterized as fundamentally *asymmetrical*, both in terms of levels of political economic development and degree of influence in EU decision-making.

This chapter analyses how this asymmetrical relation has shaped Romania and Bulgaria's strategies for influencing the EU policy-making process. If we conceive of proactive 'policy-making' as the extent to which a member state is able to influence EU decisions through normal decision-making procedures, then Bulgaria and Romania, given their lack of political leverage, relatively limited policy expertise and administrative capacity, appear to be reactive policy-takers. Yet it is worth considering how peripheral EU states like Bulgaria and Romania can use more flexible strategies to advance their interests at EU level. This chapter shows how Bulgaria and Romania, in the absence of bargaining power, utilize other means of influencing the policy debate, primarily through forming alliances with other EU member states, and in rare cases threatening the use of their veto. Acting in concert with other actors is a fundamental feature of EU decision-making. But we show how alliance formation is both more important and more fluid for states like Bulgaria and Romania: important, since it remains one of the few ways of increasing their leverage at the EU level, and fluid, since neither state can afford, given the exceptional conditions of their membership, to consistently align against core EU states.

This chapter analyses these flexible strategies and fluid alignments through a comparison of Bulgaria and Romania's positions on EU migration policy, both in terms of internal migration (the case of posted workers) and external migration (the refugee crisis). We show how in some cases Bulgaria and Romania aligned with the Visegrád Four (or V4, including Czech Republic, Hungary, Poland, and Slovakia) against the dominant preferences of core states, such as triggering a 'yellow card' to block a Commission proposal to strengthen regulations of posted workers. Yet at other times Bulgarian and Romanian leaders have chosen to align with core states, such as on EU policy on refugee relocation. Cooperation with core states is motivated in part by seeking 'loyalty rewards' (Browning and Christou 2010), such as securing Schengen entry or discontinuing the Cooperation and Verification Mechanism (CVM). The two states have also sought to create alliances with states outside the EU, such as with the so-called 'Craiova Group', a trilateral cooperation forum with Serbia. In sum, if proactive and coordinated 'policy-making' at the EU level is challenging for states like Bulgaria and Romania, given their asymmetrical relationship with the EU and limited administrative capacity, this does not preclude these states from using more reactive and flexible strategies to pursue their interests at the EU level. The chapter examines these strategies in more depth.

Romania and Bulgaria: the 'laggards' of the EU's Eastern enlargement

Bulgaria and Romania are often placed in the same category of other post-socialist 'new member states' of the EU. However, their paths to the EU have diverged from other post-socialist states in many ways. From the early 1990s it became evident that each country's transition to a functioning democratic market economy was not progressing at the same pace as in other CEE states. Romania and Bulgaria applied for EU membership in 1995. However, the Commission, determining that they had not satisfied the Copenhagen Criteria, delayed the start of their accession negotiations. The Commission cited shortcomings in institutional capacity, lack of enforcement of rule of law, mistreatment of minorities and poor quality of governance as the main obstacles to Romania and Bulgaria attaining full EU membership (Noutcheva and Bechev 2008: 116). Effectively separated from other CEEs, the two countries came to be known as the 'laggards' of the EU's astern enlargement (Noutcheva and Bechev 2008; Chiva and Phinnemore 2009; Trauner 2009). Not only did these states lag behind other CEE states in EU accession negotiations; they were subject to the strictest conditionality regime ever applied to EU applicants. Given the EU's concerns about Bulgaria and Romania's preparedness to begin EU accession negotiations, once they began the Commission became 'extremely cautious not to turn a blind eye' to domestic developments in the two countries (Andreev 2009: 377). As a result, Romania and Bulgaria had to transpose an 'unprecedented' volume of EU rules (Papadimitriou and Gateva 2009: 154).

The Commission extended this conditionality regime after Bulgaria and Romania officially joined the EU in 2007, introducing a novel set of checks and safeguards. Bulgaria and Romania's accession treaty also grants the Council of the EU the right to postpone the accession of either candidate, through a unanimous vote in the case of Bulgaria or qualified majority vote (QMV) in the case of Romania. Another tool was added, the Cooperation and Verification Mechanism (CVM), which allows the Commission to monitor the compliance of the two states on judicial reform, corruption and, in the case of Bulgaria, the fight against organised crime. Twice a year the European Commission submits both a progress report and a technical report to the European Council and European Parliament assessing the steps each state has taken to meet designated benchmarks, and identifying areas for further improvement. The Commission can suspend certain membership benefits if it deems that a state is in violation of EU conditions. The Commission used this tool in 2008, suspending nearly €600 million in aid to Bulgaria after it declared that the government had not done enough to fight high-level corruption and organized crime. Like in the previous 2004 enlargement, the accession treaty for Bulgaria and Romania permitted other member states to impose transitional restrictions on the free movement rights of Bulgarian and Romanian citizens up to seven years after accession. Most EU-15 states chose to impose restrictions, except Finland and Sweden.[1] The UK, which had opted not to impose transition periods on free movement in the 2004 round of enlargement, decided in the case of Bulgaria and Romania to apply restrictions for the full seven-year period.

This extended form of conditionality has effectively made the two states *sui generis* EU members. No other EU member state has been subjected to this type or level of scrutiny. These special EU conditions, combined with relatively weak administrative capacity, have contributed to the perception of these two countries acting more as 'policy-takers rather than effective entrepreneurs' in EU-level decision making (Chiva and Phinnemore 2009: 151). Notable exceptions exist. Romania has managed to push for the interests of Moldova at the EU level. Both states have also been active in keeping Western Balkan enlargement on the EU's agenda. Yet most Bulgarian and Romanian leaders and citizens perceive their capacity to influence the EU agenda as limited. In their study of Romania's representation in Brussels, for example, Bretea and his co-authors (2014) show that Romanian governing elites believe Romania has limited means of actively participating in the EU policy-making process and are destined to remain policy-takers. The authors conclude, however, that this perception does not necessarily match the reality of the EU's institutional architecture, which offers ample opportunities for states like Romania to be proactive in EU decision-making (Bretea et al 2014: 41). For example, Bulgaria and Romania are scheduled to hold the presidency of the Council of the EU in 2018 and 2019 respectively, which will likely coincide with Brexit negotiations. Holding the presidency is one means of strengthening their influence at EU level. This opportunity was highlighted by the President of Romania, Klaus Iohannis, who admitted that while 'Romania is often treated like a second-hand country' in EU affairs, the Brexit negotiations represent an opportunity to show that Romania is 'a serious country, with well-prepared people, that is capable of dealing with such complex situations' (Politico 2016).

The politics of posted workers: internal EU migration and Brexit

The fundamental right of EU citizens to move freely across the EU has become one of the most contentious issues related to enlargement, magnified by Brexit and the rise of anti-immigration parties across the EU. EU policies overseeing posted workers – that is, an employee who is sent by an employer based in one EU member state to carry out a service in another EU member state on a temporary basis – has revealed significant divisions between East and West European states. The 2004 and 2007 enlargements gave rise to increasing concerns expressed by West European governments, trade unions, and workers about the threat of 'social dumping' and unfair competition from the East. The 'Polish plumber' symbolized such concerns in the 2005 failed French referendum on the Constitutional treaty. Wage competition from CEE migrants went on to become a key issue in the UK referendum on EU membership, and will be a focal point in Brexit negotiations. While most West European governments support placing further restrictions on posted workers, CEE governments seek to further liberalize free movement. This section examines debates in 2016 over a proposed revision of the 1996 Posted Workers Directive (PWD), considering the roles of Bulgaria and Romania in trying to influence EU decision-making.

When the original PWD was passed in 1996, the primary concern was the posting of temporary workers from southern EU states to northern ones to carry out short term contracts. The legislation made posted workers subject to the host state's national employment and social regulations, including minimum wages. This was designed to both protect the social welfare of posted workers, and prevent the undercutting of domestic wages and social benefits. The 2004 and 2007 enlargements put posted workers back on the EU's agenda. Given that new CEE member state wages and social benefits were far lower than in the EU-15, critics feared that enlargement would spur widespread social dumping (Vaughn-Whitehead 2003). However, other actors saw enlargement as an opportunity to further liberalize the free movement of services, which historically had been subject to more domestic restrictions than the free movement of goods. In 2004, then Single Market Commissioner, Frits Bolkestein, introduced legislation that would make service providers subject to home country rules and regulations (the so-called 'country of origin' principle).

For example, a Polish plumbing firm employing Polish plumbers in France would, under these new rules, be subject to Polish minimum wage rules and social benefit obligations.

New member states supported the country of origin principle, arguing that it would strengthen the competitive advantage of lower wage countries and enhance single market competitiveness more generally (Crespy and Gajewska 2010). Most West European governments, and trade unions, were strongly opposed, however, with the Directive spurring large demonstrations in Brussels and Paris. The country of origin principle was ultimately removed from the final 2006 Services Directive (Jensen and Nedergaard 2012). Yet the Services Directive left open legal questions concerning how to balance the right to free movement of people and services with national labour and social regulations. A number of subsequent European Court of Justice (ECJ) cases weighed in on this question where litigants from new EU member states challenged restrictions on their right to free movement within West European states. For example, in the 2007 Laval case, the ECJ awarded a Latvian construction firm, Laval, damages against Swedish trade unions for organizing a blockade to protest Laval's refusal to pay Latvian posted workers Swedish industry-wide negotiated wages and benefits. An analysis of member state legal briefs submitted to ECJ hearings on the case shows CEE states, including Bulgaria and Romania (and the UK), sided with Laval, while West European governments sided with the trade unions (Lindstrom 2010).

Responding to increased pressure from certain member states and trade unions to close loopholes in EU posted worker legislation in the wake of the ECJ judgements, in 2014 the European Commission proposed, and the Council and European Parliament passed, an 'Enforcement Directive' designed to address issues related to fraud and the circumvention of rules. In his 2016 State of the Union speech, Jean-Claude Juncker went further, championing a significant revision of the PWD, promising to ensure 'equal pay for equal work at the same place' (European Commission 2016a). The revised PWD promises to address social dumping concerns by ensuring that posted workers are subject to the same employment rules, including collective bargaining agreements. The proposed legislation also targets so-called 'letter box companies' whereby firms seek to circumvent national rules by securing legal status in another EU state to recruit temporary workers to carry out contracts. More generally, the proposal was designed to address what EU Commissioner for Economic Affairs Pierre Moscovici describes as the 'surprising violence of the political and social reaction' to EU migration (Financial Times 2016).

In May 2011, 11 member states triggered the subsidiarity control mechanism, or the so-called 'yellow card' procedure. The 11 states included all the CEE member states, minus Slovenia, and including Denmark.[2] The participating parliaments argued that the revised PWD violates the principle of subsidiarity in that posted workers should be covered by national legislation. Not only did the signatories easily exceed the one third threshold; it was only the third time a yellow yard had been successfully triggered since the mechanism was introduced in the 2007 Lisbon Treaty. The composition of the parliaments was also significant, with all signatories (except Denmark) from CEE states. As Weber (2016) argues, 'this demonstrates a true coordinated effort between the parliaments, and it sets an important precedent. Alliances formed by regional or policy interests can be more efficient in following and influencing EU legislative proposals, and thus make a real impact on EU politics.' One striking feature of the triggering of the yellow card was the UK's absence from the list. This marks a notable departure from the UK's close alignment with CEE states in negotiations around the 2006 Services Directive and the subsequent ECJ cases. Indeed, in the case of the revised PWD, the UK submitted opinions with France, Italy, Portugal, and Spain arguing that the Commission's proposal was compatible with the principle of subsidiarity (European Commission 2016b).

The European Commission responded to the yellow card challenge in July 2016 arguing that the proposal would be upheld given that the posting of workers is a 'cross border issue by nature' and thus is in full conformity with the subsidiarity principle (European Commission 2016b). The Commissioner for Employment, Social Affairs, Skills and Labour Mobility, Marianne Thyssen, went on to state that 'The Juncker Commission remains firmly committed to the free movement of people on the basis of rules that are clear, fair for everybody and enforced on the ground' (European Commission 2016b). CEE leaders condemned the Commission's judgement. The Czech Minister for Europe, Tomas Prouza, remarked, 'After the Brexit vote, the promise was to work on topics that are unifying, not divisive. Having such a divisive decision is not in anybody's interest at the moment' (Financial Times 2016). Another senior CEE diplomat complained, 'This conversation has become, just like in Britain during the referendum, about "Bloody East Europeans taking our jobs"' (Financial Times 2016).

The refugee crisis: a window of opportunity?

If Bulgaria and Romania joined with other CEE states in trying, but ultimately failing, to block a Commission proposal regulating migration within the EU, this section considers their positions on EU decision-making on external migration. Having been described as the largest humanitarian crisis that the world has faced since World War II (European Commission 2016c), the 2015 refugee crisis has put serious pressures on the very architecture and functioning of the EU. The unreformed 1999 Common European Asylum System and the absence of a unitary and overarching migration and asylum policy have only exacerbated the crisis. With the EU incapacitated by conflicts amongst member states on how to respond to the crisis, EU solutions have been patchy and contested. In September 2015, the Justice and Home Affairs Council passed a Commission proposal to relocate refugees amongst member states based on an algorithm involving variables such as population size, GDP and unemployment rate. The decision was strongly opposed by countries like Hungary, Slovakia and the Czech Republic, which have attempted to push for their own solutions to the crisis through the V4

(Kyuchukov 2016). While the crisis seems to have revealed a clear division in positions between old and new member states, Romania and Bulgaria have chosen to follow different strategies. Romania initially opposed the mandatory relocation quotas, but Bulgaria has been an active supporter of the EU policy from the beginning. Nonetheless, both member states have consistently advocated for the need of common solutions and EU-wide solidarity.

Romania departed from its pattern of conforming to EU decisions by voting against the mandatory resettlement quotas in the Justice and Home Affairs Council. In a declaration following the vote, Prime Minister Victor Ponta clarified that Romania's vote represented a reflection of its national interest. At the same time, however, Ponta was careful to distance Romania from countries like Hungary and Slovakia that have adopted a more hard-line anti-European attitude on the matter (Romanian Government 2015b). The more cooperative position of the Ponta government was demonstrated by Romania choosing not to file a complaint to the ECJ against the Council's decision, as did other opponents of relocation quotas. In fact, a rhetorical battle erupted between the Romanian and Hungarian governments following Hungarian Prime Minister Viktor Orban's decision to build a wall at the frontier between the two countries, an action that the Romanian government regarded as 'anti-European' (Sebe 2015: 17). Romanian leaders were also reluctant to use the refugee crisis as a bargaining chip for furthering the country's Schengen membership aspiration, with Ponta declaring that the two issues should be discussed independently from each other (Romanian Presidential Administration 2015). Therefore, the response of the Romanian authorities has revealed an ability to defend the country's purported national interests at the EU level, while also supporting common solutions as opposed to obstructionist actions.[3]

Bulgaria shares a similarly disadvantaged position with Romania in EU-level bargaining, given the ongoing EU monitoring activities of the two countries through the CVM. Bulgarian leaders used the refugee crisis as another means of avoiding its 'peripheral position in the EU [becoming] institutionalized' (Kyuchukov 2016: 15). A crucial difference between the two countries is their geographical position. While Romania had the advantage of being located outside the main migration routes (Sebe 2015: 16), Bulgaria's location made the country more prone to becoming the route of choice for the refugees once the Balkan corridor was closed. Bulgaria's position on the refugee crisis has been consistent throughout the crisis, with Bulgaria pledging its support of relocation quotas from the start. Bulgarian President Rosen Plevneliev repeatedly advocated for common European responses and reiterated his country's commitment to European solidarity. Plevneliev declared that the worst path for the EU to take during the refugee crisis would be 'the nationalist one' and the best would be 'to act as a united family' (Bulgarian Presidential Administration 2015), as '[t]he only workable solution is the pan-European one' (Bulgarian Presidential Administration 2016b). Therefore, Bulgaria presented itself as a reliable ally of core EU member states such as Germany pushing for a more unified response to the refugee/migration crisis.

Domestic public opinion in Bulgaria does not necessarily correspond to the position taken by its leaders, however. The Bulgarian people have exhibited a 'deep scepticism, sometimes growing out to outright intolerance' against immigrants, especially those of Muslim origins (IRIS 2014: 1). Numerous anti-refugee protests have been organised in Bulgaria, even before the main wave of migrants made their way into Europe in 2015. The Islamophobic sentiment in the country reflects a longstanding expression of resentment on the part of some Bulgarians to the presence of a significant minority of Turkish Muslims. Many Bulgarians also voiced concerns about the country's economic ability to host and support a significant refugee population (Kyuchukov 2016: 1). The response of the Bulgarian leaders during the crisis thus appears to diverge from the population's view on the prospect of hosting asylum seekers. Despite this widespread opposition of Bulgarians to the settlement of refugees, the government has been 'extremely outspoken' in favour of the mandatory relocation quotas (Nicolov 2015). The Bulgarian authorities have also consistently sought to distance the country from the position of the V4, in order to prove Bulgaria's support for close European cooperation. The government has also been very responsive to the opinions of other EU member states, and immediately dropped its plans to build a wall at the border with Turkey when the plan faced European disapproval (Kyuchukov 2016: 13).

The refugee crisis also prompted Romania and Bulgaria to engage in other forms of regional cooperation in order to promote their domestic interests. With respect to EU policy on refugee relocation, neither country wanted to clearly align itself with the more obstructionist V4 countries. As an alternative, Romania and Bulgaria decided to replicate the successful model of the Visegrád states in regional cooperation and coalition building through the so-called 'Craiova group', an initiative to institutionalise trilateral cooperation with Romania, Bulgaria and Serbia. The group was founded in April 2015 during a trilateral meeting with the three countries' prime ministers in Craiova, a Romanian city equidistant from Bucharest, Belgrade and Sofia. In addition to cooperation on the refugee crisis, the group also has pledged to cooperate on energy and transport infrastructure and facilitating Serbia's accession to the EU. The intention to mimic the successful cooperation of the V4 was highlighted from the very first meeting by Romania's Prime Minister Victor Ponta, who acknowledged the success of the V4 countries in 'promoting their interests and their regional projects'. He went on to state that the goal of the Craiova group was to replicate that example, in order to 'consult each other, share positions and projects and support each other' (Romanian Government 2015a).

Unfinished business: Schengen area membership and visa free regimes

Bulgaria and Romania have been EU members for ten years, but they have not yet obtained membership to the Schengen area. While the European Parliament has already acknowledged that both countries have fulfilled the technical criteria (European Parliament 2011), their official inclusion in Schengen has been continuously delayed by other EU states, with countries like The Netherlands effectively blocking their membership on multiple occasions. Therefore, while both countries have reiterated their interest to join the Schengen area, they have encountered political unwillingness of other member states to approve their membership.[4] While Romania and Bulgaria are situated differently, the two states have been treated like a package in these negotiations, with the EU signalling that they should be accepted together (Ciucu 2012: 10). Despite the insistence of both countries that they meet the necessary conditions and should be granted Schengen membership, their membership has encountered repeated obstacles in diplomatic channels (Ciucu and Albisteanu 2015: 6). The refugee crisis presents some additional difficulties in Romania and Bulgaria achieving Schengen membership, given that the refugee crisis has created serious pressures on both the external and internal EU borders and ignited doubts about the functioning of the Schengen area. But the refugee/migration crisis also presents opportunities, namely the chance for each state to prove its ability to enforce external EU borders and to cooperate with other member states during a crisis.

Despite endorsing the EU's refugee relocation plan and pledging solidarity, Bulgaria did not attempt to directly link their continued goal of achieving Schengen membership with the refugee crisis (Kyuchukov 2016: 14). Nonetheless, during a state meeting in the company of the French President Francois Hollande, the Bulgarian President Rosen Plevneliev seized the opportunity to remind EU officials about the unfinished business of Schengen integration. Plevneliev remarked to the gathered officials that '[a]ll member states should show maximum solidarity to those who are first to bear the migration pressure because the external EU borders are not just Schengen' (Bulgarian Presidential Administration 2016a). Nonetheless, similar to the situation of Romania, Bulgaria has also failed to show its concrete commitment by neglecting to comply fully with EU asylum legislation. The Commission consequently issued two letters of formal notice regarding directives 2013/32/EU and 2013/33/EU, followed by a reasoned option from the Commission for non-compliance with the Qualifications Directive 2011/95/EU.

The threat of veto in the CETA negotiations

The issue of visa-free travel also arose in the context of negotiations on the free trade agreement between the EU and Canada, the so-called Comprehensive Economic and Trade Agreement (CETA). By 2015 Romanians and Bulgarians were the only EU citizens still required to obtain a travel visa in order to enter Canada. Bulgarian and Romanian leaders sought to use CETA negotiations to lift these restrictions. Initially, they attempted to trigger the 1289/2013 EU regulation, which would establish 'a temporary suspension of the exemption from the visa requirement for a third country' through an 'act of solidarity' of all EU member states. Summarizing the opinions of the Council and the European Parliament, the Commission deemed the application of the EU regulation as unfeasible given the high number of visa applications that the EU member states would have to process as a result and the potential negative economic impact (European Commission 2016d). The Commission's response was viewed as 'treachery' in Bulgaria and Romania, which motivated their leaders to change strategies (Euractiv 2016a). In order to press forward with the aim of achieving visa free travel for its citizens, Romania and Bulgaria have threatened that their parliaments would veto CETA if their demand was not met.

CETA, like the Transatlantic Trade and Investment Partnership (TTIP) being negotiated with the United States, is a 'mixed agreement', meaning that any agreement must be ratified by every EU member state. This made Bulgaria and Romania's hard line approach more effective. Wallonia threatening to veto CETA in November 2016 illustrated the increased power that mixed agreements give to less powerful states. After a number of bilateral and multilateral rounds of negotiations, Bulgaria and Romania obtained a commitment from the Canadian authorities for the gradual removal of visa requirements. There has also been a notable distinction in the approaches of the two member states. Being more readily available to accept a deal with Canada, the Bulgarian authorities immediately agreed with the terms proposed by the Canadian government. Romanian authorities, however, adopted a firmer position, refusing any deal with Canada unless visa requirements were removed no later than 2017. Canada lifted visa requirements for both states on 1 December 2017. The threat of veto proved to be a more effective tool in achieving visa-free travel than fulfilling the technical requirements of Schengen membership.

Conclusion

Romania and Bulgaria represent very particular cases of enlargement states, having been subjected to unprecedented EU vertical pressures. The EU's strict pre- and post-accession conditionality regimes had a lasting effect on the nature of the interaction between the two post-socialist states and the EU. During their ten years of EU membership, Romania and Bulgaria have mostly acted reactively, due to their inferior bargaining position, weak administrative capacity and relative inexperience in producing concrete EU policy proposals. However, it would be a mistake to characterize these two member states as nothing more than passive EU policy-takers. As this chapter has shown, Bulgaria and Romania have used a variety of means to pursue their policy preferences at EU level. Through our analysis of two policy issues, the refugee crisis and posted workers, we have demonstrated how Bulgarian and Romanian leaders exhibited a mix of obedience and disobedience with the EU, sometimes forging alliances with other CEE member states to obstruct EU policy proposals, and at other times actively siding with core EU member states against the more obstructionist V4. Each state has also been willing to use the threat of veto.

This chapter has shown that Romania and Bulgaria do in fact amount to more than mere policy-takers. However, under what conditions do peripheral EU states choose to cooperate with the EU on policy goals and when do they decide to obstruct these goals, whether by cooperating with like-minded states or threatening to veto EU decisions? A crucial factor is the type of EU governance shaping a particular policy area. In policy areas where the EU has exclusive competence, like free movement of workers, states are more likely to use existing mechanisms of influence, like triggering a 'yellow card' in cooperation with other states, in achieving policy goals. However, when the EU's legal competence is murkier, as in the case of refugee resettlement, we can expect states to pursue less coordinated strategies. That Bulgaria and Romania diverged from the V4 on this issue, and at the same time pursued coordination with non-EU states like Serbia, suggests that 'flexible solidarity' (Euractiv 2016b) is an apt description of EU refugee policy to date. The EU's decision to make bilateral trade negotiations like CETA a 'mixed agreement', requiring unanimous approval from all EU member states, created an opportunity for states like Bulgaria and Romania to effectively use the threat of veto to achieve their goal of lifting visa restrictions.

The vertical pressures exerted on countries like Romania and Bulgaria remain highly visible ten years after their accession to the EU, with the two states still monitored under the CVM. This mechanism became the focus of heated debate in the context of the anti-corruption protests in Romania in early 2017. Hundreds of thousands of Romanian citizens voiced their disapproval against a controversial emergency decree put forward by the government. The Romanian executive attempted to change the criminal code to decriminalize the misconduct of public officials accused of misconduct leading to financial losses of less than 45,000 euro (*The Economist* 2017). During the protests, the Commission released its latest CVM report on Romania. The Commission acknowledged that while significant progress had been made in the country's fight against corruption, more progress was required before the monitoring mechanism was removed (European Commission 2017a). Following the Commission's report, Calin Popescu Tariceanu, the president of Romania's Senate, declared that Romania should no longer cooperate under the CVM, accusing the mechanism of being discriminatory (Romania Insider 2017). In a later report, the Commission warned the Romanian government about the danger that its attempt to change the criminal code represents for the progress made in the last ten years (European Commission 2017b). While discontent with the scrutiny imposed from Brussels is increasing among the country's ruling politicians, the Commission appears committed to continue pursuing the logic of top-down pressure established during Romania's EU accession process.

While their efforts at policy-making have been largely reactive to date, our analysis suggests that these states may play a more active role in shaping EU policy in the future. On the issue of Brexit, Romania and Bulgaria will hold the Council presidencies in 2018 and 2019 when negotiations between the EU and UK will likely be in their most intense phase. Given that the UK hosts large diasporic communities of Romanian and Bulgarian migrants, each state will continue to press the EU to take a hard line on protecting the rights of EU citizens to free movement and equal treatment. Overseeing Brexit negotiations while holding the Council presidency presents a window of opportunity for Bulgaria and Romania to demonstrate their capacity to manage complex issues and to become more active policy-makers in the EU arena. Moreover, that each state threatened to veto CETA in order to achieve visa free travel to Canada sends a signal to EU leaders that they are willing to use this 'nuclear option' in any future negotiations. At the same time, by defecting from the V4 on the case of refugee resettlement, Bulgaria and Romania have demonstrated to the EU that they are reliable and loyal partners in efforts to create common EU policies to address this ongoing crisis. An open question is whether and how this loyalty will be rewarded, such as the EU approving Bulgaria and Romania's outstanding application for Schengen membership or discontinuing special conditions like CVM.

Notes

1 For a full list of transition periods imposed on Bulgarian and Romanian citizens by other EU member states, see: http://ec.europa.eu/social/main.jsp?catId=466&.

2 The subsidiary mechanism includes parliamentary chambers, thus EU member states with bicameral legislatures could potentially have two votes. In this case, 11 member states were involved in triggering the yellow card, with 14 parliamentary chambers signing on. Denmark joined the new member states arguing that the revised PWD proposal did not go far enough in protecting the Danish collective bargaining model.

3 Nonetheless, despite official Romanian government rhetoric insisting that the refugee crisis must be addressed by solidarity and common European solutions over inward-looking national preferences (Romanian Government 2015b), the response of the Romanian administration has been weak in terms of implementation. For instance, the Romanian government failed to communicate the transposition of the Asylum Procedures Directive 2013/32/EU and the Reception Conditions Directive 2013/33/EU on minimum standards and international protection in the asylum process. This led to the Commission launching two separate infringement procedures and sending two letters of formal notice (European Commission 2015).

4 In order to address the increasing restlessness of Romania and Bulgaria, France and Germany proposed a process of gradual accession of the two countries, starting with initial integration of the airspace and maritime frontiers, followed by an eventual abolition of the terrestrial borders (Ciucu 2012: 4). Yet this proposal, too, appears effectively frozen.

References

Andreev, S. A. (2009) The Unbearable Lightness of Membership: Bulgaria and Romania after the 2007 EU Accession, *Communist and Post-Communist Studies* 42(3), pp. 375–393.

Bretea, L., Tamasan A. and Mihailescu, G. (2014) *Actor pasiv sau proactive: Cum sunt reprezentate interesel romanesti la Bruxelles*. Report. [ONLINE] Available from: http://www.europuls.ro/wp-content/uploads/2014/10/RaportEuropulsActorpasivsauproactiv.pdf (accessed 14 December 2016).

Browning, C. and Christou, G. (2010) The Constitutive Power of Outsiders: The European Neighbourhood Policy and the Eastern Dimension, *Political Geography* 29(2): 109–118.

Bulgarian Presidential Administration (2015) *President Rosen Plevneliev: Europe Can Cope with the Migration Flows if it Follows the Common Rules valid for all.* [ONLINE] Press Release. 12 November. Available from: https://www.president.bg/news2902/president-rosen-plevneliev-europe-can-cope-with-the-migration-flows-if-follows-the-common-rules-valid-for-all.html (accessed 14 December 2016).

Bulgarian Presidential Administration (2016a) *President Plevneliev and Hollande: After the Referendum in Great Britain, the EU Should Be Strengthened and Get a New Dose of Trust.* Press Release. 27 June. [ONLINE] Available from: https://www.president.bg/news3297/presidents-plevneliev-and-hollande-after-the-referendum-in-great-britain-the-eu-should-be-strengthened-and-get-a-new-dose-of-trust.html (accessed 14 December 2016).

Bulgarian Presidential Administration (2016b) *The President from Arraiolos: The EU Badly Needs a Long-term and Coordinated Decision-making process on the Crises.* Press Release. 15 September. [ONLINE] Available from: https://www.president.bg/news3372/the-presidents-from-arraiolos-the-eu-badly-needs-a-long-term-and-coordinated-decision-making-process-on-the-crises.html (accessed 14 December 2016).

Chiva, C. and Phinnemore, D. (2009) Preface: The European Union's 2007 Enlargement, *Perspectives on European Politics and Society* 10(2), pp. 149–151.

Ciucu, C. (2012) Schengen: de ce nu se poate decuple Bulgaria de Romania si unde este problema reala. CRPE Policy brief no. 16 September.

Ciucu, C. and Albisteanu, R. (2015) La spartul targului? Optiunile Romaniei vizavi de Spatiul Schengen. CRPE Policy Brief no. 38 September.

Crespy, A. and K. Gajewska (2010) New Parliament, New Cleavages after the Eastern Enlargement? The Conflict over the Services Directive as an Opposition between the Liberals and Regulators, *Journal of Common Market Studies* 48(5), pp. 1185–1208.

Economist, The (2006) A Case of Enlargement Fatigue. 11 May. [ONLINE] Available from: http://www.economist.com/node/6914116 (accessed 24 January 2018).

Economist, The (2017) Hands off their DNA: Huge Protests Force Romania's Government to Reverse Itself on Corruption. 11 February. [ONLINE] Available from: https://www.economist.com/news/europe/21716570-decree-would-pardon-crooked-officials-dropped (accessed 24 January 2018).

Euractiv (2016a) *Romania will Veto the EU-Canada Trade Deal.* 14 April. [ONLINE] Available from: http://www.euractiv.com/section/trade-society/news/romania-will-veto-the-eu-canada-trade-deal/ (accessed 14 December 2016).

Euractiv (2016b) *Flexible Solidarity Becomes New Tool in Response to Refugee Crisis.* 19 September. [ONLINE] Available from: https://www.euractiv.com/section/justice-home-affairs/news/flexible-solidarity-becomes-new-tool-in-response-to-refugee-crisis/ (accessed 15 December 2016).

European Commission (2015) *More Responsibility in managing the refugee crisis: European Commission adopts 40 infringement decision to make European Asylum System work.* Press Release. Brussels, 23 September.

European Commission (2016a) *State of the Union Address 2016: Towards a Better Europe – a Europe that Protects, Empowers and Defends.* Strasbourg, 14 September. [ONLINE] Available from: http://europa.eu/rapid/press-release_SPEECH-16-3043_en.htm (accessed 15 December 2016).

European Commission (2016b) *Posting of Workers: Commission Discusses Concerns of National Parliaments.* Press Release. 20 July. [ONLINE] Available from: http://europa.eu/rapid/press-release_IP-16-2546_en.htm (accessed 15 December 2016).

European Commission (2016c) *Syria Crisis*. Humanitarian Aid and Civil Protection ECHO Factsheet. [ONLINE] Available from: https://ec.europa.eu/echo/files/aid/countries/factsheets/syria_en.pdf (accessed 24 January 2018).

European Commission (2016d) *Communication from the Commission to the European Parliament and the Council: State of Play and Ways Forward as Regards the Situation of Non-reciprocity with Certain Third Countries in the Area of Visa Policy*. COM 221 final. 12 April. [ONLINE] Available from: https://ec.europa.eu/home-affairs/sites/homeaffairs/files/what-we-do/policies/borders-and-visas/visa-policy/docs/communication_visa_non_reciprocity_en.pdf (accessed 24 January 2018).

European Commission (2017a) *Report from the Commission to the European Parliament and the Council: On Progress in Romania under the Co-operation and Verification Mechanism*. COM (2017) 44 final. 25 January. [ONLINE] Available from: https://ec.europa.eu/info/files/progress-report-romania-2017-com-2017-44_en (accessed 24 January 2018).

European Commission (2017b) *Commission Staff Working Document: Country Report Romania*. SWD (2017) 88 final. 22 February. [ONLINE] Available from: https://ec.europa.eu/info/sites/info/files/2017-european-semester-country-report-romania-en.pdf (accessed 24 January 2018).

European Parliament (2011) *Bulgaria and Romania ready to join Schengen area, says Parliament*. Press Release. 8 June. [ONLINE] Available from: http://www.europarl.europa.eu/news/en/news-room/20110608IPR20929/bulgaria-and-romania-ready-to-join-schengen-area-says-parliament (accessed 14 December 2016).

Financial Times (2016) *Brussels Bows to French Demands for Tougher Rules on 'Posted' Workers*. 20 July. [ONLINE] Available from: https://www.ft.com/content/d6235564-4e6b-11e6-8172-e39ecd3b86fc (accessed 24 January 2018).

Institute for Regional and International Studies (IRIS) (2014) Intergroup Tolerance and Xenophobia, *Bulgarian Human Security Chronicle* 5(May).

Jensen, M. D. and Nedergaard, P. (2012) From 'Frankenstein' to 'Toothless Vampire'? Explaining the Watering Down of the Services Directive, *Journal of European Public Policy* 19(6), pp. 844–862.

Kyuchukov, L. (2016) *Impact of the Refugee Crisis on Bulgarian Society and Politics: Fears But Not Hatred*. Friedrich-Ebert-StiftungAnalyses. [ONLINE] Available from http://library.fes.de/pdf-files/bueros/ sofia/12570.pdf (accessed 14 December 2016).

Lindstrom, N. (2010) Service Liberalization in the Enlarged EU: A Race to the Bottom of the Emergence of Transnational Political Conflict? *Journal of Common Market Studies* 48(5), pp. 1305–1325.

Nicolov, A. (2015) *The European Refugee Crisis: Bulgaria's Wake-up Call?* OpenDemocracy. [ONLINE] Available from: https://www.opendemocracy.net/can-europe-make-it/alice-nicolov/european-refugee-crisis-bulgaria%E2%80%99s-wake-up-call (accessed 14 December 2016).

Noutcheva, G. and D. Bechev (2008) The Successful Laggards: Bulgaria and Romania's Accession to the EU. *East European Politics & Societies* 22(1), pp. 114–144.

Papadimitriou, D. and E. Gateva (2009) Between Enlargement-led Europeanization and Balkan Exceptionalism: An Appraisal of Bulgaria's and Romania's Entry into the European Union. *Perspectives on European Politics and Society* 10(2), pp. 152–166.

Politico (2016) The Transylvanian Who'll Have a Hand in Brexit. 28 October. [ONLINE] Available from: http://www.politico.eu/article/the-transylvanian-wholl-have-a-hand-in-brexit-klaus-iohannis-romania-europe/ (accessed 14 December 2016).

Romanian Government (2015a) *Prime Minister Victor Ponta Participated in a Trilateral Meeting with the Prime Minister of the Republic of Serbia, Aleksandar Vucic and the Prime*

Minister of the Republic of Bulgaria, Boyko Borissov. Press Release. 24 April. [ONLINE] Available from http://gov.ro/en/news/prime-minister-victor-ponta-participated-in-a-trilateral-meeting-with-the-prime-minister-of-the-republic-of-serbia-aleksandar-vucic-and-the-prime-minister-of-the-republic-of-bulgaria-boyko-borissov (accessed 14 December 2016).

Romanian Government (2015b) *The Speech Delivered by Prime Minister Victor Ponta in the Plenary of the Chamber of Deputies at 'Prime Minister's Hour'*. Press Release. 5 October. [ONLINE] Available from: http://gov.ro/en/news/the-speech-delivered-by-prime-minister-victor-ponta-in-the-plenary-of-the-chamber-of-deputies-at-prime-minister-s-hour (accessed 14 December 2016).

Romania Insider (2017) *Senate President: Romania Should Pull Out from CVM*, 26 January. [ONLINE] Available from: http://www.romania-insider.com/senate-president-romania-pull-cvm/ (accessed 23 February 2017).

Romanian Presidential Administration (2015) *Conferinta de presa sustinuta de Presedintele Romaniei, domnul Klaus Iohannis*. Press Release. 23 September. Available from: http://www.presidency.ro/ro/media/agenda-presedintelui/transcrierea-conferintei-de-presa-sustinuta-de-presedintele-romaniei-domnul-klaus-iohannis (accessed 14 December 2016).

Sebe, M. (2015) *Romania's Stance in the Issue of the Refugees Crisis*. Institute of European Democrats Working Paper. [ONLINE] Available from: http://www.iedonline.eu/publications/2015/romania-refugee-crisis.php (accessed 14 December 2016).

Trauner, F. (2009) Post-accession Compliance with EU law in Bulgaria and Romania: A Comparative Perspective, *European Integration Online Papers*. Special Issue 2(13), Vol. 13, Art. 21. [ONLINE] Available from: http://eiop.or.at/eiop/pdf/2009-021.pdf (accessed 24 January 2018).

Vaughan-Whitehead, D. (2013) *EU Enlargement versus Social Europe? The Uncertain Future of the European Social Model*. Edward Elgar.

Weber, T. (2016) Third Time's a Charm? National Parliaments for Bloc Against Posted Workers Directive. Leiden Law Blog. [ONLINE] Available from: http://leidenlawblog.nl/articles/third-times-a-charm-national-parliaments-form-bloc-against-posted-workers-d (accessed 14 December 2016).

European Parliament and Council Regulation

Regulation of the European Parliament and of the Council (2013) Regulation (EU) No 1289/2013 of the European Parliament and of the Council of 11 December 2013 amending Council Regulation (EC) No 539/2001 listing the third countries whose nationals must be in possession of visas when crossing the external borders and those whose nationals are exempt from the requirement, Official Journal of the European Union, L 347/74.

10 The Baltic states in the EU

Committed europhiles or geopolitical hostages?

Liutauras Gudžinskas and Tomas Bekišas

Introduction: Baltic EU policy priorities and premises

The Baltic experience of being under direct Soviet rule as well as their uneasy proximity to Russia have so far distinguished their EU policies from other EU member states (MS). Due to heightened security concerns, their foreign and European affairs have been mostly beyond direct political competition. Furthermore, the Baltics share broadly the same attitude towards the core European issues, by persistently pursuing three common strategic European policy goals: full integration into the EU single market; enhanced cooperation with the EU MS in the Baltic Sea region in such fields as energy security; and diffusion of the EU influence eastwards.

These common priorities have been well reflected both in their EU presidency programmes and in their public EU policy strategic documents. The latter also reveal a broad support for the very process of European integration. The Baltic countries mostly favour further European integration, although most recently they became more cautious in this respect. After the adoption of the Lisbon Treaty, the Baltic countries usually emphasise the need to make use of the existing legal framework rather than to develop a new one. Nevertheless, they are keen to be at the forefront of the integration process and in general tend to avoid a scenario of multi-speed Europe (Government of the Republic of Estonia 2015; Ministry of Foreign Affairs of the Republic of Lithuania 2015; Permanent Representation of the Republic of Latvia to the EU 2016).

The Baltic countries, however, have been confronted with a critical security dilemma already during their accession to the EU. While EU membership – in addition to one in NATO – has profoundly boosted *the external* security of the Baltic countries, it has also created important challenges for their perceived *internal* security (Mole 2012). Although the Baltic elites almost unanimously chose the EU integration path, various legal requirements put forward by European institutions fuelled Eurosceptic forces within societies of these countries. It was perceived by broad societal segments that some of the EU demands neglected subtleties of an internal situation of an acceding state and thus could risk its political stability. This dilemma was aggravated by the prevalence of so-called 'survival values' focused on physical and economic security and opposed to 'self-expression' values that include social tolerance, aspiration to liberty and public expression. Except for Bulgaria and Romania, the Baltic societies distinguish themselves for the highest incidence of survival values in the EU (World Values Survey 2015).

Foremost, this security dilemma was more acutely experienced by Latvia and Estonia which have inherited a greater share of ethnic Russian-speaking minorities than a largely homogenous Lithuania. After restoring their independence, both Estonia and Latvia adopted strict citizenship legislation that deprived those inhabitants of citizenship who either came to these countries amid the Soviet occupation or were their descendants. During the negotiations on the EU membership, the EU institutions along with the Organization for Security and Co-operation in Europe have pressured both Latvia and Estonia to change their discriminatory citizenship and language laws. Legislative amendments required to ease the naturalisation process have been eventually enacted, although the integration of ethnic minorities has not been entirely successful. In both countries, there are still considerable numbers of non-citizen residents whose political and civic rights remain restrained (Auers 2015).

The institutional clash over rights of ethnic minorities created salient tensions between national and European identities within Estonian and Latvian societies. Consequently, the discord fuelled Eurosceptic voices and negatively affected the public support for the membership of the EU, which was reflected in the outcomes of national referendums on the accession to the EU arranged in 2003. While all three Baltic governments managed to frame the voting as making a historic geopolitical choice between the East and the West, only 67 per cent participating in the referendum in Estonia (with 64 per cent turnout) were for the membership in the EU. It was the lowest 'yes' vote of all the post-communist accession countries. In Latvia, the result was similar, with 67.5 per cent of the 'yes' votes on albeit a higher turnout of 72.5 per cent (Mikkel and Pridham 2004). Meanwhile, a margin in the referendum in Lithuania was much wider than in other two Baltic countries with 91 per cent voting for EU membership. However, the turnout was the lowest among all three Baltic countries with only 63 per cent participating in the referendum. Nevertheless, Lithuanian public support for the EU remains well above the EU average and is still much higher than in its Baltic counterparts (see Figure 10.1). However, as in the other two Baltic countries, political alienation (characterised by distrust of political institutions) felt by broad segments of society continues to create a space for Eurosceptic ideas in Lithuania.

Time after time it has led Lithuanian politicians to be at loggerheads with European institutions. One of such instances was an initiation of several legal measures restricting civil rights of LGBT people. While most of them were ultimately rejected or frozen, it provoked strong criticism from the European Parliament, which later adopted two resolutions condemning those legislative initiatives (Gudžinskas 2014). Other instances include protracted institutional struggles over carrying out Accession Treaty obligations such as decommissioning the Ignalina Nuclear Power Plant (NPP) and cancellation of

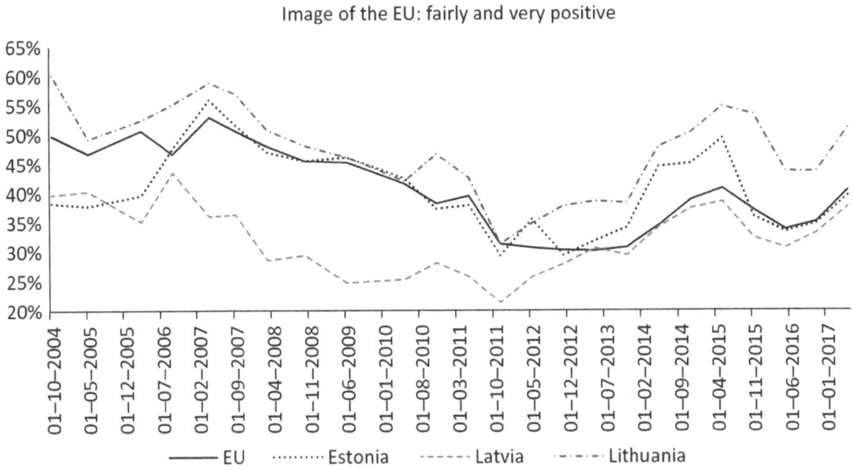

Figure 10.1 Image of the EU: share of population whose opinion of the EU is either fairly or very positive
Source: European Commission 2017d.

temporary restriction to sell land to foreigners. In both cases, there have been significant (although eventually failed) attempts to thwart implementation of these commitments by organising national referendums.

Nevertheless, there are no major political forces that would be decidedly Eurosceptic in any of the Baltic countries. Recent findings show (see Figure 10.2) that all relevant Lithuanian, Latvian and Estonian parliamentary parties are rather pro-European, and just five parties tend to show some Eurosceptic inclinations, whereas no hard-Eurosceptic parties were determined at all. This absence of coherent Eurosceptic forces corresponds perfectly with the fact that there are only small fractions of citizens in all three countries who have a fairly or even very negative view of the EU.

Moreover, any power alterations when more Eurosceptic forces replace more pro-European parties have not resulted in substantial changes in the countries' stance towards the EU. In Lithuania, after the parliamentary elections in 2012, a ruling coalition formed by Social Democrats (LSDP) together with a populist Labour Party (DP), socially conservative forces of 'Order and Justice' (TT) and Polish Electoral Action (LLRA) retained and eventually achieved the introduction of euro in 2015. Eurosceptic voices within the government were effectively quashed during this process. The pro-European stance of the Lithuanian government had not changed even after the parliamentary elections in 2016 when the Farmers and Green Union (LVZS), which was evaluated as the single most Eurosceptic party in the Baltics just before European Parliament elections in 2014, scored a surprising victory.

To some extent, however, the continuation of EU policy in Lithuania is also ensured by a directly elected president who has important powers in foreign affairs. Since regaining independence, with the tentative exception of

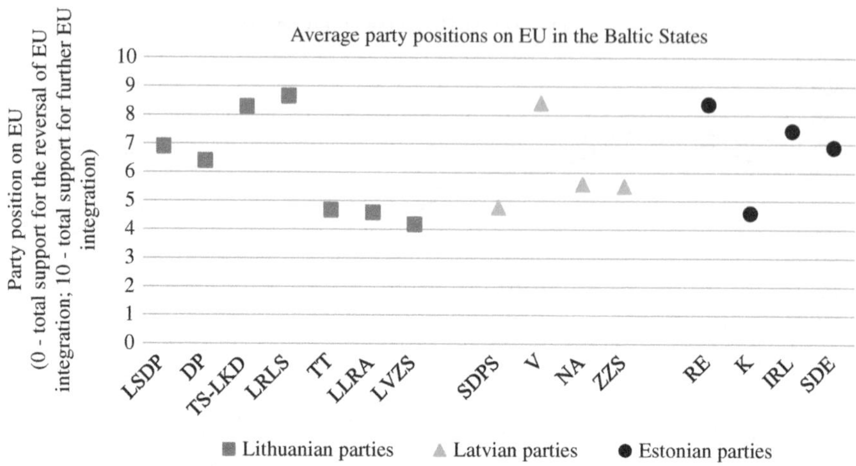

Figure 10.2 Party positions on the EU in the Baltic States in 2014
Source: Own calculations using EUVox survey data.

impeached Rolandas Paksas (2003–2004), all heads of state have been active supporters of Lithuania's integration into the EU. Furthermore, while the primary responsibilities of participation in the EU decision-making process lie within the competencies of the government accountable to the parliament, Dalia Grybauskaitė, after winning her first presidential elections in 2009, has obtained an informal right to represent Lithuania in the European Council exclusively. With this achievement, she has acquired a leading role in EU policy-making at the national level, which further enhanced the status of national EU policy as foremost falling within general foreign policy and security framework.

While the presidents are less powerful in both Latvia and Estonia, the most recent changes in the composition of their governments did not affect their pro-EU stance as well. In Estonia, after a collapse of the government led by the Reform Party (RE) in November 2016, a new ruling coalition headed by the Centre party (K), shortly announced its firm commitment to pro-Western orientation to dispel any suspicions about its friendliness to Russia (Baltic News Service 2016).

Similarly, there were no substantial changes in Latvian EU policy platform when Māris Kučinskis, a representative from Farmers and Green Party (ZZS), became the Prime Minister in 2016. On the other hand, given a strong presence of the Nationalist Alliance (NA) and relative fragmentation of pro-European forces within the government, the Latvian political representatives have been arguably the least enthusiastic supporters of further European integration among the Baltics. Moreover, a migrant crisis and subsequent EU decisions to relocate a certain number of refugees across the MS caused serious clashes within Latvia's ruling coalition in September 2015. Eventually, Latvia has accepted these obligations and, thus, diverged from Visegrád countries (V4) that opposed migrant quota allocation schemes by the European Commission (Ragozin 2015). Nevertheless, this hesitation revealed a fragmentation of pro-European forces aggravated by still existing tensions over minority rights and economic hardship affecting wide societal strata.

Participation in the Single Market

The economic development of the Baltic states since their accession to the EU in 2004 has been a story of relative success. Despite hard times during the financial crisis of 2008–2010, their economic convergence with wealthier EU counterparts has been faster in comparison with most other new MS. In fact, according to Eurostat's calculations, Lithuania's catch-up rate with the EU average has so far been the greatest spanning from 49 per cent of the EU average GDP per capita in purchasing power standard (PPS) in 2004 to 75 per cent of the EU average in 2015. Estonia and Latvia have experienced similar economic growth – respectively from 54 to 75 per cent and 46 to 64 per cent of the EU average GDP per capita in PPS in 2004 and 2015. However, there are reasonable doubts whether the Baltic developmental path is sustainable. Since 2005, Latvia has lost around 12.5 per cent and Lithuania – 14 per cent of their population. While Estonia's population has remained rather steady, its density is still the lowest among the Baltics. One of the key factors of the demographic change has been an emigration to Western Europe catalysed by a guarantee of freedom of movement within the EU. While it has contributed to a reduction of unemployment and increased amounts of remittances sent back by the emigrants to their homelands, there has been a growing concern that the ratio of economically active residents to the whole population is becoming unsustainable. Another persistent source of worry about the Baltic economies is that they have one of the highest rates of income inequality in the EU (European Commission 2017a; 2017b; 2017c).

From the outset of the post-communist transformation, the developmental model of the Baltic countries could be classified as the most neoliberal within the CEE region. It has been carried out through rapid privatisation and liberalisation reforms as well as an early introduction of a fixed exchange rate regime and tight monetary policies. At the same time, little has been done for mitigation of the social consequences of this 'shock therapy'. Such a development path has been intrinsically tied to the agenda of nation state building. Since Russia's economic and political influence was widely seen as the biggest threat to their national sovereignty and security within the Baltic societies, the political elites were less constrained by the economic and social costs of radical transformation than was the case in other CEE countries (Bohle and Greskovits 2012).

The membership of the EU has thus provided a needed shelter for the Baltics. The benefits were multiple. In addition to access to the Single Market, which has significantly boosted their international trade capabilities, the Baltic countries have received huge financial influxes both via private actors (credits from the Nordic-owned commercial banks and remittances) and via EU structural assistance, that has mostly covered the bills for public investment. Furthermore, the EU has enhanced their regulatory state capacities and overall quality of governance.

Against this background, the Baltic countries have been mainly committed to participation in the Single Market. Since their access to the EU, the ratio of their volumes of intra-EU trade in goods to GDP has increased well above the EU average. Their integration into the internal services market is less pronounced but still better (especially in Estonia) than the EU average. Baltics also transpose EU directives into the national legislation exemplary, with Estonia and Latvia being among the best performers in transposing the directives correctly (European Commission 2015b). On the other hand, being much more focused on economic competitiveness rather than on other top priorities of sustainable development, the Baltic countries have usually been sceptical about raising social and environmental standards or harmonising taxation within the Single Market. This ambivalence towards further development of the Single Market somewhat reflects the essential security dilemma described above.

While access to the Single Market has markedly revitalised the Baltic economies, its impact on the governance in this region has not been unambiguous. During the membership negotiations, the EU as a regulatory state (Majone 1996) has impelled the candidate countries to divert their resources and attention towards those public policies and regulations that are developed at EU level. Meanwhile, quality and content of welfare policies mostly left for national competence have been largely ignored during this process. Against this background, the CEE countries started to resemble a 'dysfunctional state' with rather developed capacities of market regulation but stagnant welfare systems captured by certain interest groups such as politicised professional clans keen to thwart any necessary reforms (Maniokas 2003).

This scenario has been particularly acute for the Baltic countries that from the outset have focused on pro-market policies by replacing the societal welfare contract with the nationalising-securitising project (Bohle and Greskovits 2012). Such development is characteristic to the cases of Latvia and Lithuania that had delayed necessary welfare reforms before access to the EU and are still muddling through or even gradually dismantling their social policies. Estonia's chances to avoid this trajectory are arguably better. It has been not only more resolute and eventually successful at reforming healthcare (Gudžinskas 2013) and education (OECD 2016) early but have also been more forceful and efficient at eradicating corruption (Bennich-Björkman 2006) and ensuring a higher tax morale (Kuokštis 2015) than their Baltic counterparts. These achievements may allow the Estonians to lay a firmer ground for developing an inherently inclusive and fiscally sustainable state.

An evolving divergence on state capacities between the Baltic countries could also be traced from their different paths to the eurozone. Estonia adopted the euro the earliest – in 2011. Unlike other two Baltic nations, Estonia was carrying a prudent pre-crisis fiscal policy and demonstrated much better tax collection results. A more successful fiscal consolidation enabled Estonia to achieve eurozone membership markedly earlier and in better conditions than the other two Baltic states. Meanwhile, the financial crisis affected the latter countries much more severely. Eventually, however, both Latvia and Lithuania became even more committed to join the eurozone as part of their exit from the crisis strategy. With a more favourable internal situation, Latvia managed to introduce the euro as national currency in 2014, one year earlier than Lithuania which delayed its entry mainly due to interests of domestic actors (Markevičiūtė and Kuokštis 2016).

Efforts to ensure energy security

Ever since their accession to the EU in 2004, the Baltics states' vulnerable energy situation strongly affected their EU policies. In fact, during the first decade of Baltic membership in the EU, they were almost exclusively dependent on Russian gas imports (Grigas 2013a: 63), and their electricity networks remain synchronised with Russian rather than the European power system (Grigas 2013b: 42). For this reason, the Baltic energy sectors are very sensitive to any external shocks, and thus, the three countries are often described as 'energy islands' within the EU. As any (external) energy shock could destabilise the three countries easily, the Baltic states pursue very active policies to increase their energy independence. It is not surprising then that their EU policies are also directed accordingly.

The importance of energy security is stressed clearly in strategic documents in each Baltic country. In Lithuania, parliamentary parties jointly declared that 'safeguarding of national security' is the key Lithuanian interest, and steps to increase Lithuanian energy independence are indicated as contributing to this end (Lietuvos Respublikos Seimas 2004; 2008). Latvian National Security Concept also explicitly stresses the need to create conditions for the supply of energy resources to ensure Latvian national security (Latvijas Republikas Saeima 2011). Similarly, the Estonian National Security Strategy emphasises that third countries (namely Russia) 'use energy resources as political and economic means' and details a number of steps for Estonia to increase its energy security (Riigikogu 2010). Consequently, the Baltics have taken measures in this direction at EU level as well, as is seen by their strong support for deepening the EU Energy Union and to properly implement the provisions of the Third Energy Package (TEP).

Even though the implementation of TEP provisions requires significant national efforts, the Baltic countries, and particularly Lithuania, are often seen among the most active players in this regard. In fact, Lithuania's actions to ensure its gas supply diversification was arguably the most ambitious among the three countries: it employed the strictest measures foreseen in EU legislation to unbundle ownership in its gas sector (Grigas 2013b: 36). Thus, by strategically employing tools provided by EU legislation, Lithuania broke up the dominant vertically integrated monopoly in its gas sector, diversified its gas supply and reduced Russian influence on its energy sector (Pakalkaitė 2016). In the electricity sector, the liberalisation process was easier and thus has advanced further in all three countries. However, the Baltic consumers cannot benefit from this process, unless Lithuanian, Latvian and Estonian electricity networks are connected to EU electricity markets (Grigas 2013a: 76). Therefore, in the late-2000s the Baltics raised this issue at EU level arguing that they cannot implement their obligations to open their electricity markets fully and asked for EU support to increase the region's electricity interconnectivity.

Estonia took such steps in 2006 when it finished the first interconnection between the Baltic and Nordic electricity markets. This link, however, was not sufficient to fully integrate Baltic electricity markets with that of the EU. Thus, several other projects were completed (or are still being implemented) under the Baltic Energy Market Interconnection Plan (Pacevičiūtė 2016). Hence, by starting to implement the provisions of the TEP but without all the necessary resources, the Baltics cornered the EC to support their efforts to ensure their region's electricity interconnectivity. In this way, the three countries started an irreversible process of their integration into the EU electricity network (Godzimirski, Vilpišauskas and Švedas 2015). In this context, however, it is important to note that the Baltics remain integrated within the Russian-controlled electricity system, which also includes Belarus and Russia (BRELL). As the Baltics want to reduce their energy dependence from Russia fully, these countries have also initiated preliminary discussions on synchronisation of their electricity networks with the European Continental Network by 2025 (Adomaitis 2014) and, thus, can be expected to put a lot of effort into convincing the EC to support this initiative both financially and politically (European Commission 2015a).

Even though the Baltics are often seen as having one voice and uniform interests, this is not always the case. A notable disagreement took place between Lithuania and Latvia in the late 2000s regarding the construction of *NordBalt* interconnector between the Baltics and Sweden, which prolonged the completion of the project for one year (European Commission 2013). A similar situation was seen when all three Baltic countries placed bids to build partially EU-funded regional LNG terminals (Vedler 2012). Another point exemplifying Baltics' rivalry is related to the construction of Astravets (Astravyets/Ostrovets) (Belarus) nuclear power plant (NPP) just 50 km from Vilnius. Lithuania sees this plant as a threat to its national and environmental security and, thus, has put its safety on the top of its agenda (Baltic News Service 2017b). It has been pushing for other EU MS support in this regard but has suffered some roadblocks when dealing with neighbouring Latvia (Baltic News Service 2017a). Latvian reluctance here may be explained by either pragmatic calculations about a possibility to secure a favourable deal with Minsk on using Latvian seaports for international trade or by annoyance with some previous Lithuanian decisions in fields of energy (concerning a disagreement on the *NordBalt* interconnector and regional LNG terminal) and transport (i.e. Lithuanian delays in implementing the *RailBaltica* project).

Involvement in the EU's external relations

The Baltics see bringing democracy and stability to their Eastern neighbours as another key strategy for increasing their external security by EU means. All three states have declared the EU's Eastern Partnership (EaP) to be their foreign policy priority (Vilson 2015: 49). The Baltic governments usually portray their contribution to this process as evidence that they can be EU 'policy-shapers' (Tulmets 2011) generating added value for the whole of Europe (Stonytė-Toločkienė 2015: 292). However, the EaP is also a way for the Baltic countries to reduce Russian influence in the region by promoting European values and in this way not only create a more predictable neighbourhood but also strengthen their national security (Made 2011: 67). Considering aggressive Russia's stance against Ukraine and its confrontation with NATO after 2014, the latter motive seems to be more relevant (Raik 2016).

For this reason, it is not surprising that the Baltics have participated actively in the development of the EaP and invested heavily in signing Association Agreements with Ukraine and other Eastern partners in 2013. They also led EU's response to the conflict in Ukraine by pushing for sanctions against Russia. This behaviour reveals that the Baltic states construct their EU policies not only to strengthen their neighbouring countries and ensure their closer ties with the EU but also to deter and contain Russia. However, this comes at a price – as EU actions on its external dimension and especially its steps on Russia require MS unanimity, the Baltics seeking support on this front tend to streamline their positions on other issues, which was perfectly exemplified by their response to the migration crisis.

The migration crisis, which struck Europe in 2015, created one of the most challenging situations that the EU has ever faced. Overwhelmed by hundreds of thousands of illegal immigrants at their borders, individual MS initiated unilateral actions that threatened the viability of the core principles of the EU. A solution of migrants' resettlement and relocation was later developed when the MS pledged to accept thousands of immigrants from the most crisis-affected countries. Even though the Baltics initially opposed the proposal on migrant quotas as well, they adjusted their positions later and started to resettle and to relocate asylum-seekers under the EU programme. In fact, in early 2017, the EU included the three Baltic countries among the other few MS that were on the right track to meet their legal obligations to relocate a specific number of asylum-seekers (European Commission 2017e). This change to the Baltic position is not incidental, however. Observing a tough critique from their Western partners towards the V4, the Baltics evaluated the risks of losing credibility within the EU more carefully. Estonian political elites even painted the picture of the loss of the NATO security umbrella and exposure to security threats from Russia if Estonians do not accept asylum-seekers under the EU programme (Viljar and Markus 2015). This narrative of 'solidarity for the sake of security' was also noted in Latvia and Lithuania (Henry, Byrne and Milne 2015; Lyman 2015). Therefore, they agreed – although without enthusiasm – with migrant quotas assigned to them and continue to implement them even despite prevailing unfavourable public opinion.

A seismic shock hit the EU when David Cameron lost a national referendum on the United Kingdom's (UK) membership in the EU in June 2016. It is widely agreed that Brexit will have a profound effect on the EU and each MS. With regard to the Baltics, in the short term, the UK's departure from the EU will negatively affect Baltic trade with the UK. This is especially the case if the British side (re)introduces import tariffs and non-tariff trade barriers post-Brexit. Moreover, Brexit may create legal problems for large Lithuanian and Latvian diasporas in the UK during the negotiations and just after them. In the long term, however, Baltic worries regarding Brexit are mostly twofold: (i) loss of an important ally in the EU's political process; (ii) fear that it could unleash the disintegration of the EU. Even though the loss of an important like-minded partner may negatively affect the Baltics' negotiation strength during discussions on new Single Market initiatives or when drafting common EU positions on Russia, the second factor seems to be more important here. While the Baltics would be interested in keeping the Single Market open for the UK, there is a concern that such a deal would encourage other EU MS to renegotiate their status within the EU and thus weaken it. *Ceteris paribus*, the three countries will likely follow a current approach of resisting any proposals for turning the Union towards a Europe à la carte.

Although the Baltics see the EU and most of its policies as a way to strengthen their national security by increasing their distance from Russia, not all EU-level initiatives are supported by these countries that, at first sight, would do exactly that. For instance, the Baltics are rather reluctant to support any efforts to create the EU defence union or the EU army. These ideas were put back on the EU agenda just after the UK made its decision to leave the EU as an example that the EU can still deliver. However, those discussions were met with rather strong opposition from the Baltics. Such a response is strongly related to Baltics' fear that any EU-level defence or military initiative would proportionally reduce NATO involvement in the region. As the three countries see NATO, and particularly the United States within it, as a guardian of their security, Lithuania, Latvia and Estonia will continue to oppose any EU integration initiatives that duplicate or weaken NATO in this regard. Following this argument, however, it can be expected that the three countries could support those EU defence and (or) military initiatives that supplement NATO activities or cover areas which are not handled by NATO (Gregory and Fouquet 2016).

Conclusion

National security concerns have heavily influenced the Baltic countries' attitude towards the EU. Such securitization is hardly a coincidence as the overall post-communist transformation of the Baltic countries has been intrinsically linked with their determination to pull away from the influence zone of the former occupying power. The geopolitics have informed their constitutional arrangements, democratisation patterns, development of economic model and eventually choices of international cooperation. After over a decade of direct participation in the European integration process, the key EU policy priorities of the Baltic countries remain oriented towards strengthening their external security. Recent fluctuations in the West and Russia's increasing aggression in the East have further deepened this trend.

On the one hand, it makes the Baltic countries inherently committed to the idea of European integration. Their decidedly pro-Western orientation has significantly contributed to generating political will for necessary domestic reforms to increase governance transparency and effectiveness. Strong engagement for participation in the Single Market has contributed to economic growth and competitiveness. The rise of international credibility has also ensured availability of capital flows to be used for inducing further development.

Nevertheless, such a developmental path entails tensions. Not all obligations arising from the membership in the EU are perceived favourably by the Baltic societies. There have been two primary sources of these misfits and their ensuing societal dissatisfaction. One of them is instigated by the clash between domestic and European institutions over the protection of minorities' rights. It is especially acute in the cases of Latvia and Estonia who had to amend citizenship and language legislation to guarantee more favourable conditions for the local Russian-speaking population. Deep-seated social distrust, based on their embedded societal survival values, however, impedes all three Baltic societies from accepting similar related demands from European institutions wholeheartedly. Another misfit denotes imbalance between the EU emphasis on market regulation and popular expectations for well-developed welfare services. The EU-induced regulatory state model has reinforced the Baltic developmental market-oriented path and created additional disincentives for restructuring welfare policies. This is a more serious issue for Latvia and Lithuania than for Estonia, which was more resolute in pre-accession reforms of the public sector and thus more successful in developing efficient and fiscally sound governance.

Domestic political problems affect the Baltic countries' participation at EU level. Despite notable achievements, the Baltics are still more reactive rather than proactive actors in the EU decision-making process. The Baltic EU policies have largely been a projection of their concerns regarding external security. While they have been quite successful in utilising the possibilities provided by EU membership, the three countries remain highly vulnerable to any future failures of European institutions and broader geopolitical fluctuations.

References

Adomaitis, N. (2014) Baltic Power Grids to Synchronize with European System by 2025, Reuters, 12 December. [ONLINE] Available from: www.reuters.com/article/us-baltic-power-idUSKBN0JQ1CY20141212 (accessed 2 March 2017).

Auers, D. (2015) *Comparative Politics and Government of the Baltic States*. Basingstoke and New York: Palgrave Macmillan.

Baltic News Service (2016) First Coalition Talks: Open Agreement Expected. *Eesti Rahvusringhääling*, 11 October. [ONLINE] Available from: news.err.ee/119647/first-coalition-talks-open-agreement-expected (accessed 2 March 2017).

Baltic News Service (2017a) Lithuanian Energy Minister Sees Some Positive Shift in Latvia's Stance on Belarus' N-plant. *The Baltic Times*, 23 February. [ONLINE] Available from: www.baltictimes.com/ lithuanian_energy_minister_sees_some_posi tive_shift_in_latvia_s_stance_on_belarus__n-plant/ (accessed 2 March 2017).

Baltic News Service (2017b) Vytautas Landsbergis: Lithuania Experiencing Nuclear Blackmail. *The Baltic Times*, 17 February. [ONLINE] Available from: www.baltictim es.com/vytautas_landsbergis __lithuania_experiencing_nuclear_blackmail/ (accessed 2 March 2017).

Bennich-Björkman, L. (2006) Building Post-communist States: Political Corruption and Strategies of Party Formation in Estonia and Latvia. In: S. Eliaeso (ed.) *Building Democracy and Civil Society East of the Elbe: Essays in Honour of Edmund Mokrzycki*. New York: Routledge, pp. 288–305.

Bohle, D. and Greskovits, B. (2012) *Capitalist Diversity on Europe's Periphery*. New York: Cornell University Press.

European Commission (2013) *Proceedings of the Conference on Energy Security: Outlook and Perspectives in the Baltic Sea Region*. [ONLINE] Available from: www.lei.lt/energy-se curity-conference/Conference_proceedings.pdf (accessed 2 March 2017).

European Commission (2015a) *Joint Press Statement by the European Commission and the Energy Ministers of Estonia, Latvia and Lithuania*. 19 February 2015. [ONLINE] Available from: ec.europa.eu/ energy/en/news/joint-press-statement-european-commission-and-energy-ministers-estonia-latvia-and-lithuania (accessed 2 March 2017).

European Commission (2015b) *Single Market Scoreboard: Transposition*. [ONLINE] Available from: ec.europa.eu/internal_market/scoreboard/_docs/2016/ transposition/ 2016-scoreboard_transposition_en.pdf (accessed 2 March 2017).

European Commission (2017a) *Commission Staff Working Paper: 2017 European Semester: Country Report – Estonia*. [ONLINE] Available from: ec.europa.eu/info/ publica tions/2017-european-semester-country-reports_en (accessed 2 March 2017).

European Commission (2017b) *Commission Staff Working Paper: 2017 European Semester: Country Report – Latvia*. [ONLINE] Available from: ec.europa.eu/info/publications/ 2017-european-semester-country-reports_en (accessed 2 March 2017).

European Commission (2017c) *Commission Staff Working Paper: 2017 European Semester: Country Report – Lithuania*. [ONLINE] Available from: ec.europa.eu/info/ publica tions/2017-european-semester-country-reports_en (accessed 2 March 2017).

European Commission (2017d) *Eurobarometer Interactive Search System: Image of the European Union*. [ONLINE] Available from: ec.europa.eu/COMMFrontOffice/ publicop inion/index.cfm/Chart/index (accessed 2 March 2017).

European Commission (2017e) *Ninth report on relocation and resettlement*. [ONLINE] Available from: ec.europa.eu/home-affairs/sites/homeaffairs/files/what-we-do/ poli cies/european-agenda-migration/20170208_ninth_report_on_relocation_and_reset tlement_en.pdf (accessed 2 March 2017).

Godzimirski, J.M., Vilpišauskas, R. and Švedas, R. (2015) *Energy Security and the Baltic Sea Region: Regional Coordination and Management of Interdependencies*. Vilnius: Vilnius University Press.

Government of the Republic of Estonia (2015) *Estonia's European Union Policy 2015–2019*. [ONLINE] Available from: riigikantselei.ee/sites/default/ files/content-editors/ Failid/eesti_el_poliitika_eng.pdf (accessed 2 March 2017).

Gregory, V. and Fouquet, H. (2016) Baltics Press EU to Beef up Defense after Trump Campaign Threats. Bloomberg, 16 November. [ONLINE] Available from: www. bloomberg.com/news/articles/2016-11-16/ baltics-press-eu-to-beef-up-defense-a fter-trump-campaign-threats (accessed 2 March 2017).

Grigas, A. (2013a) Energy Policy: The Achilles Heel of the Baltic States. In: Grigas, A., Kasekamp, A., Maslauskaitė, K., Zorgenfreija, L. and Buzek, J. (eds) *The Baltic States in the EU: Yesterday, Today and Tomorrow*. Paris: Notre Europe – Jacques Delors Institute, pp. 65–86.

Grigas, A. (2013b) *The Politics of Energy and Memory between the Baltic States and Russia* 2nd edn. Abingdon and New York: Routledge.

Gudžinskas, L. (2013) Development of Health Care in Lithuania and Estonia: Similar Conditions, Different Results, *World Political Science Review* 9(1), pp. 385–406.

Gudžinskas, L. (2014) *The Impact of the EU on LGBT Rights Development: Reframing the Political Field in Lithuania*. In: ECPR (European Consortium for Political Research), General Conference. Glasgow, 3–6 September 2014. [ONLINE] Available from: ecpr. eu/Events/ PaperDetails.aspx?PaperID=22043&EventID=14 (accessed 2 March 2017).

Henry, F., A. Byrne, and R. Milne (2015) Eastern Europe Moderates its Opposition to Refugee Quotas. *Financial Times*, 3 September. [ONLINE] Available from: www.ft. com/content/e0a5abde-517a-11e5-b029-b9d50a74fd14 (accessed 2 March 2017).

Kuokštis, V. (2015) Cooperating Estonians and 'Exiting' Lithuanians: Trust in Times of Crisis, *Post-Soviet Affairs* 31(6), pp. 557–575.

Latvijas Republikas Saeima (2011) *Par Nacionālās drošības koncepcijas apstiprināšanu*. [ONLINE] Available from: vestnesis.lv/ta/id/227460-par-nacionalas-drosibas-koncep cijas-apstiprinasanu (accessed 2 March 2017).

Lietuvos Respublikos Seimas (2004) *Dėl pagrindinių valstybės užsienio politikos tikslų ir uždavinių 2004–2008 metais*. [ONLINE] Available from: www3.lrs.lt/ pls/inter/w5_ show?p_r=5042&p_k=1 (accessed 2 March 2017).

Lietuvos Respublikos Seimas (2008) *Dėl 2008–2012 metų Lietuvos užsienio politikos principų, strateginių gairių ir tikslų*. [ONLINE] Available from: www3.lrs.lt/ pls/inter/w5_ show?p_r=5042&p_k=1 (accessed 2 March 2017).

Lyman, R. (2015) Opposition to Refugee Quotas Softens in Europe's Old Communist Bloc. *The New York Times*, 23 September. [ONLINE] Available from: www.nytimes. com/2015/09/24/world/europe/opposition-to-refugee-quotas-softens-in-europes-old-communist-bloc.html?_r=1 (accessed 2 March 2017).

Made, V. (2011) Shining in Brussels? The Eastern Partnership in Estonia's Foreign Policy, *Perspectives* 19(2), pp. 67–79.

Majone, G. (1996) *Regulating Europe*. London: Routledge.

Maniokas, K. (2003) *Europos Sąjungos plėtra ir europeizacija: Vidurio ir Rytų Europos valstybių įsijungimas į Europos Sąjungą*. Vilnius: Eugrimas.

Markevičiūtė, A. and Kuokštis, V. (2016) Race to the Euro: Why Latvia Joined Earlier Than Lithuania, *Baltic Journal of Political Science* 5(5), pp. 5–20.

Mikkel, E. and G. Pridham (2004) Clinching the 'Return to Europe': The Referendums on EU Accession in Estonia and Latvia, *West European Politics* 27(4), pp. 716–748.

Ministry of Foreign Affairs of the Republic of Lithuania (2015) *Lietuvos ES politikos 2015–2020 metų strateginės kryptys*. [ONLINE] Available from: www.urm.lt/uploads/

default/documents/uzienio_politika/ES/Lietuvos ESpolitikos2015–2020strategines_kryptys.pdf (accessed 2 March 2017).

Mole, R. (2012) *The Baltic States from the Soviet Union to the European Union: Identity, Discourse and Power in the Post-Communist Transition of Estonia, Latvia and Lithuania.* London and New York: Routledge.

OECD (2016) *PISA 2015 High Performers: Estonia.* [ONLINE] Available from: www.oecd.org/pisa/PISA-2015-estonia.pdf (accessed 2 March 2017).

Pacevičiūtė, I. (2016) *Towards the Energy Union: The BEMIP and the Case of Lithuania.* [ONLINE] Available from: www.iai.it/sites/default/files/ iaiwp1706.pdf (accessed 2 March 2017).

Pakalkaitė, V. (2016) *Lithuania's Strategic Use of EU Energy Policy Tools: A Transformation of Gas Dynamics.* Oxford: Oxford Institute for Energy Studies. [ONLINE] Available from: www.oxfordenergy.org/ wpcms/wp-content/uploads/2016/09/Lithuanias-Strategic-Use-of-EU-Energy-Policy-Tools-A-transformation-of-Gas-Market-Dynamics-NG-111.pdf (accessed 2 March 2017).

Permanent Representation of the Republic of Latvia to the EU (2016) *Latvian Priorities for the European Union's Agenda in 2016.* [ONLINE] Available at: www.mfa.gov.lv/en/brussels/priorities (accessed 2 March 2017).

Ragozin, L. (2015) Latvians Find Unity in Rejecting Refugees. Politico.eu, 25 September. [ONLINE] Available from: <www.politico.eu/article/latvia-migration-asylum-crisis-baltics-eu/> (accessed 2 March 2017).

Raik, K. (2016) Liberalism and Geopolitics in EU–Russia Relations: Rereading the Baltic factor, *European Security* 25(2), pp. 237–255.

Riigikogu (2010) *National Security Concept of Estonia.* [ONLINE] Available at: <www.mfa.ee/sites/default/files/content-editors/JPA_2010_ENG.pdf> (accessed 2 March 2017).

Stonytė-Toločkienė, I. (2015) Lietuva ir ES Rytų politika: tarp permainų ir tęstinumo. In: Jakniūnaitė, D. (ed.) *Kaip kalbėsime apie 2004–2014 m. Lietuvos užsienio politiką?* Vilnius: Vilniaus universiteto leidykla, pp. 291–318.

Tulmets, E. (2011) Introduction: Identity and Solidarity in the Foreign Policy of East Central European EU Members: Renewing the Research Agenda, *Perspectives* 19(2), pp. 5–25.

Vedler, S. (2012) Estonia's Battle for the Baltic LNG Terminal. *The Baltic Times*, 17 May. [ONLINE] Available from: www.baltictimes.com/news/articles/31270/ (accessed 2 March 2017).

Viljar, V. and R. Markus (2015) Europe's Refugee Crisis in 2015 and Security Threats from the Baltic Perspective, *Journal of Politics and Law* 8(4), pp. 254–262.

Vilson, M. (2015) The Foreign Policy of the Baltic States and the Ukrainian Crisis: A Case of Europeanization? *New Perspectives* 23(2), pp. 49–76.

World Values Survey (2015) *Cultural Map – 6th wave, 2010–2014.* [ONLINE] Available at: www.worldvaluessurvey.org/WVSContents.jsp (accessed 2 March 2017).

11 The new kid on the block

Croatia's EU membership in the shadow of the eurozone crisis

Will Bartlett

Introduction

In the latter half of the twentieth century, the Socialist Republic of Croatia was a constituent republic of federal Yugoslavia. During this period, a system of social, rather than state, ownership prevailed under which most industrial companies were run as self-managed enterprises within which managers had a high degree of autonomy to trade on the market; employees were involved in management through the institution of the Workers' Council. Within these constraints, managers were able to make independent decisions relating to their business operations, although politicians influenced employment and investment plans. In the late 1980s, well before the collapse of the Yugoslav state, the process of economic transition had begun under the so-called Marković reforms, which began the privatization of the socially owned enterprises.

Croatia became an independent country in 1991 and was soon engaged in armed conflicts with the Yugoslav army and with rebel forces within its own territory (Tanner 1997; Goldstein 1999). Privatisation of the socially owned enterprises continued even during the wars, resulting in the sale of a large portion of their assets to new owners who were politically connected to the new ruling party, the Croatian Democratic Union (HDZ). The privatisation programme came under severe criticism from Croatian economists who characterised the new system as one of 'crony capitalism' (Bićanić 1993). This strong connection between the political and managerial elites persists until the present day, and could be characterised as a form of 'political capitalism' (Holcombe 2015). The legacy of communism in Croatia has been the strong interconnection between political and economic elites, and the strong role of personal connections in business success. Political capitalism involves a system of mutual interconnection between political and industrial elites. There are good grounds for calling the form of capitalism that has emerged in Croatia political capitalism, in the sense of its strong links between the business elite and the political elite.[1]

The political and institutional context of post-socialist Croatia was thus formed in part by the legacy of the past as well as by the policies pursued by various governments through the period of transition. During this period, until the end of the 1990s, the dominant political force in the country was the nationalist Croatian Democratic Union (HDZ), led by President Franjo Tudjman, who had overseen the drive to independence and installed an authoritarian political system. Tudjman's death in 1999 ushered in a period of transition to a more liberal form of democracy under the Social Democratic Party that briefly held power in the early 2000s. Elections in 2003 brought to power a reformed and pro-EU HDZ under the leadership of Ivo Sanader, laying the groundwork for the country's eventual EU membership.[2] The country became a member of the EU in July 2013 under an SDP government that had been elected to power in 2011 under the leadership of Zoran Milanović. During this period, the authoritarian nature of the political system gave way to a more liberal democracy, although the system of political capitalism under which the political and economic elites were closely intertwined only deepened.

Since the onset of the eurozone crisis in 2009, the economy has been subject to a deep recession with six years of negative GDP growth. Croatia has languished in recession in each subsequent year. Due to the high level of euroisation of the economy, monetary policy became an ineffective policy instrument and fiscal policy remained as the only viable instrument of macroeconomic policy. Yet, the use of fiscal policy to stimulate the economy has gradually become more and more limited due to the growing level of public and external indebtedness (Deskar-Škrbić et al 2015; Ćorić et al 2015).

After a long accession process, Croatia joined the EU in 2013. On joining the EU, the country's external debt was approaching 100% of GDP. By mid-2015 this had increased to 115% of GDP. This poor economic performance indicates deep structural problems and difficulties in adjusting the economy in the wake of the initial recession and reveals an underlying problem of weak competitiveness of the Croatian economy. Partly, this may be due to the weakness of entrepreneurial activity and corresponding policies.

Under political capitalism, new and aspiring entrepreneurs often face difficulties in establishing their businesses. This weakness has hindered the ability of the economy to respond to economic shocks and has undermined economic competitiveness. It is hardly surprising, therefore, that the economy only recently escaped from the long six-year recession that began in 2009.

Privatisation and the creation of political capitalism

During the communist period, companies in Croatia were autonomous from the state but operated under a system of social ownership and workers' self-management. The property transformation law of April 1991 provided for the compulsory privatisation of all socially owned enterprises and the elimination of social ownership.[3] Paradoxically, privatisation resulted in a large proportion of assets of the formerly socially owned firms being taken into state ownership. The process was supervised by the Croatian Privatisation Agency, which had the power to install managers in loss making enterprises who could then initiate privatisation. Companies that failed to submit a privatisation plan were taken over by the Croatian Development Fund and effectively became owned by the state. Workers' councils were abolished and replaced by supervisory boards with a government representative, alongside representatives from the local municipality, the Chamber of Commerce, and employees (Ostović et al 1994). The Development Fund also received the revenues accumulated from shares sold in the process of privatisation and two thirds of any unsold shares; the remaining unsold shares were transferred to the Pension Fund and the Disability Insurance Fund. The Development Fund appointed managers in companies in which it owned more than 20 per cent of the shares, and in this way obtained a strong influence over the companies in its portfolio[4]. Through the Fund, the state ended up controlling many large enterprises. Moreover, companies, including state owned companies, could also buy shares. For example, the state owned petroleum company, INA, gained control over a large part of the economy in this way. The state also directly took over ownership and control of over one hundred important large companies including major public utilities and installed new managers, most of whom were members of the ruling party (Bićanić 1993). In 1993, the Agency and the Fund were merged as the Croatian Privatization Fund, controlled by a management board consisting of political appointees or politicians and one trade union representative (Ostović et al 1994).

Many of the privatised companies were acquired by 'a narrow elite made up of those who had the capital to buy the most attractive parts of the socially owned assets' (Čučković 1995: 87). Many of the new owners were wealthy expatriates or local businessmen with close links to the ruling party or members of it. Managers with connections to the ruling party, government officials or politicians were able to get loans to support management buy-outs (Bićanić 1993). In addition there was a close relationship between the political and economic elites. Ministers, members of parliament and top civil servants were appointed to the supervisory boards or became company directors. The daily newspaper Nacional wrote that 'from the very beginning of privatisation, the goal of the governing party has [been] to distribute the national wealth and power specifically according to political lines to individuals through which the HDZ would be able to retain its power, even if it were to lose the elections, over the better part of the nation's financial and economic resources' (Pleše 1999).

The HDZ created a system in which the largest and most profitable enterprises were transferred to an elite group of privileged owners with party connections. Non-privatised enterprises were brought under the control of the party and the state through controlling shares held by the Privatization Fund, which appointed politically well-connected directors. Some of the new owners of larger companies and company groups were involved in asset stripping the privatized companies, causing widespread public concern. The coalition government that came to power in 2000 led by the SDP carried out a review of the privatisation process and discovered numerous irregularities. However, little action was taken. The new government turned to the privatisation of public utilities, selling a stake in Croatia Telecomm to Deutsche Telecomm, and a stake in the INA oil and gas company to the Hungarian MOL. The HDZ returned to power in

2003 and continued with the sale of assets from the portfolio of the Croatian Privatisation Agency. However, this process gradually came to a halt and the state continued to hold assets in many semi-privatised companies.

Under the system of political capitalism, Croatia has a low growth potential linked to poor productivity rooted in a weak business environment. There was little support for the development of a new entrepreneurial and innovative small business sector (Čučković and Bartlett 2007). Yet, productivity is lower in companies that are under state ownership or partial state ownership compared to private companies. The productivity gap is estimated to be about 32 per cent for those companies under majority state ownership and 12 per cent for those under minority state ownership (EC 2017a: 51). The gap can be explained by the preferential treatment of these companies in obtaining bank loans, which has enabled them to maintain high levels of employment compared to the companies in the private sector. This allocative inefficiency reduces the growth potential of the economy (EC 2017a). Other research supports this view that unfinished privatisation is a significant obstacle to improved productivity performance of the economy (Vukšić 2016). These findings reflect the functioning of the system of political capitalism in which companies closely connected to the ruling party receive favourable treatment through loans and subsidies, enabling them to provide jobs to the supporters of the ruling party, which in turn reduces their overall productivity levels.

Economic performance before and after the crisis

The initial decline in GDP was due to the negative shock-waves of the global financial crisis followed by the eurozone crisis that began in the autumn of 2009 following the revelation of the massive debts of the Greek state. Croatia was badly affected due to her high dependency on international trade, and especially on trade in services related to the tourism sector (Bokan et al 2009). Since then, Croatia's recovery has been slower than that of the EU (see Figure 11.1). The Croatian recession was not only deep but also long lasting; it did not come to an end until 2015, after six years of negative growth. The deep recession had two main causes. First, the fixed exchange rate prevented the monetary authorities from depreciating the *kuna* as a way to improve economic competitiveness. This policy has become ingrained due to the high level of euroisation of the economy Ozsoz et al 2010; Galac 2012. Following the entry of European banks, the volume of loans made or indexed to the euro expanded hugely and a depreciation of the currency would place these borrowers, whether corporate or personal in a difficult financial condition. This means that any increase in economic competitiveness of the Croatian economy should come through internal devaluation, i.e. a reduction in unit labour costs, just as in the periphery countries of the EU such as Greece and Portugal. Second, macroeconomic austerity policies were reinforced by the requirements of the EU's Excessive Deficit Procedure, which has been strongly deflationary. This has required fiscal consolidation, through reduced budget deficits, a

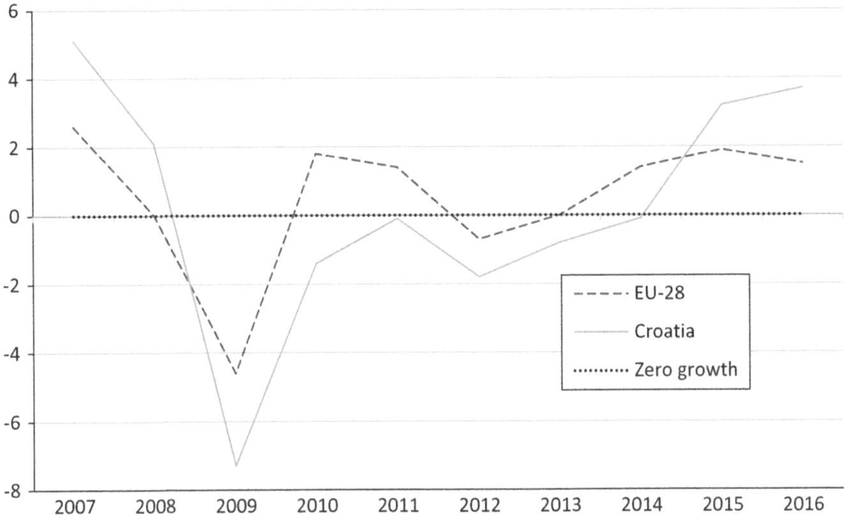

Figure 11.1 GDP growth rates in Croatia and EU-28
Source: Eurostat online data variable code [nama_10_cpc].

procedure likely to involve a reduction in aggregate demand having a deflationary impact on the economy. The deflationary policy could be expected to support internal devaluation and a shift of resources from satisfying domestic demand to increasing export capacity and an improved competitiveness of the economy at the price of economic recession, as has indeed occurred.

The downturn has had serious social consequences. The unemployment rate almost doubled from a low of 8.6 per cent in 2008 to a peak of 17.4 per cent in 2013, while youth unemployment rose to 50 per cent. In the words of the European Commission this high level of unemployment has placed a 'strain on the social fabric' (EC 2014a: 27) while low employment rates were damaging growth prospects. The unemployment rate began to fall in 2014 as economic recovery took hold. However, much of the reduction in unemployment came from the emigration of young workers to find jobs abroad after Croatia joined the EU. Moreover, the quality of new jobs that have been created is low, as most new jobs created have been temporary jobs. In 2016 after two years of recovery, the unemployment rate was still 13.3 per cent, almost five percentage points above the EU average. At the same time real wages, which had increased from 3,799 kuna per month in 1999 to 5,572 kuna in 2008, flat lined for the next six years.[5] In 2014 real wages were just 5,514 kuna. In the following two and a half years real wages began to increase, reaching to 5,707 kuna per month in 2016 (about 770 euros).

In an early response to the crisis, in 2010 the HDZ government headed by Jadranka Kosor announced a policy of fiscal consolidation and austerity as advocated by the International Monetary Fund (IMF 2010). The declared intention was to reduce expenditure on public administration and social

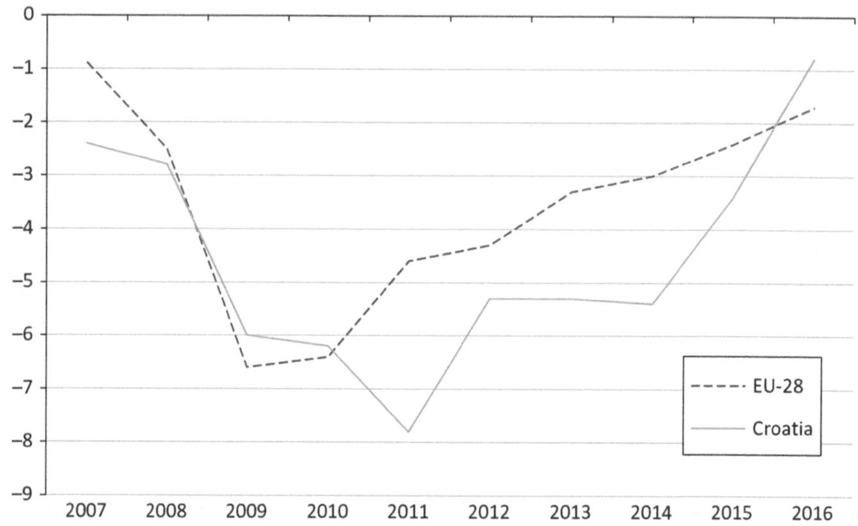

Figure 11.2 General government deficits, Croatia and EU-28 (% of GDP)
Source: Eurostat online data variable code [gov_10dd_edpt1].

programmes, enact structural reforms to enhance labor force participation and improve the business environment, and introduce income and wage policies to improve competitiveness in the context of a broadly stable exchange rate. A fiscal responsibility law required the government to reduce budget expenditure by one percentage point each year until a primary balance in the general government budget was reached, after which the cyclically adjusted primary deficit was to be kept at around zero[6].

However, the announced austerity measures were never effectively implemented. Governments maintained public expenditure at high levels due to the need to maintain public sector employment under the system of political capitalism. Under this system, parties that win elections aim to reward their voters with jobs in public enterprises or partially privatised enterprises in which the state holds a majority or minority stake and positions of influence on supervisory committees. Stubbs and Zrinščak also point to the role of clientelism in the welfare system, which privileged social welfare payments to war veterans and to individuals who were able to claim unjustified benefits through political connections formed at the level of local governments (Stubbs and Zrinščak 2015). The inability to reduce the government budget deficit had direct consequences for the share of public debt in the economy, which increased from 40 per cent of GDP in 2008 to a peak of 87 per cent of GDP in 2014, far in excess of the target set within the EU Stability and Growth Pact of 60 per cent of GDP and leading to immediate corrective action after Croatia joined the EU.

Although these policies were not successfully implemented, the economic downturn led to dissatisfaction with the government and the SDP led by Zoran

Milanović came to power in December 2011. The new government's policy aim was to shift the economy onto an investment-led growth path, while reducing taxes and social contributions on labour to encourage employers to hire more workers.[7] Additional reforms in the labour market and to social contributions were to be introduced to provide further incentives to the supply side of the labour market. In addition, an investment programme was envisaged that would raise capacity and improve productivity, and would be accompanied by redistribution of income to lower wage earners to boost consumption and aggregate demand. Unfortunately, few of these plans came to fruition.

In its first budget in 2012, the new government announced measures of fiscal consolidation that involved cuts to the public sector wage bill, reductions in state subsidies, and reductions in public health spending. VAT was increased by two per cent, combined with a two per cent reduction in social health contributions designed to ease the burden of social contributions on wages and boost employment. The government continued the previous policy of fiscal consolidation announcing plans to reduce public expenditure by one percentage point per year.

Labour market reforms were adopted in 2013 focused on fixed-term employment contracts, and on shortening and simplifying the procedures for collective dismissal. Employers could now take on workers under fixed-term contracts lasting for more than three years. Procedures for dismissal during the probationary work period were relaxed so that a probationer could be fired without cause. New rules introduced in January 2014 made it easier for an employer to dismiss a worker, and increased working time flexibility through the introduction of flexible part-time contracts. All these measures were introduced by the SDP government in the lead up to EU accession.

Croatia's EU membership

Croatia joined the EU in July 2013, and soon afterwards the Milanović government came under strong pressure to introduce further economic reforms. The EU had adopted a system of 'new economic governance' in 2010 in response to the eurozone crisis. As a member state, Croatia immediately became involved in the 'European Semester' process beginning in November each year with the publication of an annual Alert Mechanism Report (AMR) for all EU member states. The third annual AMR, published in November 2013, identified a severe macroeconomic imbalance in Croatia that required further investigation through the process of an in-depth review (IDR). Even before the results of the IDR were announced, Croatia was placed in the Excessive Deficit Procedure (EDP) in January 2014.[8] From that point on, several important instruments of economic policy were effectively handed over to the European Commission.

The IDR was published on 5 March 2014, and concluded that Croatia was experiencing an 'excessive' macroeconomic imbalance that required specific monitoring and strong policy action (ECFIN 2014). The IDR identified a range of serious problems, including large external liabilities, declining export performance, highly leveraged firms, and fast growing government debt. It also revealed that state owned companies had not been restructured, were highly indebted and were only weakly profitable. It also concluded that Croatia has the lowest activity and employment rates in the EU, while the business environment ranked below the average of all the EU's post-communist states. In April 2014, Croatia submitted its 2014 National Reform Programme and its 2014 Convergence Programme to the European Commission. The latter outlined a strategy to correct the excessive deficit by 2016 and move the economy onto a path of sustainable growth. The Commission made a series of recommendations on reforms to achieve the 2016 fiscal target. The main ones were that Croatia should reduce public sector wages, social security expenditures and subsidies, and that more effective control should be placed on government expenditures. The projected aim was to reduce the deficit from 4.9 per cent of GDP in 2013 to 3 per cent of GDP by 2016, a deadline imposed by the EDP. In fact, the targets were over-achieved, with the budget deficit falling to 3.4 per cent in 2015 and 0.8 per cent in 2016.

The Commission's recommendations were highly effective in bringing about a reduction in public expenditure (Figure 11.3). Previously, the government had resisted such policy advice, since within the system of political capitalism high levels of public expenditure can be used to reward loyal voters to the ruling party with public sector jobs and other discretionary forms of expenditure. Close connections between the political elite and the business elite ensure that the interests of politically connected companies are rewarded with favourable legislation and subsidies to favoured industries. This also requires high levels of public expenditure and the flexibility that this provides to the ruling party to reward its cronies. The downside of this arrangement is the misallocation of resources, and the consequent allocative inefficiency that leads to low productivity and low growth performance. However, the European Commission is not tied into this system and its recommendations are not biased by connections to particular political parties or particular business interest groups. After accession, the European Commission gained greater influence over the direction of economic policy and was able to encourage the government to reduce public expenditure, especially on social benefits and on the public sector wage bill ('compensation of employees') (see Figure 11.3). Combined with an upturn in tax receipts as the economy began to recover in 2014, this led to an elimination of the pubic sector budget deficit by 2016.

Croatia's EU membership has also had a positive impact on external competitiveness with the share of exports of goods and services to GDP rising above the share of imports to GDP for the first time in decades, leading to a balance of trade surplus of around 3 per cent of GDP by 2016. This has underpinned a current account surplus, which has in turn led to a reduction in the high levels of external indebtedness of the economy, which peaked at 108 per cent of GDP in 2014, and has begun to fall since then, reaching 91 per cent of GDP in 2016. The boost to exports that resulted from Croatia's EU entry was remarkable, and contributed to bringing the long period of recession to an

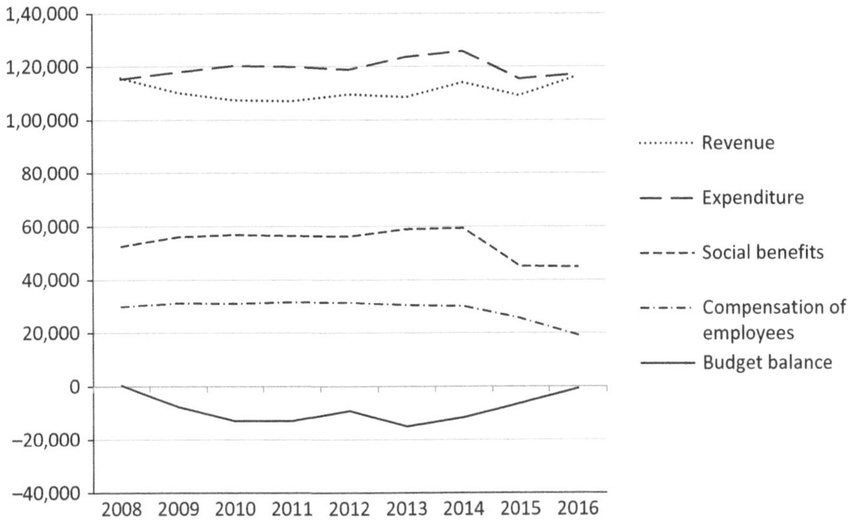

Figure 11.3 Central government budget (million kuna)
Source: Croatian National Bank online data

end. To a large extent the export recovery was due to the recovery of the eurozone from the crisis period, and could easily be reversed if external conditions change. It also reflected improved earnings from the tourism sector, which are also volatile. Therefore, the economy remains vulnerable to external events.

Croatia also benefitted from an increase in FDI inflows after joining the EU. During the long recession from 2009 to 2013, FDI inflows had fallen to an average of just 2.8 per cent of GDP. In 2014, FDI inflows shot up to 6.4 per cent of GDP reflecting an increased optimism among investors. Although the inflow appears to have tailed off in 2015, it is reasonable to expect that the improved economic prospects will attract increased attention of foreign investors in the future.

Due to the continuing economic crisis, the SPD government lost popular support and in the 2015 elections the HDZ was returned to power in coalition with a small insurgent party Most (Bridge) in a government led by a 'neutral' businessman, Tihomir Oresković. In June 2016 the government collapsed following Oresković insistence that the chairman of the HDZ, Tomislav Karamarko, should resign due to his close connections to the Hungarian oil company MOL, which has a large stake in the Croatian oil company INA – a further example of the role of connected actors within the system of political capitalism. New elections were called in the autumn of 2016, which returned the HDZ with a small majority under the leadership of its new chairman Andrej Plenković. The new government continued with a programme of the structural reforms recommended by the Commission under the EU Excessive Deficit Procedure, involving reforms to the labour market, welfare spending, and the education and health systems.

In March 2016 the Commission concluded that Croatia was still suffering from excessive macroeconomic imbalances and called for a new in-depth analysis (EC 2017b). This concluded that two thirds of the public debt was exposed to currency risk. However, since the budget deficit had been reduced to well below the 3 per cent benchmark, the Commission decided to abrogate the 2014 decision on the existence of an excessive deficit in Croatia, removing Croatia from the Excessive Deficit Procedure (EC 2017b), and transferring the country from the 'corrective arm' of the Stability and Growth Pact to the 'preventive arm' of the Pact.

However, the Commission also warned that private sector debt, which amounted to 115 per cent of GDP, was heavily exposed to currency risk. In other words, since almost all the Croatian debt is in foreign currency, any depreciation of the kuna would lead to a greater debt burden on the economy. A study carried out by the Croatian National Bank in 2017 found that around one third of corporate debt is unsustainable, reducing the willingness of businesses to carry out investment and posing a threat to financial stability (Martinis and Ljubaj 2017). The problem is especially severe in large and non-exporting companies. The vulnerability of the private sector is illustrated by the case of Agrokor, Croatia's biggest company accounting for about 15 per cent of GDP and with 40,000 employees in Croatia.[9] The example also illustrates the continuing operation of the system of political capitalism in Croatia. In early 2017, Agrokor became effectively bankrupt due to enormous debts to creditors and suppliers, valued at 6 billion euros that proved to be too great to sustain. The government quickly passed a law permitting the state to bail out the company through a bankruptcy protection system for systemic enterprises that are 'too big to fail'. This prioritised payments to suppliers who would not otherwise have been protected under existing bankruptcy laws. The company owner and CEO, Ivica Todorović, resigned and the company was put under administration, with a view to its restructuring and eventual sale of profitable parts of the business to new owners. The arrangements for the rescue demonstrate deep links between the government and the company as the Minister of Finance, Zdravko Marić had been Agrokor's executive director for capital markets until 2016. The company came to an agreement with the creditors to restructure its debts, but the government stands ready to bail out the company if the agreement with the creditors should fail. Remarkably, the government itself is a creditor through the Croatian Bank for Development HBOR, which provided a secret loan to the company, which is now frozen under administration procedures.[10]

Labour market reforms

One of the key concerns of the European Commission has been the poor performance of the labour market, especially for youth and for older workers (EC 2014b). An increasing number of young people are neither in education, employment nor training, while the proportion of people at risk of poverty and social exclusion has increased to levels significantly above the EU average. Despite growing unemployment, spending on and coverage of active labour market measures are below average in the EU. Nevertheless, various attempts at labour market reforms have been made relating to active labour market policies, conditions for early withdrawal from the labour market and employment protection legislation. Overall, these reforms have reduced the protection of workers and worsened working conditions.

Under the terms of a Social Welfare Act that entered into force on January 2014 social welfare beneficiaries are required to participate in 'social inclusion activities'. The maximum accumulated amount of benefits has been limited to the level of the minimum gross salary. On the positive side, a transitional period of three months has been introduced for welfare claimants who find a job, so that new employees do not lose all their benefits when they start work. New rules allow the continuation of pension payments if a retiree takes on a part time job.

Tax reforms

Personal income tax rates were reduced in 2015 and again in January 2017, reducing the progressivity of the tax system through a set of measures designed to change the balance of taxation away from labour and towards capital. The overall effect was to reduce the upper personal income tax rate from 40% to 36% while raising the threshold at which this came into effect. Although the lower tax threshold has been increased, taking an additional 560,000 low-income persons out of income tax altogether, the overall impact has been to increase income inequality (EC 2017a). Most of the gains are concentrated in the top two deciles of income earners. The Gini coefficient increased by 0.4 percentage points after the 2015 reform, and again by 0.3 percentage points following the 2017 reform. The corporate income tax rate (profit tax rate) was reduced from 20 per cent to 18 per cent, and to 12 per cent for small businesses and farmers. These changes may have had some positive effects on investment. During the crisis the investment rate had fallen from a peak of 28 per cent of GDP in 2008 to just 21 per cent of GDP in 2010 and then stagnated. Following the introduction of the tax reforms investment began to pick up again in 2016 (EC 2017a).

While these tax changes were introduced, the government refused to implement a recurrent property tax recommended by the Commission, that could both raise additional revenue and be justified from a distributional point of view as a tax on wealth (EC 2015: 12). Instead the government proposed to upgrade the system of communal fees. However, following further pressure from the Commission, the government has scheduled the introduction of a recurrent property tax for 2018, as announced in the National Reform Programme for 2016.

Conclusions

Following independence and during a damaging period of armed conflict in the early 1990s, Croatia developed a system of political capitalism that created strong links between the political and business elites through a privatisation process that left the state in control of a large part of the economy. The close connections between these elites reduced competition on the domestic market and undermined the productivity and growth capacity of the economy. During the 2000s the economy grew strongly on the basis of foreign credits obtained through the banking system which was by then mainly under the ownership of EU banks. With the onset of the eurozone crisis these sources of foreign resources collapsed, as did the inflow of foreign direct investment. With a highly euroised economy, the instruments of monetary policy became ineffective and fiscal policy took the burden of adjustment. The ruling parties within the system of political capitalism made use of high levels of government expenditure to provide resources for clientelistic allocation of resources to politically connected companies with partial state ownership in the form of subsidies and jobs for political party members, which in turn reduced the productivity of these companies compared to private sector companies. Unwilling to reduce public expenditure, the falling tax revenues associated with recession conditions created a large budget deficit and a consequent rapid growth on the public debt. Private debt also increased, and total external debt reached more than 100 per cent of GDP by the time Croatia joined the EU in 2013. During this time real wages stagnated and unemployment increased to high levels.

On joining the EU, Croatia was immediately placed in the Excessive Deficit Procedure in early 2014, with harsh austerity measures becoming mandatory under the pressure of the recommendations of the European Commission, through the Council, to reduce public expenditure at last. Unaffected by the political and economic connections between domestic elites, the EU had an interest in stabilising Croatia's growing debt and imposing real cuts to public expenditure. These were implemented mainly through cuts to welfare programmes and to the public sector wage bill from 2014 onwards. At the same time labour market reforms were implemented that undermined the position of workers in the labour market. Unemployment decreased but this was largely due to the young people taking advantage of the free movement options available through EU membership, and many young skilled workers left the country to find jobs elsewhere. Moreover, many of the jobs that were created following EU membership were low quality temporary jobs. Accompanying these reforms, tax reforms cut the top rate of income tax and reduced corporate income tax (profit tax), privileging the upper income deciles and inequality further increased.

The collapse of Agrokor at the beginning of 2017 illustrated the dire state of the economy overburdened by enormous debts, threatening the stability of the financial system. The system of political capitalism was well illustrated by the connections between politically connected loans that had been made to Agrokor through the Croatian development bank HBOR, and the previous tenure of the finance minister as a senior executive in the company. At the time of writing, the full impact of the restructuring process on small farmers and suppliers from the food processing industry was uncertain.

Yet Croatia's membership of the EU also brought with it some positive developments, with an improvement in the external position due to growth of exports of goods and services leading to a trade surplus and the return of foreign direct investment inflows on the back of the boost to investor confidence due to the EU accession. Yet these gains may be fragile as the FDI inflow soon relented, and the gains to trade are dependent on a continued recovery of the EU market. The question facing Croatian decision makers is whether real institutional reforms can be made that involve removing the system of political capitalism that is holding back productivity, innovation and entrepreneurship, and replacing it with a more vibrant competitive capitalism that would be capable of building a modern knowledge intensive, high technology economy for the future.

Notes

1 Cvijanović and Redžepagić (2011) characterized the former socialist system in Croatia as one of 'political capitalism' and the system that emerged from it as 'clientelistic' or 'crony' capitalism. In my view, it is misconceived to call the former system a capitalist system. Certainly, there was a high degree of political control over enterprise autonomy, and this was carried over into the emerging capitalist system in the 1990s.
2 Ivo Sanader was subsequently jailed for corruption, an event indicative of the nature of the political elite in Croatia.
3 Employees were offered discounts on the purchase of shares depending on the length of service, while the general public could buy shares at their full price.
4 'The fund has … great powers and no direct accountability. In its portfolio it has shares from almost all enterprises in the economy, making it the largest asset owner…it appoints managers and can initiate privatization when and how it sees fit. Bićanić 1993: 428.
5 Real wages are calculated with respect to 2015 prices, author calculations from online data obtained from the Croatian National Bank.
6 This was part of the Croatian Recovery Programme introduced in April 2010.
7 Ministry of Finance (2012) *Economic and Fiscal Policy Guidelines for the Period 2013–2015*, Zagreb
8 This procedure is within the 'corrective arm' of the Stability and Growth Pact.
9 'Croatia's Agrokor Business Empire too Big to Fail?' *Deutsche Welle*, 9 May 2017.
10 'State Provided Previously Undisclosed Indirect Loan to Agrokor', total-croatia-news.com, 25 July 2017.

References

Bićanić, I. (1993) Privatization in Croatia, *East European Politics and Society* 7(3), pp. 422–439.

Bokan, N., Grgurić, L., Krznar, I. and Lang, M. (2009) The Impact of the Financial Crisis and Policy Responses in Croatia. *Working Papers W-22*. Zagreb: Croatian National Bank.

Ćorić, T., Šimović, H. and Deskar-Škrbić, M. (2015) Monetary and Fiscal Policy in a Small Open Economy: The Case of Croatia, *Ekonomska Istraživanja* 28(1), pp. 407–421.

Čučković, N. (1995) The Privatization Process and its Consequences for the Distribution of Welfare: The Case of Croatia, *Moct-Most* 5(3), pp. 75–90.

Čučković, N. and Bartlett, W. (2007) Entrepreneurship and Competitiveness: The Europeanisation of Small and Medium-sized Enterprise Policy in Croatia, *Southeast European and Black Sea Studies* 7(1), pp. 37–56.

Cvijanović, V. and Redžepagić, D. (2011) From Political Capitalism to Clientalist Capitalism? The Case of Croatia, *Zbornik radova Ekonomskog Fakulteta Rijeci* 29(2), pp. 355–372.

Deskar-Škrbić, M. Šimović, H. and Ćorić, T. (2015) The Effects of Fiscal Policy in a Small Open Transitional Economy: The Case of Croatia, *Acta Oeconomica* 64, pp. 133/152.

EC (2014a) *Alert Mechanism Report 2015*, COM(2014) 904 final. 28 November. Brussels.

EC (2014b) *Council Recommendations on Croatia's 2014 National Reform Programme*, COM (2014) 412 final. 2 June. Brussels

EC (2015) *Croatia: Review of Progress on Policy Measures Relevant for the Correction of Macroeconomic Imbalances*. December. Brussels.

EC (2017a) *Country Report Croatia Including an In-Depth Review on Prevention and Correction of Macroeconomic Imbalances*. Commission Staff Working Document, SWD 76 final. 22 February. Brussels.

EC (2017b) *Recommendation for a Council Decision Abrogating Decision 2014/56/EU on the Existence of an Excessive Deficit in Croatia*. COM 529 final. 22 May. Brussels.

ECFIN (2014) *Macroeconomic Imbalances Country Report: Croatia 2014*, Occasional Papers 179, Brussels: European Commission DG Economic and Financial Affairs.

Galac, T. (2012) Global Crisis and Credit Euroisation in Croatia. *Working Papers W-33*. Zagreb: Croatian National Bank

Goldstein, I. (1999) *Croatia: A History*, London: Hurst & Co.

Holcombe, R. G. (2015) Political Capitalism, *Cato Journal* 35(1), pp. 41–66.

Martinis, A. and Ljubaj, I. (2017) Corporate Debt Overhand in Croatia: Micro Assessment and Macro Implications. *Working Papers W-51*. Zagreb: Croatian National Bank.

Oštović, D., Gračanin, B. and Mateša, Z. (1994) Privatisation Report – 1994, Fifth CEEPN Conference on Economic Transition, Bled, 2–13 December.

Ozsoz, E., Rengifo, E.W. and Salvatore, D. (2010) Deposit Dollarization as an Investment Signal in Transition Economies: The Cases of Croatia, the Czech Republic and Slovakia, *Emerging Markets Finance & Trade* 46(4), pp. 5–22.

Pleše, M. (1999) HDZ has Completely Destroyed the Croatian Economy, *Nacional* 202, 29 September.

Stubbs, P. and Zrinščak, S. (2015) Clientelism and Social Welfare in Croatia: Clientelism and the Limits of 'Europeanisation', *European Politics and Society* 16(3), pp. 395–410.

Tanner, M. (1997), *Croatia: A Nation Forged in War*. New Haven: Yale University Press.

Vukšić, G. (2016) Effects of Private Ownership, Trade, and Foreign Direct Investment on Labor Productivity Growth in Transition Economies: Evidence from the Croatian Manufacturing Industry, *Emerging Markets Finance and Trade* 52, pp. 322–335.

Part III

The Visegrád cooperation – challenges for a semi-institutionalised regional group

12 Internal and external aspects of the Visegrád 4 cooperation

Tomáš Strážay

Introduction

The Visegrád group celebrated its twenty-fifth anniversary in 2016. Despite the fact that the V4 had to overcome several problems over the past quarter-century, it has proved to be the most efficient regional initiative in a broader defined Central Europe and one of the most efficient models of regional cooperation in the European Union. The V4 also successfully managed to pursue the joint interests of V4 countries on EU level.

Thanks to the fact that the EU is supportive of the maintenance and developing of regional groupings, the V4 had favorable conditions to develop after 2004. The Treaty of Nice provided the V4 with the same number of votes in the Council as France and Germany had altogether, which gave the V4 real power. The widely spread attitude among the old member countries, however, is that the V4 has served more as a blocking coalition than a real policy shaper. This attitude was even strengthened in the course of the migration crisis when the V4 got the label of the most obstructive grouping of countries in the entire EU, due to its opposing attitude towards the quotas on the redistribution of refugees. The question is how the V4 should demonstrate its focus on a positive agenda and solutions which would have validity for the entire EU. Ideas good enough to attract the attention of other member states would naturally integrate V4 in the decision-making process at EU level. Otherwise, by pursuing a narrowly defined regional interest, the role of the V4 can become rather marginal.[1]

The chapter also examines the notion of solidarity, which has had a crucial meaning both for the V4 and EU. The main research question in this respect is if the concept of regional solidarity that is now pursued by the V4 countries in relation to the migration crisis is compatible with the solidarity concept in the EU and the consequences any discrepancy might have on the role of the V4 in the EU and on relations between the two.

V4 as an informally institutionalized regional initiative

The establishment of the International Visegrád Fund (IVF) in the year 2000 changed the institutional setting of the Visegrád cooperation. Until then the V4 was a regional initiative with no formal institutional anchoring. In effect it was more a coalition of the willing than a well-structured regional grouping. Though the IVF changed the status quo, its establishment did not have a dramatic impact on the functioning of the V4 at all. This was due to the fact that the mission and main focus of the Fund was defined quite narrowly – the main aim was to strengthen the civic dimension of V4.

The IVF remains the only V4 standing institution, which means that cooperation is not coordinated by any body (such as a secretariat) and decisions adopted on the V4 level in fact are not legally binding. Weak institutionalization is what distinguishes the V4 from other well-established regional initiatives in the EU, such as Benelux or Nordic cooperation. Such institutional arrangements also make V4 more flexible, which can certainly be perceived as an advantage, especially in times of quickly changing reality. Last but not least, weak institutionalization enables the V4 to survive difficult periods, when the V4 countries do not necessarily speak with one voice. Thanks to the fact that the V4 countries are not obliged to always look for a compromise or joint solution, they can simply concentrate on those areas where they find a joint interest.

The practical lack of formal institutions, however, is compensated by a high number of informal ones. These include regular meetings of the representatives of individual V4 countries on all levels, different working groups, as well as high number of informal ties and contacts in both governmental and non-governmental sectors. The institute of the Visegrád Group presidency can also be mentioned as an example.

Four dimensions of cooperation

Political cooperation

Since the very beginning the Visegrád cooperation was mostly based on political cooperation. Stakeholders in the region are, however, somewhat divided when identifying decisive factors that led to the establishment of V4. While some consider V4 to be an autonomous regional initiative, founded and driven by local stakeholders, others rather stress the importance of external pressure that led to the establishment of a coalition of otherwise quite different countries. All in all, it can be argued that V4 managed to contribute to the stabilization of Central Europe and therefore satisfied the expectations of external stakeholders in Western Europe and in the US, while on the other hand there certainly was a governing elite in each of the V4 countries that was supportive for deepening cooperation with Central European neighbours.

More than 25 years of cooperation has confirmed that V4 remains predominantly a political animal. Even the IVF, despite its declared support for the civic dimension, is run by political nominees and supervised by the ministries of foreign affairs (MFAs) of the Visegrád countries. A prerequisite for any Visegrád initiative is the participation of all four countries, as decisions at the V4 level are taken only if the representatives of all countries reach a consensus. In practice, the Visegrád modus operandi includes three possibility outcomes:

1 All V4 countries agree on the same position from the outset.
2 Their positions differ slightly and they reach a compromise.
3 They differ and maintain their original positions without reaching a compromise (Strážay 2015).

The flexible character of cooperation enables V4 to continue its existence regardless of which out of the three options mentioned above prevails. Nevertheless, it can be argued that for the viability of any regional initiative the joint positions are important, especially as regards strategic issues.

Cooperation on the EU level

After their accession to the EU, the V4 countries developed a mechanism for cooperation and coordination at EU level. V4 meetings prior to EU summits have already become a tradition. The successful coordination of positions on EU-related issues has also enhanced the reputation of V4 countries among the other EU members. The EU itself is perceived by V4 countries not only as a modernization project or source of funds, but as an opportunity to shape various policies and pursue regional interests. The significance of the V4 was for instance demonstrated during the debate over the EU budget 2014–2020 and cohesion policy, and in the case of the climate and energy package. A coordinated position towards illegal migration also shows the ability of the V4 to respond jointly to common challenges (Visegrád group 2015a).

Sectoral cooperation

V4 cooperation has also gained a significant sectoral dimension. Progress has been achieved in the fields of energy, infrastructure, and security and defense, though in all these areas there is still a long way to go to achieve tangible results. Another important field of cooperation is the EU neighbourhood policy, with its specific focus on the Eastern neighbours, and enlargement policy.

As regards energy, a regional gas market is still in preparation and the North/South energy corridor is not yet completed. The V4 countries, however, remain strong supporters of the Energy Union. The development of infrastructure is considered a strategic priority of all V4 countries. The creation of the High-Level Working Group during the 2013/14 Hungarian V4 presidency may be regarded as an important step underlining the importance of the topic. Despite an interest in developing cross-border connections, in practice little has been done so far. The only new highway connection built within the V4 area in the last 25 years is that connecting the Czech Republic and Poland.

Security and defense represents another challenge for the V4, especially when one takes into account the worsening security situation in the Eastern neighbourhood and threats coming from the South. The creation of the V4 EU battle group, which was put on standby in the first half of 2016, can be considered a test of the ability of the V4 to cooperate in the area of the so-called hard security.

Neighbourhood and enlargement policy represents an area in which the V4 claims to create added value for the EU. The Visegrád group has supported the enlargement policy intensively, especially regarding the Western Balkans. The V4 countries have also become advocates of the EaP countries, and have developed and divided responsibilities in terms of their cooperation with Ukraine (Visegrád group 2015b).

With regard to economic development, all the V4 countries are in the process of catching up with the 'old' EU members. Faster economic growth than the EU average is a prerequisite for faster convergence. The V4 countries are therefore strong supporters of innovation technologies and the digital agenda in all sectors of society.

The civic dimension of cooperation, especially in the fields of research, innovation, education, and culture, is supported through the programs of the International Visegrád Fund. The IVF, which turned 15 years old in 2015, has an irreplaceable role among V4 activities and instruments. Though awareness of the V4 has been increasing year by year, and IVF programs attracting more applicants, a systematic strategy that would focus on public awareness in V4 countries is still in preparation.

Cooperation with non-V4 countries

In general, cooperation with third (non-V4) countries and groupings may be regarded as another important pillar of V4. Cooperation within the framework of the V4+ formula already includes a long list of countries, both European and non-European. In a number of cases, the cooperation has become systematic and continuous – for example V4+Eastern Partnership, V4+Western Balkans ministerial summits, and V4+Japan, just to mention a few. On the other hand, new formats of cooperation are appearing every year – V4+France and V4 +Turkey may be cited as recent examples.

Factors undermining the internal cohesion of the V4

Bilateral relations

Bilateral cooperation between individual countries plays an important role in V4. In the 1990s, for instance, the V4 suffered from worsening bilateral relations between Slovakia and Hungary. This is no longer the case, however good neighborly relations and intensive bilateral cooperation particularly between the V4 countries remain prerequisites for the successful performance of the Visegrád group. In addition, regional issues to a large extent generate the content of bilateral meetings. Naturally, the aim of discussing regional issues at the bilateral level is not to divide the V4, but to develop ideas that may be adopted by all V4 countries.

V4 countries on different orbits of European integration

The V4 countries can be found on different integration levels within the EU. While Slovakia reached full integration with the adoption of the euro in 2009, the date of the largest V4 country's accession to the eurozone is still unknown. Though Poland has tried to follow and join in those actions initiated within the Euro group, the accession to the eurozone was not perceived as a priority even by the Civic Platform government. Besides the current configuration of political elites, which is not supportive of the adoption of the single currency, the rather negative stance towards accession to the eurozone of a significant portion of the Polish economic elite also plays an important role here (National Bank of Poland 2014). In addition, the accession to the Eurozone will have to be preceded by constitutional change. Thanks to the pro-integration course of the current Czech government, it is more likely that the Czech Republic will become the second V4 country to be a member of the eurozone, although not in the near future.

Differences in perceiving threats

Differences in the size and geopolitical position of the four countries, together with their differing historical experience, have had an impact on how each country perceives the threats facing the external neighbourhood and neighbouring countries. Though the V4 countries recognize the Eastern neighbours of the EU as a priority, their respective levels of engagement and sensitivity to the ongoing security crisis in Eastern Ukraine are markedly different. Among the four Poland is being considered as the most critical of Russia and emphasizes the importance of hard security, in which the development of proper capabilities and their deployment plays an important role.

Generally, the prevailing perception of Russia within the V4 countries is different. In Slovakia, for instance, Russia is perceived rather as a cooperative partner than as a foe. Though the total Slovak export to Russia is only half of that to Poland (Statistical Office of the Slovak Republic 2015), the fact that the Slovak state budget receives huge revenues from the transiting of Russian gas to the West plays an important role in the rhetoric of Prime Minister Fico and other ministers. The situation in Poland is different – though the country's export to Russia was hit hard by the introduction of sanctions, Russia's investment presence in Poland is almost nonexistent. In addition, Poland plays much less of a role as a transit country for Russian gas than Slovakia. In Slovakia, a significant part of the population does not share anti-Russian attitudes – although, as one recent opinion poll showed (Duleba 2014), the respondents did not want Russia to interfere in the domestic affairs of Ukraine. Nevertheless, it is important to mention that despite their differences, Poland and Slovakia, along with the other two V4 countries, did manage to adopt several joint declarations condemning the annexation of Crimea by Russia, and supporting the European orientation of Ukraine (Visegrad group 2015c).

Different perspectives on regional cooperation

All V4 countries are committed supporters of the Visegrád cooperation and aware of the benefits it brings. Being the smallest Visegrád country, the V4 provides Slovakia with an opportunity to pursue its national interests at regional as well as EU level. Therefore, the V4 has been the first choice for Slovakia when it comes to the discussion of regional issues or EU policies. Recently, the V4 has had increasingly important economic significance for Slovakia – together, the V4 countries are the most important trade partner for Slovakia, even bigger than Germany, which is the most important individual partner. Membership of the eurozone naturally pushes Slovakia to look for other partners beyond V4, since the Czech Republic, Hungary and Poland are currently not insiders. On the other hand, Slovakia recognizes the importance of the Single Market and is therefore opposed to any dividing lines that would separate eurozone members from the rest of the EU.

Though Poland – the biggest V4 country – has also taken part in other regional initiatives, such as the Weimar triangle, most frequently it is the V4 that is its first option for consultations. Being the biggest V4 as well as a middle-sized EU country, it naturally has slightly different preferences than other V4 countries with respect to some issues. However, there has been a systematic attempt to push Poland among the bigger and more powerful EU members, as the example of the Weimar triangle shows. By forming a coalition with its Southern neighbours in the framework of Visegrád cooperation, the position of Poland got strengthened. In some cases, Poland (though with the support of its Visegrád partners) instrumentally used the V4 as the platform for building broader coalitions with other EU countries, most frequently under the V4+ formula.

Warsaw seems recently to have preferred extending the Visegrád cooperation to other partners, although without the formal enlargement of the V4. The current Polish government led by the PIS party focuses almost exclusively on new EU members from the 2004 and 2007 enlargement groups, finding more commonalities with them than in the case of old EU members. This is also the case of the Three Seas Initiative that is being intensively promoted by Poland and Croatia. However, an intensive focus on exploiting the V4+ format might draw attention away from cooperation within a closed V4 format. Another danger poses itself in relation to persisting differences in the positions of V4 countries towards some issues of strategic importance, including perception of Russia or the future of the EU, which could result in a lack of trust within the group, if all V4 consultation mechanisms are not exploited properly.

Besides the Visegrád group, all V4 countries participate actively in a number of other regional initiatives. Some of them encompass all four countries (the Central European Initiative can be mentioned as an example), while others do not. EU macro-regional strategies may be mentioned as an example here: while Slovakia, together with the Czech Republic and Hungary, is part of the Danube strategy, Poland takes part in the Baltic strategy. Membership of different initiatives, however, does not automatically undermine the interests of the Visegrád group, or deepen internal dividing lines. A lot depends upon there being a good communication strategy within the V4 – if this fails, some V4 partners could feel excluded. For instance, the process of establishing the so-called Austerlitz triangle encompassing Austria, the Czech Republic and Slovakia, which was highly promoted by the Czech government, triggered feelings of exclusion in Poland and Hungary. Warsaw and Budapest perceive the Austerlitz initiative as a possible alternative to the V4 for the Czech Republic and Slovakia.

Visegrád inspirational? Potential for coalition building at EU level

Though the V4 countries managed to obtain the support of other non-V4 EU members for some initiatives, the last 12 years showed that they performed more as policy-takers than policy-shapers. One also has to distinguish between the recognition of the V4 in the EU and the real coalition potential of the group. Though the former seems to have increased over the course of the last few years, the potential of V4 to serve as the core of pan-European initiatives is far from exhausted. Some of the areas where V4 had and/or continues to have a significant coalition potential are identified below.

Cohesion policy

Since all of the V4 countries are net beneficiaries of the EU cohesion policy, they all will have a strong interest in profiting from the membership in the future. An informal group of 'friends of cohesion policy' also includes other new member states, namely the three Baltic countries, Romania, Bulgaria, Slovenia and Croatia. It is therefore not surprising that the V4 countries pay significant attention to the drafting of the new EU budget. However, it is still unclear how the cohesion policy after 2020 will look, taking into consideration possible institutional and procedural changes in the EU and impact of the Brexit effect. One of the reasons for the weakening of the friends of cohesion policy coalition could be the transition of some countries from the group of net beneficiaries to net contributors. In this regard, especially the Czech Republic and Slovenia are the most frequently mentioned examples.

Climate-energy package

The position of the Visegrád countries on an EU 2030 climate and energy policy can serve as an example of their influence. The opposition of the Visegrád group (and Romania and Bulgaria) to the proposed renewable and energy efficiency targets was reflected in the final version of the package. From their point of view, 'the introduction of any legally binding renewable energy and energy efficiency targets at EU or national level is not desirable' (Visegrád group 2014). The probability that the V4 countries will change their attitudes significantly on the necessity of a quick increase of renewables in their energy mixes is quite low, so the Visegrád group is likely to remain the guardian of rather conservative views on climate and energy policy into the future.

Energy policy and energy security: Nordstream 2

The V4 countries share a joint interest regarding energy security. All of them also declare the aim to diversify the routes and suppliers of the two most important commodities – gas and oil. At the same time, all V4 countries are supporters of the single EU energy market and Energy Union. The high interest in energy security is related to the fact that all V4 countries are – though to a different degree – dependent on Russia as the main supplier of gas and oil, but also nuclear fuel. Their negative experience from the year 2009, when Russia stopped delivering gas through Ukraine for approximately two weeks is another reason why energy policy and energy security ranks so high among the priorities of the Visegrád group. In order to attain a broader regional impact and to make the North–South energy infrastructure really work, cooperation with other non-V4 countries in the region is necessary. Therefore, there also is potential to build broader regional coalitions in this field in the future.

One example of a successful demonstration of V4´s coalition potential was the joint letter of the representatives of eight EU member countries addressed to the European Commission (Sytas 2016). In the letter, the leaders of the V4 countries, Estonia, Latvia, Lithuania and Romania expressed their objection to the intention to build the Nordstream 2 gas pipeline through which Russia would be shipping gas to Germany. The objection concerned the fact that the new pipeline would strengthen the position of Russia in the EU gas market and would increase energy risks in the broadly defined region of Central Europe. Another reason was that it would omit traditional transit countries, namely Ukraine and Slovakia, which would decrease their revenues significantly.

Migration policy

The firm stance of the V4 countries on the redistribution quotas worsened their reputation in some old EU member countries, while on the other hand the Visegrád group as such became more known in the EU. Until now, the V4 countries found support for their position among some politicians, but not among other EU countries. They also were not successful in terms of gaining support for their concept of flexible solidarity. Nevertheless, in the wake of the victory of some populist political leaders in non-V4 EU countries that share the same attitude, the V4 might become more efficient in creating coalitions on the migration issue. The same could happen if the flow of migrants started to increase dramatically. For the time being, the migration issue is rather used to demonstrate the cohesiveness of the Visegrád group, since it can be considered as a powerful binding factor for the governments of the V4 countries. The fact that this issue is a dividing factor in the EU is not even mentioned in the region.

Enlargement policy and relations with the Eastern neighbours

In terms of enlargement policy the main task for the Visegrád group and other like-minded countries is to find a way to convince those in the EU who are suffering from so-called enlargement fatigue that enlargement policy simply pays off and has the potential to continue to be one of the most successful EU policies. Similarly, the support for reforms and transformation of Ukraine, Moldova and Georgia, as well as technical assistance to Eastern partnership countries should be a domain in which the V4 countries could become the core of the coalition of supporting countries. Under certain conditions they could also play an important role in the redefinition of relations between the EU and Belarus.

Brexit: challenge and opportunity

Though the V4 countries were openly supportive for the *remain* option in the UK referendum, they now have to cope with a different political reality after June 2016. Brexit represents a challenge for the whole EU, the V4 countries included. With the UK becoming a third party for the EU, there is an even stronger need than at any time before to establish a joint platform between the V4 and the UK to discuss issues of joint interest. These would comprise issues which are equally attractive for the V4 countries and for the UK. Such an instrument can also become valuable for the EU as such.

Solidarity: the crucial concept

Since the very beginning the Visegrád cooperation has been based on the idea of solidarity and its only real standing institution – the International Visegrád Fund – is based on the equal contribution, equal rights principle, which also means solidarity. The sticking to the principle of solidarity pays off not only for Slovakia, but also for other V4 countries, including Poland, since it enables their voices to be heard in Brussels.

The old EU members actually perceive the demonstration of regional solidarity as an attempt to preserve narrowly defined regional interests. V4 as such is therefore often presented as the blocking coalition of unsatisfied newcomers. The words of French President Nicolas Sarkozy of 2009 to a large extent reflected the views of several political leaders representing the EU-15 (Mahohny 2009). From their perspective, the new member countries should rather be silent and adopt the solutions presented by their more experienced partners in the EU. One of the arguments is that all new member states are net beneficiaries of the EU budget and therefore take out more than they contribute. The strict opposition of the V4 countries to redistribution quotas was often presented as an example of a serious break of the principle of solidarity in the EU. As a result, the V4 received a label of a problematic grouping inside the EU.

On the other hand, solidarity with the new members is not implemented unconditionally in the EU. New member states are highly underrepresented in EU institutions, which can be also demonstrated in the case of the European External Action Service (EEAS). The lack of solidarity is being used as an argument of the V4+ group of countries, for example, in case of the Nordstream 2 project that is supported by Germany and some other EU-15 members.

These two narratives regarding solidarity – regional versus European – are to a large extent contradictory. The more Brussels emphasizes the need for European solidarity and criticizes the V4 countries, without implementing the principle of solidarity in practice, the bigger the resistance on the side of new member countries will be. This is already visible in the Polish and Hungarian cases. The real challenge in the years to come is to find ways for the convergence of regional with EU level solidarity.

Visegrád recycleable? Future challenges and opportunities

All V4 countries have invested a significant amount of energy into the V4 brand, and it would be a mistake in the future not to use the potential that the V4 is offering. However, in order to face future challenges efficiently, the V4 needs to adapt to new circumstances. There is no interest in transforming the V4 into a block which would always speak with one voice – emphasis is rather placed on the V4 being a flexible and modern regional initiative, with added value for both the EU and NATO.

The V4 countries continue to identify with the 'three nos': no to further institutionalization, no to the enlargement of the group, and no to more slowdown in cooperation (Strážay 2011). Despite the EU's ongoing institutional reforms, the V4 is not likely to move towards stronger institutionalization. A weak institutionalization also helps the V4 to overcome potential divergences in political positions, also moderates differences resulting from a different level of integration of the V4 countries in the EU. The International Visegrád Fund will remain the most robust Visegrád institution, while the creation of other standing institutions – as the example of the Visegrád Patent Institute shows (Visegrád 2015d)[2] – cannot be neglected. However, these will have more technical than political value. What may further develop are informal institutions and instruments of cooperation: official and semi-official meetings of governmental representatives, presidencies, high level working groups, advisory platforms, etc.

In order to remain viable, the V4 should remain a group of four countries. The acceptance of any new country to the informal club would most probably deteriorate the decision-making process within the V4. On the other hand, the V4 should remain open to cooperation with any country, or group of countries, via the V4+ formula. Non-V4 EU members represent the most natural allies for the V4 and partners for bigger coalitions, needed for the successful presentation of regional (V4) interests at the EU level.

In order to avoid any future slowdown in cooperation, V4 countries are recommended to return to the origins of Visegrád cooperation. This implies that the V4 should hearken back to the values and principles that were established at the very beginning of its existence. Emphasis should be placed especially on the deepening of regional cohesion and trust among the V4 countries. In addition, the slogan *return to Europe*, so powerful in the 1990s, has certain validity today. The V4 should not only continue being a well-recognized trademark, but an integral part of the overall European architecture.

Notes

1 The Lisbon Treaty has changed the distribution of votes in the Council. While the combined votes of the V4 countries were equal to the votes of France and Germany together, the implementation of the Lisbon Treaty pushes the V4 to look for additional partners in the EU.

2 The Visegrad group (V4) countries establish a joint Patent Institute, http://www.visegradgroup.eu/calendar/ 2015/the-visegrad-group-v4.

References

Duleba, A. (2014) *Kríza na Ukrajine ako imulz pre východnú politiku SR a EÚ*. Bratislava: Research Center of the Slovak Foreign Policy Association.

Mahohny, H. (2009) Sarkozy Warns Visegrad Countries not to Make a Habit Of Pre-summit Meetings. EUObserver, 4 November. [ONLINE] Available from: https://euobserver.com/news/28928 (accessed 1 October 2017).

National Bank of Poland (2014) Ekonomiczne wyzwania integracji Polski ze strefą euro. November. [ONLINE] Available from: http://www.nbp.pl/aktualnosci/wiadomosci_2014/20141120_raport_wyzwania_integracji_ze_strefa _euro.pdf (accessed 27 August 2015).

Statistical Office of the Slovak Republic (2015) *Celkový dovoz a celkový vývoz podľa kontinentov a ekonomických zoskupení krajín v roku 2014–2015*. [ONLINE] Available from: http://statdat.statistics.sk/cognosext/cgi-bin/cognos .cgi?b_action=cognosViewer&ui.action=run&ui.object=storeID%28%22i10B2CB52FFF44B319DA31F65A3FFE155%22%29&ui.name=Celkov%C3%BD%20dovoz%20a%20celkov%C3%BD%20v%C3%BDvoz%20pod%C4%BEa%20kontinentov%20a%20ekonomick%C3%BDch%20zoskupen%C3%AD%20kraj%C3%ADn%20v%20roku%202014%20-%202015%20[zo0002ms]&run.outputFormat=&run.prompt=true&cv.header=false&ui.backURL=%2fcognosext%2fcps4%2fportlets%2fcommon%2fclose.html (accessed 26 August 2015).

Strážay, T. (2011) *Visegrad:Arrival, Survival, Revival' Two Decades of Visegrad Cooperation*. Bratislava: International Visegrad Fund.

Strážay, T. (2015) *Exploring Possibilities of Deepening the internal cohesion of the V4: Polish and Slovak Perspectives*. Slovak Foreign Policy Association. [ONLINE] Available from: http://www.sfpa.sk/wp-content/uploads/2015/09/Internal-Cohesion-of-the-V4_SK-and-PL-perspectives.pdf (accessed 1 October 2017).

Sytas, A. (2016) *EU Leaders Sign Letter Objecting to Nord Stream-2 Gas Link*. 16 March [ONLINE] Available at: http://uk.reuters.com/article/uk-eu-energy-nordstream/eu-leaders-sign-letter-objecting-to-nord-stream-2-gas-link-idUKKCN0WI1YV (accessed on 1 October 2017).

Visegrád group (2014) *Joint Statement of the V4 Foreign Ministers of the Environment of the Visegrád Group and Bulgaria and Romania*. 30 September. [ONLINE] Available from: http://www.visegradgroup.eu/calendar/2014/joint-statement (accessed 1 October 2017)

Visegrád group (2015a) *Joint Statement of the Heads of Government of the Visegrád Group Countries*. 19 June. [ONLINE] Available from: http://www.visegradgroup.eu/calendar/2015/joint-statement-of-the (accessed 31 August 2015).

Visegrád group (2015b) *Slovakia and V4 to Assist Ukraine*, December 17. [ONLINE] Available from: http://www.visegradgroup.eu/slovakia-and-v4-to (accessed 26 August 2015).

Visegrád group (2015c) *The Visegrad Group Joint Statement on the Eastern Partnership*. 14–15 May. [ONLINE] Available from: http://www.visegradgroup.eu/calendar/2015/the-visegrad-group-joint (accessed 31 August 2015).

Visegrad group (2015d) *Countries Establish a Joint Patent Institute*. [ONLINE] Available from: http://www.visegradgroup.eu/calendar/ 2015/the-visegrad-group-v4 (accessed 1 October 2017).

13 The dual crisis and 'regionalization' in the Visegrád states

The identity politics of East-Central Europe in the new world order

Attila Ágh

Introduction: the Visegrád states in the emerging new world order

In the mid-2010s the drastic change in geopolitical situation around the EU's Eastern borders has produced a serious challenge for the EU and particularly for the Visegrád States (Visegrád 4, V4). It can be termed as the dual crisis, since it began with the Ukrainian conflict and continued with the refugee crisis. It is important to emphasize that these two crises are different, although their effects on the Visegrád states have converged. The Ukrainian crisis has been provoked by the new aggressive behaviour of Russia in wider Europe, while the refugee crisis has erupted with the mass immigration of people from the Middle East and further regions. Altogether, their direct and indirect effects have had repercussions for the V4 and have impacted upon them by deepening their identity conflicts within the EU.

In general, in the mid-2010s there was a fundamental change in the entire world system with the collapse of the old world order (OWO) and the emergence of the new world order (NWO). This chapter deals first with the comeback of geopolitics and the ensuing securitization of European governance in wider Europe at the time of the emerging NWO. The main focus of this chapter is the effect of this dual crisis on the Visegrád states and the strong identity politics generated in this security community. Hence, the analysis of the V4 story comprises two levels, the first dealing with the new global policy of the EU in wider Europe and its impact on V4, and the second with the controversial regionalization of V4 due to both the wider effects of NWO and the direct effects of dual crisis.

Thus, this chapter overviews first the global situation of the EU and its external Europeanization during the emergence of NWO. Within this global transformation it describes the new geopolitics as well as the dual crisis in general and their implications for V4 in particular, especially in the case of Eastern Partnership (EaP) as the Eastern part of the European Neighbourhood Policy (ENP). Second, it analyses the V4 common historical trajectory that has recently produced divergent regional process from the EU mainstream. The previous divergence within V4 under the impact of dual crisis has turned to a rather controversial convergence with regionalization and securitization in East Central Europe (ECE). The chapter concludes with the warning that this attitude of the V4 states – with special regard to Hungary and Poland as the key actors in this process – contains the threat of further peripheralization and the deepening of the core-periphery divide.[1]

The radical transformation of the world system in the mid-2010s has changed the global landscape beyond recognition in this New Cold War. The world system has entered a new cycle, from the old world order (OWO) – that began around 1990 – to the new world order (NWO) with the return of geopolitics and new security challenges. Although these transformations have been predictable, since they followed the timing of the Kondratieff long cycles, they have still been unexpected for many global actors and their experts. Similar radical transformations took place about 25 years ago, at the turn of the eighties and nineties with the collapse of the bipolar world. It was celebrated in Western scholarship as 'The end of history' in Fukuyama (1992) with great illusions. The former system of OWO was beneficial for global development: it removed superpower competition and reduced the traditional military security threat worldwide. The global situation in the last quarter-century was especially favourable for the democratization of the V4 states because the EU as a civil superpower could act in normative way promoting democracy both globally and in its neighbourhood. Thus, with the democratization of EaP a much larger wider Europe also appeared on the EU's horizon. In this period, the EU had the ambition to embrace the continent as a whole through External European Governance.[2]

The new world order and its implications for wider Europe

The original aim of the ENP in 2004 was the creation of a 'ring of friends' and to encircle itself with 'well-governed countries'. The EU envisioned not only increasing economic contacts with the neighbouring countries, but first of all general democratization through external governance. In the optimistic spirit of the so called coloured revolutions in the East democratization came to the fore in the EaP with the six Eastern states in 2009. Therefore, Europeanization meant institution-building at both state and civil society levels with the EU's role as the 'centre of gravity'.

In general, EaP has demonstrated that the EU has deep concerns regarding wider Europe. The analysis of wider Europe is a nested game or two-level game with intensive external–internal linkages, reflecting the dynamics of both the international and domestic politics in the countries concerned. This specific Eastern policy needs a new conceptual framework based on the two analytical pillars of (i) External Europeanization and/or external governance with promotion of democracy, (ii) Deep and Comprehensive Free Trade (DCFT). External Europeanization has evolved in a historical process, in the several stages of subsequent agreements. The EU expected a relatively quick adjustment of the EaP countries to the EU due to its normative challenge. Even the intensive economic contacts acted supposedly to promote welfare and prosperity, and – through many spill-over effects –also fostered the democratic order as an easy dream about democracy promotion. The idea of an institution transfer to EaP dominated in External Europeanization, without raising the issue whether these new institutions remained on the surface as mere formal-legal facades or could become an organic part of society. The EU in its relations with outsiders seemed to favour the top-down governance approach based on rule transfer and conditionality. EaP as a 'Europeanization light' followed the model of Eastern enlargement with its genetic failure of the formalistic-legalistic approach due to its naive belief in its automatism.

The EaP was too general, not specific and differentiated enough. The institutional reforms remained shallow and ineffective, since the proper workings of these big formal institutions would have necessitated deep structural reforms. They would have to be based on the network of many smaller informal institutions and the civic patterns of behaviour that were missing in the EaP region. Furthermore, their emergence would have needed much more time and a much more favourable international environment. Although the EaP was a big step forward compared to ENP in specifying relationships and financing instruments in the East, nonetheless the content of the partnership structure remained vague, and the dual – multilateral and bilateral – track approach proved to be controversial. The added value of the strategic partnership was still not defined properly either: 'In summary, as the research indicates, EU "politics of inclusion" remain patchy and inconsistent, making it difficult for the neighbours to commit themselves to the European course of reform. (…) All neighbours felt that they were "caught" between the EU and Russia' (Korosteleva 2011: 14, 15).

In principle, all European countries must have a 'European perspective'; even the six EaP states to whom membership has not yet been offered. Therefore, the regionalization drive in EaP has been rather weak. Europeanization rhetoric has lured the EaP with the promotion of democratization versus the pragmatic EU interests in 'deep trade', but with no concrete vision of regional specificity or security dimensions.. Thus, there has been a deep contradiction between the abstract-normative approaches of promoting the European values and the shallow pragmatism of advancing EaP prosperity through 'deep trade', which can only deliver benefits in the long run (Adarov and Haylik 2016: 5). This situation can be termed as a 'carrot crisis' (Ágh 2010) in the EaP by not providing enough incentives for structural reforms because the perspective of the EU membership has been too remote and increasingly not credible. The strategic designs for EaP – reduced sometimes to slogans – were not real programs of Europeanization and they collapsed when Russia returned to regional expansion and the Ukrainian crisis began. This hybrid war has triggered identity politics world-wide with the start of geopolitical regionalization.[3]

Thus, the EaP has been a policy failure for these countries in between. The big Eastern crisis with the expansionist Russia and declining EaP region has come as a surprise to the EU because the Europeans have lost the habit and the expertise to analyse the world in geopolitical terms in the relatively relaxed period of the multipolar era. As a result, after Russian aggression the EaP has been detached from the EU's enlargement philosophy and come to resemble a more classic foreign policy. Indeed, the European External Action Service has increasingly become involved, and the Eastern policy as regional security has come to the fore. The Riga Summit (2015) has focused on the Ukrainian crisis and the Riga Declaration has called for 'multilateral and bilateral security dialogue' in the EaP (EaP 2015: 8). The Riga Summit has usually been described as a non-event and/or survival summit with ongoing stagnation in the EaP. After this failure of external Europeanization securitization has been the priority in the EaP, and beyond (CEU-CENS 2015).

The Riga Summit has meant a turning point towards pragmatism and crisis management. As the European Neighbourhood Watch (ENW 2015: 1–2) has noted, after the Russian aggression it has become clear that

> the EU had a moderate influence on the affairs of its neighbours (…) In the face of new challenges, the long term goals of the ENP have been complemented by a short term objective: the stabilization of the neighbourhood in security and economic terms (…) The "new" ENP will be a crucial testing ground for the EU's relatively new "comprehensive" approach, which aims to bring together all available tools and policies – security, diplomacy, technical support and financial instruments.

Hence, after the Riga Summit the EU has realized more and more that it should not promise too much if wishes to retain credibility. Given the contentious issues in the high-intensity crisis, the new policy has needed to cobble together a comprehensive package to save the EaP. Thus, a new security concept has been gaining ground in the EU, exploring the inherent fragilities and deep-seated structural factors in wider Europe.

The crisis of 'globalization cum regionalization' (Ágh 2010) in ENP following the global crisis has also demonstrated the weaknesses of the EaP and indicated the end of the OWO. In earlier European studies these issues remained under-researched or forgotten; after the security-sensitive bipolar world it was thought that (traditional-military) security issues would disappear forever. The 'end of history' principle of Fukuyama was applied at global level as the final victory of democratization-liberalization without Huntington's idea of 'return wave'. Altogether, the OWO created two decades of favourable external conditions for EU development; facilitating both deepening and widening. This was the embodiment of 'the ever increasing integration' idea of the EU in general, but also encompassed the accession of New Member States and the extension to the EaP in particular. Nonetheless, behind the success of the EU as a global player, there was a tension between the EU as an economic giant and a political dwarf, with a constant effort to create a common foreign and defence policy without real success. Still the EU security document, the European Security Strategy was very optimistic in both the 'desecuritization' (European

Commission 2003) of global policy and the normative value of democracy promotion. Finally this period produced a series of contradictions: the decline of BRICS, the failure of the Arab Spring and the tension along the Muslim arch with the Middle East crisis and Turkey's interventionism.

The new power politics in the 2010s has produced the return of geopolitics (Kagan 2015) as an accelerated securitization process with new security challenges. In the geopolitical approach to global security and migration – or to the complex security issues from social security to military security – the research on the NWO has surfaced high on the agenda. The incoming dual crisis has triggered deep divergences within the EU foreign policy, but the main tendency of the securitization of the EaP policy and the ensuing rediscovery of the geopolitics has been clear. The wider Europe policy has proved to be an opening towards a new kind of foreign and defence policy in the emerging NWO and has offered a model for addressing the new challenges. Its main ideas have returned in the EU documents, like securitization, stabilization, comprehensive approach, more flexibility/differentiation and new partnership approach. The change from OWO to NWO needs a new vocabulary and new concepts in the EU, almost 'reinventing the wheel' in rediscovering security policy in the age of cyber war and the various sorts of hard and soft security.

This reconceptualization of European security policy has taken place in the recently published key EU document, *A Global Strategy for the European Union's Foreign And Security Policy*, hereafter called *Global Strategy*, based on 'principled pragmatism' with a restriction of normative approach and promotion of democracy (European Commission 2016). The new vulnerability of the EU following the wider Europe crisis has also been expressed in strong words: 'We have learned the lesson: my neighbour's and my partner's weaknesses are my own weaknesses' and 'Internal and external security are ever more intertwined: our security at home entails a parallel interest in peace in our neighbouring and surrounding regions.' (European Commission 2016: 4, 14). As the analysts have emphasized,

> In the last five years, it has become commonplace for European ministers and Commissioners and the EU High Representative for Foreign and Security Policy to admit with apparently repentant modesty that the EU model no longer hold quite the same way over other regions that it once did.
> (Youngs 2016: 6)

Thus, the EaP crisis has played a big role in the preparation of the larger framework for the EU global strategy. First, this crisis around the EU borders has given the EU security policy a sharp shock. Second, the inherent problems of wider Europe have been the key issues for the new conceptual framework of global strategy. In this new 'fragile world' terrorism, hybrid threats, economic volatility, climate change and energy insecurity as the returning expressions of *Global Strategy* are the main characteristics of the new world system. Above all the Russian aggression has provoked a hot crisis in the EaP region: 'Russia's violation of international law and the destabilisation of Ukraine, on top of protracted conflicts in the wider Black Sea region, have challenged the European security order at is core.' (European Commission 2016: 33). Consequently, the main conceptual pillars of the new strategy have come from the EaP crisis management proposals: 'resilience to crisis' as strategic priority, 'principled pragmatism' as guide to external actions and the suggestion of creating 'cooperative regional orders' (European Commission 2016: 9, 15–16, 32).

The 'perverse' regionalism and the 'alienation' of Visegrád states

The V4 states are nowadays at a critical juncture because the destabilizing effects of global politics have appeared on their borders, first as the Ukrainian and then the refugee crisis. Moreover, after the last quarter century the contrast between the high expectations of the populations and the controversial results of the catching up process is very big in the V4 states. This situation has resulted in the 'alienation' of V4 from the core in their identity perceptions and created some kind of 'perverse' regionalism. It has come to the surface in their sharp divergence from the EU mainstream during the polycrisis, which has also been expressed in an exchange of angry public messages in the last few years.

The original expectation was that Europeanization in the V4 countries would be a big success story, producing both regional convergence with the core and a common 'voice' in their interest representation in the EU transnational decision-making mechanism. In the OWO period the V4 states believed in the successful catching up process, but they were looking for separate ways of development in the individual ECE countries without any meaningful cooperation. It had become an over-competitive situation of a 'lose–lose' game. The regionalization drive still appeared in the V4 states, which had a common historical trajectory and some kind of Central European identity. On 15 February 1991 they established their regional organization as a security community based on a shared identity and common interest. The V4 was a rather thin regional organization framework with constant family quarrels, yet it had some advantages given the states' similar positions and converging interests even in the pre-accession process and then more so, later, within the EU. Regarding the OWO period as a whole, there was some convergence between the EU and the V4 in GDP terms. However, the EU did not design 'cooperative regional orders' (Global Strategy 2016: 32) for NMS and in European studies it meant an overwhelming dominance of generalist approaches to Europeanization and democratization. In transitology there has been a clear neglect of area studies concentrating on regional/national specificities. Therefore, the V4 states felt more and more neglected and marginalized. Accordingly, they focused on their own national specificities with many polite references to the generalities of European Studies, but without realizing that they had a common historical trajectory in the last quarter century. Therefore, in the long history of the OWO period there was sometimes a feeling that the V4 was falling apart. In general, the most important function of the V4 group was its discussion platform, even if the partner states did not reach common conclusions. Their basic common interest was to maximize the regional influence of V4 in the EU by increasing their potential to make a collective impact on the EU policy agenda. This effort was successful from time to time at their meetings before the EU Summits.[4]

The return of the V4 states to a more intensive regional approach only came with the realization of the common crisis in the 2010s. Detailed datasets from top ranking institutions were able to expose the common trends and problems in the Visegrád region, influencing their change in direction. The common frustration in V4 due to its failure to catch up with process and the identity crisis has led to the re-emerging Central European narrative in the widening core–periphery divide. The new great transformation can be attributed to the cultural and geographic character of Central Europe that was the key narrative back in the eighties at the change leading to OWO. In this new situation, the regionalization process of the V4 has been intensified. It has however been a perverse regionalism, since the new (semi-)authoritarian regimes have murmured the mantra of national sovereignty when the EU has called them for common action in the refugee crisis. The real contrast between the OWO and NWO periods is broadly that the external EU-V4 and the internal V4 relationships have changed to the opposite direction. Paradoxically, under the impact of dual crisis the earlier convergence in the external EU-V4 aspect has turned to divergence, while the earlier divergence in the internal V4 aspect has become convergence. These are the main tendencies, which appear in a very tentative and controversial way, yet still they are the dominant directions in the emerging NWO system. In NWO, there has been a manifest divergence from the EU in switching from cooperation to confrontation, with active deviation from the EU mainstream. It has led to a search for collective – old and new, national and regional – identities. The appearance of new enemies as a 'blame-game' has taken various forms of EU-populism in the V4 states. Their deep resentment can be seen in the V4 Declaration of the Prague Summit which took place on 4 September 2015 as a founding document of this 'perverse' regionalization. The Prime Ministers of the Czech Republic, Poland and the Slovak Republic therefore reiterated their full support to Hungary in tackling this challenge (Visegrád group 2015).

However, in the first stage of the dual crisis the inherent weaknesses of this group from the OWO period turned from bad to worse, since the V4 common security interests were seriously damaged by their diverging approach to the Russian intervention. Nonetheless, they have common vital interests in the EaP policy because the instability in the EU Eastern neighbourhood is a deep concern for the V4 states, combined with energy security in various ways (Dostál 2015: 6). In 2015 in a series of 'Debating V4' the central question was 'Does the V4 have a future?' that has pushed many analysts to bury the V4 group. Nevertheless, the V4 states have 'diverging voices, converging policies' in the Ukraine–Russia conflict, as Kucharczyk and Meseznikov (2015a) have emphasized. They have supported the sanctions, although only Poland did so vigorously. The other three states – especially Hungary – rather reluctantly. Poland strongly opposed Russia's new politics, while the other V4 states developed much more reconciliatory behaviour, the Czech Republic and Slovakia mostly for economic reasons, and Hungary due to the special ties of the Orbán government with Putin's Russia.[5]

The close contacts between the Hungarian and Russian leadership raised concern in the Czech Republic and Slovakia as well. Thus, the Austrian challenge to the V4 proved to be attractive and it led to a new alliance in the Slavkov meeting on 29 January 2015, leaving aside both Poland and Hungary. It demonstrated the increasing isolation of the Hungarian government due to its pro-Russian course and praise for the alleged success of Putin's Russia in Orbán's speeches. Accordingly, the top challenge for the V4 states was to overcome their internal debates deepened by the Ukrainian crisis. Overall, the common historical trajectory of the V4 states has mirrored long-term trends in their cooperation as a result of their common worries concerning the situation in wider Europe and the geopolitical dimension with complex regional security interests. It can only be somewhat modified by quickly changing short-term interests such as the family quarrel about the sanctions against Russia. Although originally change to authoritarian rule by Putin after 2011 and the ensuing expansionism of Russia caused a split in V4 their convergent long term tendencies have prevailed. As the editors of the book quoted above have concluded: 'We can only hope that the V4 governments will rise to the occasion and – despite populist temptations on the domestic front – remain united in their support for a sustained and principled EU response, which also happens to be in their long-term best political interests.' (Kucharczyk and Meseznikov 2015b: 210).

Therefore, the Ukrainian crisis has to be separated from the refugee crisis in both the EU and the V4 behaviour, and consequently in relations between the V4 and the rest of the EU. The intensification of the refugee crisis in summer 2015 and the Law and Justice Party (PiS) victory in Poland in October 2015 marked a big change in 'East–West' relationships within the EU. At this new historical juncture the internal divergence among the V4 states from the sunny days of OWO has turned to a tentative convergence in the rainy days of the emerging NWO. Under the conditions of NWO strategic design has again been put high on the agenda of the V4 states in a new form. They have formed a geopolitical region, based on the common regional identity conceptualized in the Central European narrative. Alienation from the EU core has led to deep resentment of other European populations. The feeling of being different has been reaffirmed through Europeanization with V4 populist governments blaming Brussels for all failures in the last quarter-century, including the management of the dual crisis. Deeply critical of how the EU has handled the refugee crisis, regionalism has been gaining ground in the V4, and 77 per cent of Hungarians and 65 per cent of Poles think that they have to solve their own problems (Pew 2016: 3). The V4 states in their new region-building drive diverge more and more from EU mainstream crisis management, although the double speech – the wordings used by V4 governments for domestic and EU audiences – has remained different from country to country. Hence, it is necessary to emphasize that this new effort of the V4 is double-faced and contradictory in its geopolitical region-building. It shows the signs of slow strategic regionalization and securitization of the V4 states. On the positive side cooperation and collective identity has increased. At the same time it also risks peripheralization by turning away more and more from EU mainstream developments.

In the second stage of the dual crisis, the start of the refugee crisis, the partial disunity seems to turn more to the unity in the V4 group resulting in common reactions to this new crisis. The main turning point of the second stage was the victory of Law and Justice Party (PiS), the nativist conservative party in Poland that soon led to a 'union' between Orbán and Jaroslaw Kaczynski. At their meeting on 6 September 2016 in Krynica they pledged to wage a 'cultural counter-revolution' against the 'declining West' that allegedly wanted to 'eliminate historical identities' (Foy and Buckley 2016). Although there are many dividing lines among the V4 states, given the diverse political and economic interests on one side and the different cultural traditions and historical experiences on the other, this identity crisis with its constant references to national sovereignty has given the group common ground. There have been many family quarrels in V4 that can easily be detected from the official declarations of their governments, but the alienation from the EU mainstream has penetrated the public mind and the decisions of the V4 governments.

The V4 refusal of the common actions in the treatment of the refugee crisis has erupted assertive reactions in the Western media with a justified anger. The core of the EU has reacted to this divergence with angry words. In the often quoted *Economist* article there has been a reference to the unholy alliance in the 'Bad Visegrád': 'Anti-migrant sentiment has unified the "Visegrád group" of Hungary, Poland, Slovakia and the Czech Republic (…) Its turn towards illiberalism presents Europe with a problem' (The Economist 2016). This basis for regional cooperation is indeed a controversial case in the EU as the group looks collectively for 'the security of their national identity' in the refugee crisis. All V4 governments have issued 'apocalyptic warnings of the consequences of allowing Muslims into their countries and purported threats to host societies in the areas of security, economics and cultural identity' (Kucharczyk and Meseznikov 2015b: 207). As Stefan Lehne has noted, 'Even more negative were the reactions in Central European member states, which had lived in relative isolation for decades and whose societies were unprepared for large influxes of foreigners' (Lehne 2016: 1). Although throughout the 2010s there has been mounting criticism in European studies on the V4 deviation and about Orbán's velvet dictatorship, but without explaining the special V4 situation: 'if major institutions of liberal democracy in one member state radically deviate from the EU's member states' constitutional traditions, and undermine the rule of law, this is an issue that the EU needs to address directly' (Bugaric 2014: 25). Altogether, beyond the fair criticisms in European studies the basic question of what has led to the alienation/deviation of V4 from the EU mainstream and the role of the negative externalities in this process has hardly been raised.

The EU has been taken by surprise in the NWO not only by the particular nature of these crisis waves, but also by the reactions of the V4 to these challenges because the EU has not been aware of the real crisis situation in the aftermath of the global crisis. In fact, their specific 'polycrisis', the cumulated, long term socio-economic and political crisis has produced these reactions in V4. The EU has not realized that the relative failure of the catching up process after the first ten years of membership has created mass dissatisfaction and resentment in the V4 populations, and it has not dealt seriously with the trend of declining democracy in the V4 either. The EU has paid a big price in the Euro-crisis for neglecting the special problems of the South, and it may pay an even bigger price nowadays for the forgotten crisis of the East.

Conclusion: the V4 region's alternative to Europeanization or peripheralization

In its response to the alienation of the V4, the EU has walked into a blind alley between the high walls of EU 'pragmatism' and the limits of EU legal procedures about the violation of European rules and values. As an EU internal crisis management approach, the 'principled pragmatism' advocated by the *Global Security* document is not enough. This extreme case of differentiated integration has had a serious detrimental impact both on the EU as a whole and on its relationships with the V4 region. The EU authorities finally have to face this divergence in the V4 governments and have to take effective measures at least against the serious violations of the European rules and values. This danger became acute when Poland also turned towards a populist-authoritarian direction. The EU has to push the V4 countries more energetically towards a convergence with mainstream European developments.

The V4 divergence from the EU mainstream has been considered an unpleasant side effect, but it has proved to be a *systemic failure*. The V4 can be diverted from the European rules and values by the new authoritarian regimes through re-inventing their past and offering this new past instead of the new EU future. It is a vital issue whether the V4 states can stop and turn back this de-Europeanization and de-democratization process. If not, the deepening core–periphery divide will lead to their further peripheralization in the EU. It is clear however that in the near future the V4 states have to also find a common position by deepening their process of regionalization. In this process Poland has to take the lead as the biggest V4 country for regional interest representation in the EU. It can take place, however, only after the overcoming the populist, anti-democratic turn in the region, by opening the window of opportunity to move towards a more integrated EU. Without a common representation of their interests in the EU, they will be marginalized within the EU as its stagnating semi-periphery in this period of intensifying globalization and sharpening global competitiveness. Russia is reclaiming the lost area between East and West in the emerging NWO, so in this 'new Yalta Pact' the Visegrád states may become a 'no man's land', a buffer zone protecting the West from Russia and Russia from the West. Thus, the success of the competitive core can only be a pyrrhic victory for the EU without a cohesive and convergent Europe.

Notes

1 I have dealt with the emergence of NWO in several papers (e.g. Ágh 2016a, b, c, d) and further developed in this chapter. In fact, ECE is the V4+1 formation with Slovenia.
2 This section continues the analysis of Ágh and Kovács (2016) that covered wider Europe until the Riga Summit. The EaP states are Armenia, Azerbaijan, Belarus, Georgia, Moldova and Ukraine. Russia was not ready to join the ENP.
3 The aggression against Ukraine was directly about Russian and Ukrainian identity, but by implication, it reinforced both Baltic and Central European identities (Ágh 2016d).
4 The rich body of literature on the V4 cooperation in OWO has been overviewed in the paper of Törő et al (2014) that has also discussed the activities of the V4 states in EaP matters.
5 With Russian aggression, 'traditional' military security has also returned to world politics in a modernized way. The Ukrainian crisis has concerned closely the V4 states, among others; according to conservative estimates there are more than one million Ukrainian migrants in these countries.

References

Adarov, A. and P. Havlik (2016) Benefits and Costs of DCFTA: Evaluation of the Impact on Georgia, Moldova and Ukraine. Bertelsmann Foundation (ed.) Joint Working Paper, December 2016. [ONLINE] Available at: http://www.bertelsmann-stiftung.de/fileadmin/files/BSt/Publikationen/Graue Publikationen/EZ_Studie_Benefits_and_Costs_of_DCFTA_2017_ENG.pdf (accessed 21 July 2017).

Ágh, A. (2010) Regionalisation as a Driving Force of EU Widening: Recovering from the EU 'Carrot Crisis' in the East, *Europe-Asia Studies*. 62(8) October, pp. 1239–1266.

Ágh, A. (2016a) The 'Securitization' of the EaP Policy in the EU: The External Europeanization in the Wider Europe, *Journal of Comparative Politics* 9(1), pp. 36–58.

Ágh, A. (2016b) The Increasing Core-Periphery Divide and the New Member States: Diverging from the European Union's Mainstream Developments. In: Magone, J. Laffan, B. and Schweiger, C. (eds) *Core-Periphery Relations in the European Union: Power and Conflict in a Dualist Political Economy*. London: Routledge, pp. 117–129.

Ágh, A. (2016c) Core-Periphery Divide in the EU Transformation Crisis: The Regional Challenge of the Visegrád Four, *Yearbook of East-Central European Institute* 14(2), pp. 113–130.

Ágh, A. (2016d) Cultural War and Reinventing the Past in Poland and Hungary: The Politics of Historical Memory in East-Central Europe, *Polish Political Science Yearbook* 45, pp. 32–44.

Ágh, A. and Kovács, A. (2016) EU Cohesion Policy in the Eastern Partnership Region: A Case of External Europeanization. In: Piattoni, S. and Polverari, L. (eds) *Handbook on Cohesion Policy in the EU*. Cheltenham, UK: Edward Elgar Publishing, pp. 399–412.

Bugaric, B. (2014) Protecting Democracy and the Rule of Law in the European Union: The Hungarian Challenge, LSE Europe in Question Paper Series, LEQS Paper No. 79, July. [ONLINE] Available from: http://www.lse.ac.uk/europeanInstitute/LEQS/LEQSPaper79.pdf (accessed date 24 January 2018).

CEU-CENS, Central European University (2015) Eastern Partnership Beyond the Riga Summit: Rethinking Cooperation. No. 11. [ONLINE] Available from: https://publications.ceu.edu/sites/default/files/publications/eu-frontiers-policy-paper-no11-eap.pdf (accessed 21 July 2017).

Dostál, V. (2015) *Trends of Visegrád Foreign Policy, Praha: Association for International Affairs*. [ONLINE] Available from: https://www.amo.cz/wp-content/uploads/2015/11/Trends-of-Visegrád-foreign-policy.pdf [accessed 21 July 2017].

EaP, Eastern Partnership (2015) *Joint Declaration of the Eastern Partnership Summit*. Riga, 21–22 May 2015. [ONLINE] Available from: http://www.consilium.europa.eu/hu/meetings/international-summit/2015/05/21-22/ (accessed 9 September 2015).

Economist, The (2016) *Illiberal Central Europe: Big, bad Visegrád*. 30 January. [ONLINE] Available from: http://www.economist.com/news/europe/21689629-migration-crisis-has-given-unsettling-new-direction-old-alliance-big-bad-visegrad (accessed 21 July 2017).

European Commission (2003) *A Secure Europe in a Better World: European Security Strategy*. Brussels, 12 December 2003. [ONLINE] Available from: https://www.consilium.europa.eu/uedocs/cmsUpload/78367.pdf (accessed 21 July 2017).

European Commission (2016) A Global Strategy for the European Union's Foreign and Security Policy, June. [ONLINE] Available from: https://europa.eu/globalstrategy/en/global-strategy-foreign-and-security-policy-european-union (accessed 21 July 2017).

European Neighbourhood Watch (2015) *Editorial*. No. 121. [ONLINE] Available from: https://www.ceps.eu/ system/files/NWatch201_0.pdf [accessed 21 July 2017].

Foy, H. and Buckley, N. (2016) Orban and Kaczynski vow 'cultural counter-revolution' to reform EU. 7 September 2016. [ONLINE] Available from: http://www.ft.com/cms/s/0/ e825f7f4–74a3–11e6-bf48-b372cdb1043a.html#axzz 4Jed295EY (accessed 21 July 2017).

Fukuyama, F. (1992) *The End of History and the Last Man*. New York: The Free Press.

Kagan, R. (2015) The Weight of Geopolitics, *Journal of Democracy* 26(1), pp. 21–31.

Korosteleva, E. (2011) The Eastern Partnership Initiative: A New Opportunity for Neighbours? *Journal of Communist Studies and Transition Politics* 27(1), pp. 1–21.

Kucharczyk, J. and Meseznikov, G. (eds) (2015a) *Diverging Voices, Converging Policies: The Visegrád States' Reactions to the Russia-Ukraine Conflict*, Prague and Warsaw. [ONLINE] Available from: https://pl.boell.org/sites/default/files/diverging-voices-converging_policies _Visegrád-states-russia-ukraine-conflict.pdf (accessed 21 July 2017).

Kucharczyk, J. and Meseznikov, G. (2015b) Afterword: The V4 Reassembled – but to What End? In: J. Kucharczyk and G. Meseznikov (eds) *Diverging Voices, Converging Policies: The Visegrád States' Reactions to the Russia-Ukraine Conflict*. Prague and Warsaw: Heinrich Böll Stiftung, pp. 207–210. [ONLINE] Available from: https://www.boell.de/sites/default/files/2015-diverging_voices_ converging_policies.pdf (accessed 21 July 2017).

Lehne, S. (2016) *The Tempting Trap of Fortress Europe*. 21 April. [Online] Available from: http://carnegieeurope.eu/2016/04/21/tempting-trap-of-fortress-europe/ixdx (accessed 21 July 2017).

Magone, J., Laffan, B. and Schweiger, C. (eds) (2016) *Core-Periphery Relations in the European Union*. London: Routledge.

Pew (2016) Europeans Face the World Divided. 13 June. [ONLINE] Available from: http://www.pewglobal.org/2016/06/13/europeans-face-the-world-divided/ (accessed 21 July 2017).

Piattoni, S. and Polverari, L. (eds) (2016) *Handbook on Cohesion Policy in the EU*. Cheltenham: Edward Elgar.

Törő, C., Butler, E. and Grúber, K. (2014) Visegrád: The Evolving Pattern of Coordination and Partnership After EU Enlargement, *Europe-Asia Studies* 66(3), pp. 364–393.

Visegrád group (2015) V4 Prague Declaration: Joint Statement of the Heads of Government of the Visegrád Group Countries. 4 September. [ONLINE] Available from: http://www.visegradgroup.eu/ calendar/2015/joint-statement-of-the-150904 (accessed 21 July 2017).

Youngs, R. (2016) How We Can Reframe the Debate About Europe's Populist Threat. [ONLINE] Available from: http://blogs.lse.ac.uk/europpblog/2016/11/17/how-we-can-reframe-the-debate-about-europes-populist-threat/ (accessed 24 January 2018).

14 Cooperation or integration?

The new defence initiatives in the Visegrád group

Anna Molnár and Zoltán Szenes

Introduction

The Visegrád group – following in the footsteps of historical alliances[1] – was founded by three countries on 15 February 1991. The declaration was signed by Václav Havel, the President of Czechoslovakia, Lech Walesa, the President of Poland and József Antall, the Prime Minister of Hungary. The main goals included in the declaration were the (i) full restoration of independence, democracy and freedom, (ii) the elimination of the existing social, economic and spiritual aspects of the totalitarian regime, (iii) the construction of a parliamentary democracy, a modern constitutional state, respect for human rights and freedoms, (iv) the establishment of a modern free-market economy and (v) full involvement in the European political, economic system, as well as the system of security and legislation. The declaration also states that: 'in accordance with the interests of the particular countries they shall harmonize their activities to shape cooperation and close contacts with European institutions and shall hold regular consultations on the matters of their security' (Visegrád Group 1991).

This group is not a formal international organization with a fully-fledged institutional structure. It does not have a legal personality, or rules of decision-making procedures and not even a permanent secretariat. The cooperation is still very flexible, and thus it offers the possibility of a platform for regular meetings of different actors. The official prime ministerial summits take place on an annual basis following the presidency change on 1 July. The declared security and defence cooperation did not appear explicitly among the goals of the V4 group, only the full involvement in the European Union (EU) and the necessity of regular consultations on the matters of their security was underlined. NATO accession became a V4 goal in 1994 (although the foundation charter was not amended officially), when NATO launched its Partnership for Peace programme and invited the East Central European countries to join. In January 1994, the defence ministers agreed on broadening their cooperation with the goals of the Euro-Atlantic cooperative and the aim of achieving full NATO membership. The Partnership for Peace (PfP) programme was started by the NATO summit organized in Brussels on 10 and 11 January 1994 and the Euro-Atlantic Partnership Council (EAPC) and Organization for Security and Cooperation in Europe (OSCE) countries were invited to participate (NATO 1994).

In the course of the development of the V4 group, 1999 was the first year to see significant change when the Czech Republic, Poland and Hungary became members of NATO. A new milestone came in 2004, when all V4 countries became member states of the EU and Slovakia obtained NATO membership. As the V4 managed to achieve their goal it became necessary to revise the situation of the cooperation and to adjust the objectives to the new international environment and to the alliance membership (EU and NATO). The new situation opened new possibilities for defence cooperation as well. This chapter discusses the major V4 defence cooperation issues focusing on: the military strength of the four countries, the experience of the V4 EU Battlegroup and the future in light of the Permanent Modular Force. We excluded questions about defence of the Schengen Area from our discussion because they belong to law enforcement cooperation.

Following the analysis of the foreign and security policy of the V4 countries the next part of the chapter focuses on the military strength of the V4 countries and the different situations of their armed forces. The third part will describe the evolution of defence cooperation and the policy change in this field. During the last few years the apparently prosperous defence oriented cooperation has simultaneously shown the strong and the weak points of the V4 cooperation: the flourishing formulation of common standpoints regarding Trans-Atlantic and EU cooperation and the slow and difficult decision-making process in the course of the fulfilment of concrete defence policy programmes. (The proposal of creating the Battlegroup was drafted for the first time in 2007.) This duality and imbalance have characterized the nearly quarter-century long history of the Visegrád group. The next part will concentrate on the process of creating the V4 EU Battlegroup in 2016. Last but not least we will focus on future goals, for example moving towards the creation of the Permanent Modular Force.

The foreign and security policies of the V4 countries

Poland enjoys dominance among the Visegrád countries: the size and importance of the country (its territory is the 58th and its population is the 60th in the world, and its economic performance is 55 per cent of the whole V4) far exceed the same parameters (Table 14.1) of the three other countries. As a result, there has been an anticipation that Warsaw should fulfil its leading function. However, the Polish government hardly accepts this role (Michelot, Pomlényi, Strázay and Visvizi 2016) as it aimed to become an interlocutor of European Great Powers instead of helping the advocacy of smaller states. Poland considers important not only the East–West foreign policy (Germany, Russia, the Baltic states and Eastern Partnership), but the North–South axis as well. This medium-power politics has urged the Poles to develop extended military programmes, which are too big to be appropriate for the smaller partner states.

Table 14.1 The main geopolitical data of the V4 countries

Name	*Area (km²)*	*Population 2017*	*GDP (USD) billion 2016*	*GDP/pers. (USD) 2016*	*Gross debt (GDP %) 2016 Q1*
CZ	78.886	10,555,130	185.16	20.374	40.40
PL	312.685	38,563,573	477.07	14.090	52.00
HU	93.030	9,787,905	121.72	14.043	77.20
SVK	49.035	5,432,157	87.60	17.973	56.20
Total	533.636	64,338,756	871.55	16.620	55.15

Source: www.worldometers.info[2]; www.tradingeconomist.com[3]; ec.europa.eu[4]

The political relationships of the V4 states are varying, but their policies regarding the EU sometimes come into conflict with EU institutions. Poland has been the most pro-European, but its relationship with the EU has changed since the Law and Justice Party came to power. The Czech Republic's traditional euro-scepticism is well known, the 2013 government crisis distracted attention from the questions of foreign and security policy. The regional relationships of Slovakia still bear the marks of its foreign policy of the 1990s, the links to Russia, the nationality issue and several other unsolved problems. Hungary has also reinforced its relations with Russia.

All of these similarities and differences in interests and opinions as well as the disharmonious approaches and viewpoints can be seen in the security perception and conviction of the V4 countries and in their intention for regional defence cooperation. Several analyses clearly demonstrate that the V4 countries have similar but differing security perceptions (Weiss 2012; Madej 2013). The similarity derives from alliance membership and the divergence from the different geopolitical situation, interests, priorities and historical experience (Balogh 2013, Bartha 2015).

In 2013, a European comparative study (de France and Whitney 2013)[5] divided the four Visegrád states into three categories following an analysis of national strategic documents: the Czech Republic belongs to the group of strategic countries; Hungary is a globalist, and Poland and Slovakia were rated as localists. Beyond the three types of classification, there are significant differences in security policy thinking and actions. The Czech strategic documents examine the changes of the strategic environment in detail, which serve as a basis for defining the strategic goals, as well as the means and resources necessary for achieving them. Hungary is considered to be a globalist as the broad-spectrum task system of its national security strategy is not supported by the necessary means and resources; its document lacks a specifying and prescriptive character. As for the Polish and Slovak localists thinking, there are approaches and policies which focus on the immediate environment and the country itself, and which tend to pay less attention to broader contexts (global, NATO or EU level).

Poland is the most Atlanticist among the four, as the United States appears in its policy on NATO and at EU levels. Warsaw has the strongest military cooperation with the United States. The US 3rd Armored Brigade arrived in Poland in January of 2017 as part of the NATO forward presence concept. In the military platform area, the most important element is the installation of American patriot air defence missiles with American personnel in 2010. The new level of cooperation is the development of the Polish air defence missile system. The Polish government plans to spend 8.4 billion dollars on the project including the accomplishment of the European missile defence shield until 2018. For the procurement of American air defence missiles and their possible production in Poland, Warsaw conceived the Wisla Project. Besides the selected Polish defence industrial company only developed Western firms are part of this project.[6]

Polish security policy ambitions are supported by their Weimar partners too, which was proved by the participation of Germany and France at the 2013 Gdansk Summit. Poland could obviously have had a bigger chance of keeping the Visegrád cooperation on the right track, if it had not benefitted from the enhanced cooperation of the two most important states of the EU.

Previously Warsaw aimed to develop good neighbourhood relations with Russia, but their relationship is controversial and sometimes dismissive; the old historical fears are still present and reinforced after the Ukrainian crisis. Warsaw is the loudest follower of NATO's Article V among the V4 countries; and the Visegrád champion of military capability development. In July 2016, Warsaw hosted the NATO summit. There is a Western- and Eastern-European geographical attachment in the ongoing Polish military cooperation programmes, too. From 1999 there has been a joint Polish-German-Danish corps headquarters in Szczecin, which is now part of NATO's command system (CS). In 2013 Poland offered a considerable amount of military forces to the multinational operation headquarters set up in Ulm, Germany, which is destined for the preparation and command of the EU Battlegroups. The Poles are committed to cooperation in a NATO framework with the Baltic states, and they ~~also~~ support the EU programme of Eastern Partnership. In 2016 they set up a joint brigade with the Ukrainians and the Lithuanians,[7] and in 2017 they will probably also take part in the creation of the NATO brigade in Romania.

The Czech security policy primarily focuses on the questions of economy and energy security, cyber threats and the new response to migration. The foreign policy of Prague aims to compensate Central European small statehood position with active multinational relations.[8] For Prague, after Germany and the United States, Poland and Slovakia are the most important partners. The economised Czech defence policy is quite rational; it adapts the size, tasks and development of the armed forces to the resources and it aims to achieve complex defence by combining NATO and national capabilities.[9] The Czechs were the first who started the multi-nationalization of forces (CRBN 2002). They undertake specialization on a political level and participate in all great NATO projects (AWACS,[10] AGS,[11] missile defence) in fields where they cannot develop military capabilities on a national basis. In the last few years, there has been a more powerful approach to cooperation between the Czech Republic and Slovakia in certain programmes (Molnár and Szilvágyi 2016).

As Slovakia is located at the periphery of NATO and the EU, the Slovak foreign and security policy – similarly to the Polish one – is highly geopolitically oriented. Despite localism, in the last few years, the Euro-Atlantic and EU commitment of Bratislava and the global elements of security policy have strengthened significantly, especially during the EU presidency of Slovakia during the second half of 2016. The annually organized GLOBSEC conference in Bratislava is a good example for this. Slovakia has always had the best Russian relations among the V4 states even if it does not agree with Russia on everything, but it does not share the Polish fears. The Slovak security strategy regarded V4 as the most important regional organization, but its defence strategy does not include references to the defence cooperation.

With respect to the Visegrád cooperation, the Hungarian security policy documents do not provide much detail. The 2012 national security strategy[12] and national military strategy[13] define Hungary as a global-minded trans-Atlantist state, which besides the new security challenges puts great emphasis on economic security issues. The Hungarian foreign policy strategy considers energetic, economic and military security of the broadly interpreted Central Europe including the Visegrád countries. Similarly to the other partner states, the Hungarian military strategy does not include the concept of V4 military partnership, the goals of joint military development nor any joint military capabilities aimed to be achieved. Maybe this is the reason why the active Hungarian-V4 relations are carried out primarily within allied or multinational limits and bilateral relations.

The defence cooperation of the V4 has to handle the geopolitical differences of the member states as well. Though the V4 countries form a France-size contiguous geographic area (533,000 km^2), the Carpathian Mountains cut through the Visegrád states, creating different geopolitical interests. This division also appears in the alliance, because NATO does not have Northern and Southern regions anymore. However, this is still a reference point for organizing different levels and types of relations. The fact that Poland, the Czech Republic and Slovakia belonging to the Northern region and Hungary to the Southern, fundamentally determines the scope of Euro-Atlantic cooperation (presence at headquarters, exercises, the geographic limits of programme development, the priorities of Partnership for Peace etc.). This division is still observable in the different geopolitical interests too. For Poland the Northern and Eastern Partnership, and the Northern Sea region have the primary importance. The Czech Republic pays attention to the global rearrangement processes, but its orientation is determined by the Western and Eastern neighbourhood and the Western Balkans. In the case of Slovakia, the Central and Eastern European focus is strong, but it also regards the Balkan and South Caucasus as important regions. Hungary attaches its foreign political identity to broader Central Europe, where besides Visegrád cooperation, the Central

European Defence Initiative (CEDI) also has a highly significant role (Csiki, Németh and Tálas 2012). The Central European Defence Cooperation, launched in 2011, embraces Austria, the Czech Republic, Croatia, Hungary, Slovakia and Slovenia. The participating states concentrate on the already existing neighbourhood military cooperation (Slovak–Hungarian peacekeeping, Hungarian–Romanian peacekeeping battalion, Italian-Slovenian-Hungarian combined brigade, Tisza engineering battalion) and its potential development. Whether there are enough resources for different geopolitical forms of cooperation and how to ensure synergy between the V4 and Central European Defence Cooperation are still unknown.

A new geographical split in the V4 countries' attitudes towards the Ukraine crisis and opinions about the Russia–Ukraine conflict has evolved. The geopolitical assessment of the conflict differs from partner to partner.

The military strength of the V4 countries

The different situations of the armed forces of the V4 countries, the disparity in financing, developing and their involvement in international tasks (crisis management, alliance and multilateral projects, the modernization of military technology) are affecting the V4 defence cooperation. The four states all together have smaller armed forces (163,600) than for instance Israel (176,500). In a military respect with regard to general power potential, Poland dominates: the strength of the Polish armed forces is 60 per cent; its defence budget is 65 per cent of the V4. Warsaw has only a one third share (31.8%) in peacekeeping operations. Among the V4 countries, Poland is the only country who has started to invest 40 billion dollars in the modernization of the armed forces. In an international military comparison, only Poland has a significant military capability. According to GFP[14] it has the 19th most powerful armed force in the world and it is in sixth place in the European context. The differences in size hinder cooperation in many respects, which could only be solved if Warsaw took the lead in military cooperation at all points and the other states accepted it. Regarding the qualitative parameters (military standard, interoperability, asymmetric combat capability, and expeditionary warfare) the four countries are in a similar situation, though undoubtedly the Poles and the Czechs lead the way and they are followed by the Hungarians and the Slovaks (Table 14.2). The problems of the professionalization of the armed forces are common, as – except Slovakia – all of the countries have switched over to a volunteer military force and their concepts of development are close to each another. There is also a significant difference in financing of the forces, which does not only hinder everyday cooperation, but makes more difficult the mid- and long-term cooperation, too.

In addition, there are significant differences between the defence budgets of the V4 countries: while Poland (25.79 per cent) and Slovakia (19.2 per cent) meet the modernization requirements of NATO, as 20 per cent of defence budget should be spent on procurement and research and development, the

Table 14.2 The most important characteristics of the V4 armed forces (2017)

Country	*Size of military force (pers.)*	*Defence expenditure (billion $)*	*Defence expenditure (GDP%)*	*Participation in peacekeeping missions (pers.)*
CZ	21,950	2.119	1.07	354
PL	**99,300**	**9.997**	**2.01**	**648**
HU	26,500	1.355	1.05	775
SVK	15,850	1.090	1.19	256
Total	163,600	15.371	1.33	2033

Source: Military Balance, 13 February 2017; NATO, 4 June 2017.

Czech Republic (7.23 per cent) and Hungary (13.0 per cent) do not follow the adopted guidelines (NATO 2017). Not only everyday cooperation, but also medium- and long-term cooperation is hindered seriously by this fact.

The evolution of defence cooperation

The policy change in the defence cooperation goes back to 2004, when the prime ministers reinforced the importance of cooperation after joining the Euro-Atlantic Organizations. The Prime Ministers' Summit in Kroměříž (Czech Republic) laid out the new principles for the future V4 cooperation after achieving NATO and EU membership. It was the first case when defence policy requirements were set up to address cooperation in the areas of crisis management, regional partnership, the European Security and Defence Policy, counter-terrorism, and defence industry.

The first qualitative change in the Visegrád defence policy took place in 2012 and 2013 when seven high-level meetings (heads of government, ministers of foreign affairs and defence ministers) formed the new defence cooperation policy, which is still fundamental for the defence programmes. The Litoměřice programme (2012) envisioned the future cooperation in the areas of capability development, interoperability, common training, prospective common procurement, as well as partnership and cooperation in Afghanistan. Besides the actual programs, the V4 states identified the new areas of cooperation for capability development. Beyond the projects, it is not difficult to recognize the intention of creating the supportive arms and enabling capabilities required for the Visegrád Battlegroup. The programme also aimed to contribute to Connected Forces Initiative (CFI) training and offered military forces in the spirit of NATO Smart Defence and the EU Pooling and Sharing Concept. This was the first V4 Ministers of Defence Declaration in which NATO requirements and contributions dominated, called 'Responsibility for the strong NATO'.[15]

In May 2013 the meeting of the foreign ministers issued a joint security and defence policy communiqué entitled 'For a more effective and stronger CSDP'. The partner states laid great emphasis on the further development of common

European defence on the basis of common political will, financial realities and multinational principles: 'Strengthening CSDP should go hand in hand with reinforced partnership with NATO.' (Visegrád group 2013). The document defines tasks in three fields for supporting the European defence: (i) strengthening the efficiency of visibility of the Common Security and Defence Policy (CSDP), (ii) military capability development and (iii) reinforcing the European defence industry.[16]

The Litoměřice programme was developed further by the decisions of heads of government in the following meetings: 22 June 2012 (Prague), 16 March 2013 (Gdansk), 14 October 2013 (Budapest), 24 June 2014 (Budapest), 31 October 2014 (Bratislava), 19 June 2015 (Bratislava), 17 December 2015 (Prague) and 15 December 2016 (Brussels). In the sequences of Prime Ministers meeting particularly the Budapest summit (24 June 2014) had an important role because a new opening in V4 defence cooperation was approved (Visegrád group 2014). The new long-term objectives included (i) capacity-building, public procurement and the improvement of military-industrial cooperation, (ii) the creation of multinational units and cross-border air defence cooperation, and (iii) improvement of education and training activities.

The Slovakian Presidency of 2014/2015 echoed the new opening and developed a new long-term plan calculating the changed security environment, the new requirements of NATO and EU and the V4 efforts to meet the new challenges, risks and threats. It was no longer sufficient to contribute only to 'Smart Defence' and Pooling and Sharing programmes, because as a response to Russian aggression in Ukraine in 2014, NATO Summits (Wales 2014, Warsaw 2016) approved the Readiness Action Plan (RAP), the Framework Nation and Forward Presence Concept. These new NATO decisions requested a both individual and collective V4 responses. In addition, there was a decision to establish a Visegrád footprint in the Baltics. A similar process was going on in the EU; focusing on the CSDP requirements and migration crisis in the home defence. The Slovakian action plan paid great attention to coordination in defence planning, which it considered as a necessary element for common acquisition of military platforms. The program also suggested the establishment of a new joint V4 Battlegroup in the second half year of 2019, which was reinforced in February by the defence ministers (Visegrád group 2017).

Joint training exercises are also not new in the plan, but the new opening suggested developing a medium-term training strategy in order to provide V4 visibility in NATO and EU exercises. The action plan covers education as well and suggests a V4 Military Education Platform (VIGMILEP), which will not be connecting with the military dimension of ERASMUS and education cooperation among Central European defence academies and universities. New areas in the action plan are joint air space management tasks (joint air space protection, air space bilateral defence agreements). It also calls for the creation of a Gripen Joint Training Centre supported by three of the V4 countries. Improvement of strategic communications is also vital in the plan from the V4 point of view. According to the 2015 poll, the majority of the population does not know about the V4 organization: Only 37 per cent of Czechs, 26 per cent of the Hungarians, 37 per cent of Poles, and 54 per cent of Slovak had actually heard of the Visegrád cooperation (Visegrád group 2015). That is why the V4 leaders decided to establish a separate tab (Defence Visegrád Cooperation) on the V4 website which publishes news and novelties.

V4 EU Battlegroup 2016

Undoubtedly, among the V4 defence programs the common EU Battlegroup (BG) caused the greatest stir (Friedman 2014, Weiss 2012) in terms of international press coverage and among experts. The decision-making process of the Visegrád partners was quite long: the idea of creating a V4 EUBG first appeared at the meeting of the chiefs of defence staff in 2007 in Sliač, Slovakia. Still in that year, the V4 defence ministers made public the possible establishment of the force in 2015. Although the V4 defence ministers repeatedly expressed their 'continued determination' between 2007 and 2011, further conceptual work was suspended due to the slow progress of the feasibility analysis and the low degree of political will (Paulech and Urbansková 2014).

However, after 2012 a new discussion started about the Battlegroup. Many saw the initiative as the flagship project of the V4 cooperation, while others considered this offering as a simple obligation. The sceptics argued that the offer came too late, as nowadays it is impossible to make as much political profit out of this CSDP contribution as it was possible a few years ago. Even the concept itself has become criticised as the Battlegroup has never been used, not even when it should have been (for instance in 2008 in order to give the EUFOR Chad/RCA a hand).

Regarding the future of this tool a question was raised: 'Use it or lose it?'(Andersson 2015) The experiences gained in the last years raised several questions concerning the use and the functioning of the concept, despite the defence agenda of the European Committee in December 2013 which provided, in theory, relevant answers to questions of a 'more flexible and effective' Battlegroup concept.[17] After the publication of the EU Global Strategy on Foreign and Security Policy (EUGS) in 2016 the concept, the system of financing and the question of deployment should be rethought in order to make it more flexible.

The basis of the Battlegroup constitutes a combined arms battalion task force, which is complemented by supporting elements and attachments (Horváth, Szenes and Szép 2007). Due to the potential great distance and rapid deployability, the planning of transportation and the logistical support of the forces became highly important. Based on the experience of the originally proposed number of servicemen (1,500) is not enough, the V4 EU Battlegroup for instance was composed of 3,700 people. In order to define the tasks, the power and the composition of the battlegroups, the EU worked out five illustrative scenarios. Because of these five scenarios, the battlegroups can be used for conflict prevention, the division of combatants by force, stabilization, reconstruction and military assistance, rescue operations and humanitarian operations. The battlegroups can be deployed in order to react quickly in a crisis situation. They can also be used for carrying out assignments deriving from the treaties of the EU. The future and the success of the BG concept depend on the implementation of the goals of the Global European Foreign Policy and Security Strategy. Two biannual EU Battlegroups are on duty in a stand-by position with five to ten days readiness level. Their use is planned for 30 days, which can be extended by two months.

The battlegroup arrangement is a challenging task, because the preparation (e.g. the forces-generation) are time- and resource-consuming, particularly in case of small and medium countries with lower national defence budgets. It is not accidental that in the initial period (2005–2006), the battlegroups were set up by the big countries alone and multinational formation started to spread later. The more countries arrange a joint battlegroup, the more challenging the task becomes, even if in such cases a framework nation is always appointed. The multinational solution is strongly supported by the EU as one of the goals of the battlegroup concept is to facilitate capability development, the enhancement of joint cooperation and the improvement of interoperability. Nations which are close to each another and countries which have collectively maintained a multinational military force in peacetime, can arrange battlegroups more easily. Such a joint military cooperation exists in several places in Europe, for instance the combined Italian, Slovenian and Hungarian Multinational Land Force (MLF) which has already fulfilled EU Battlegroup tasks twice and led Battlegroup operations in the first and the second semester of 2017 under the Defence Cooperation Initiative (DECI, Hungary, Austria, Croatia, Italy and Slovenia).[18]

Nevertheless, the arrangement of a V4 EU Battlegroup has resulted in a new challenge for the V4 countries despite them already having taken part in such formations individually. In the second half of 2010 the Czech Republic and Slovakia arranged a common EU Battlegroup and in the first half of 2011 a German, Latvian, Lithuanian and Slovakian Battlegroup operated with Polish leadership. However, a joint V4 BG military force had not been created before. There was an agreement from the beginning that the framework nation role would be performed by Poland, which already had experience in this field. The framework nation has always great responsibility as it has to coordinate planning, national and joint training, the compilation of forces and services, and it has to lead the Battlegroup forces in the field. The framework nation also needs to fill the gap where shortage appears.

The Visegrád Battlegroup has been the cherished ambition of the V4 countries from when it was first proposed in 2004. It was also proposed that in case of positive experiences, the partner states would repeat the Battlegroup offer every three years in order to maintain and develop related important multinational projects (logistics, heath care institutions, strategic air transport, joint procurements and services). The Polish Presidency already included this ambition into the program in 2016: 'Continue the preparation of the V4 EU Battlegroup for the stand-by in the second half of 2019, with the potential to build a V4 Modular Force at a later stage'[19]

The General Staff of the V4 partner states started planning the Visegrád Battlegroup in 2014. They agreed at the beginning to divide the task force into eight modules: combat subunits, combat service and support, special operations (SOF), logistics, health care, engineer support, civil-military relations (CIMIC) and NBC forces, which were provided by different nations The V4 BG had 3,700-strong force and approximately 50 per cent of it was provided by Poland, the framework nation; 20 per cent by the Czech Republic; 18 per cent by Hungary and 12 per cent by Slovakia. The Poles reorganized the Cracow Land Operation HQs into the EU Operational Force HQs, which performed the command and control arrangements during the duty period of V4 BG.[20] Every nation gave an equal number of soldiers to the mechanized infantry battalion and~~also~~ established a national support element in order to carry out the logistical support of their own forces. The combat and service support elements were divided among the participating countries: the Poles provided the combat support forces, the Czechs were responsible for logistics and medical support, the Slovakians for the protection against weapons of mass destruction, and the Hungarians for technical (engineering) support, civil-military relations, and special operation forces.

The planning and preparation phase was finished by the first half of 2014, and then the training period started, first in modules and later in battlegroup size. The seriousness of the offer was also shown by the fact that the certification exercise of V4 BG, the Common Challenge 2015 was arranged together with the Very High Readiness Joint Task Force (VJTF) in exercise Trident Junction 2015. The creation of the V4 BG required serious efforts from the participating countries.[21] As a result of the nearly two-year period of preparation, coordination and implementation, the V4 BG was on standby successfully for six months in the second half year of 2016, but it was not used, not deployed.

Although the experiences of the preparation and creation of the V4 EUBG have not yet been publicly assessed, the press gives us the opportunity to summarise many lessons learnt. On the political level, it was important to practice decision processes that were well thought-out. What can or can't a nation do alone? What sort of tasks might a battlegroup contribute to? What conditions are required for its deployment? Are there any legislative implications for the eventual use of the group? Every member state had to think over what it could undertake and what tasks needed to be done in order to complete its contribution. It became visible on a V4 level, what the different armies were capable of and what shortfalls remained even after the adding of forces and assets. For example, contributing companies seemed to be easy compared to the size of the national armies, yet when NATO requirements were overlaid on the above mentioned capabilities, flaws and deficiencies were revealed that could only be handled by determining national limitations. The involved parties tried to eliminate shortfalls via expedited procedures. During the preparation, for instance, the creation of a Close Air Support (CAS) capability was commissioned in Hungary, which cost €9.1 million. Poland realized that it was necessary to establish an independent EU operation headquarters for regular EUBG contributions because the Corps HQs in Szczecin had become the NATO headquarters in the meantime, responsible for the Baltic region (MNC-NE), resulting in constant activity. That is why it was suggested that it would be practical to turn the Cracow Land Component Command HQ into a sixth EU Operation Headquarters.[22] Every member state acquired important experience related to standby duties and compatibility with other tasks (watch-keeping capability, military training and exercise as well as border management) which was not easy anywhere. NATO exercises were taking place with full intensity in 2016. The NATO Anaconda Exercise involved the participation of 34,000 service members in Poland in July. The testing of stand-by capabilities is important because the Very High Readiness Joint Task Force (VJTF) will have been engaged for three years (preparation, operational readiness, post-mission availability) in the strengthened NATO Response Force (NRF). Every member state has to consider how much to contribute in which field (EUBG, NATO NRF, VJTF, exercises and operations), because the requirements for force generation have multiplied due to the collective defence tasks. Therefore, it is completely rational that the V4 endeavours to find common solutions and develop a kind of Visegrád footprint if they can harmonize the differing interests, ambitions and possible solutions. For example, Poland has already announced that it will assume a VJTF framework nation task until 2020, and would like to include in it the V4 partner states (Bodnárová 2013). In February 2017, the V4 defence ministers accepted the suggestion and identified the 2020 rotation of the NATO VJTF under the Polish command as an important opportunity for V4 to tighten its cooperation.[23]

Thus, the experience of the EU Battlegroup proves very useful not only in the EU but in NATO as well. The V4 countries already decided that they will prepare for the next V4 EUBG in 2019. Operational headquarters in Krakow have proved V4's readiness and ability to contribute to other multinational formations. The robust composition and the establishment of the V4 EUBG means it can be exercised for NATO tasks by contributing to NFR and VJTF. It can also be useful in the activities of the NATO Force Integration Unit (NFIU) as well as in missions linked to rotational deployment.[24]

Moving to the permanent modular force

In addition to V4 EUBG, the Visegrád long-term vision aims to establish more multinational units. The advantage of the functioning peacetime military units is that they have permanent joint command and designated affiliated units, subunits, and their function gives the opportunity to analyse gained experience, disseminate best practice, and increase efficiency of training and leadership. It is easy to offer a continuously available permanent force both for NATO and the EU and in favour of the United Nations. NATO´s Smart Defence Concept and the EU´s Pooling and Sharing Concept suggest establishing peacetime multinational military formations. This is because modern warfare is dominated by the coalition character of the forces, the common international command language (in Western alliances, English, but in the Shanghai Cooperation Organization, Russian) and the highest possible capability for interoperability. In countries with a high degree level of force integration (Benelux, NORDEFCO, Baltic) a wide variety of command and control solutions exist, from which the Visegrád countries selected the permanent modular design power (Permanent Modular Force, V4PMF). The permanent force has at least peacetime joint command and designated or permanent subordinated forces. Modularity means that the smaller battalion- or company-level elements can be mixed and matched by the brigade's commander to suit the particular mission. The common interest here obviously would be to create a V4PMF, which would immediately be offered to the EU and NATO Response Force and NATO Readiness Action Plan (Suplata 2013).

The Slovak Presidency (2014/2015) accepted the possibility of setting up a permanent modular force and included the declaration of Bratislava. Development and discussion of the modular concept of power has already begun in 2014, which continued during the Czech (2015/2016) and the Polish (2016/2017) presidencies. It is expected that the concept will be approved by the prime ministers and defence ministers during the Polish presidency. The conceptual discourse of the concept takes place in the V4 existing defence policy forums based on the Slovakian so-called non-paper materials. It is agreed that the long-term V4 training and exercise strategy should develop around the V4 Battlegroup and the V4PMF. An agreement was also achieved regarding the organizational designs, which have to follow NATO and EU standards. There is also no question about the need to examine a number of areas: V4 foreign and security policy, legal aspects, national contributions, force management, operations, training, sharing practices and multinationality before taking the final decision (Suplata and Nad 2014). The considerations should cover the latest NATO decisions taken in Wales and Warsaw related to collective defence. During the discussions, the timeline to set up the permanent modular force was also agreed.

In Phase I (2016–2020) the V4 countries will establish again a new V4 EUBG (in the second half of 2019) and the Polish-led VJTF (land component in 2020). If the V4PMF targets are met, during the second phase (2021–2025) a joint brigade-level headquarters (HQ V4PMF) will be established. The modular force structure will be created in the third phase (2026–2030) with different possible command and control relations: permanent or semi-permanent peace period subordination or just using the affiliation solution like in the case of the Multinational Land Force led by Italy which involved Hungary and Slovenia.

Despite the long-term plans and the political and military agreement, a lot of uncertainty about the V4 Permanent Modular Force still remains. Obviously, much will depend on the medium-term security environment, the durability of the Eastern Russian threats, the Alliance concepts and the political will for their realization. Technically, a V4PMF could be set up relatively quickly, as we see today in the case of Romanian Multinational Division headquarters, or the Black Sea brigade. All depends on how strong the pressure or political ration will be or, how difficult it will be to reach a consensus on policy issues, since military-technical solutions will be easier to achieve. However, no doubt that in the light of Brexit the V4PMF could have serious implications for European military capabilities.

Conclusion

The cooperation of Visegrád countries has been shaped by several factors from the beginning and the group's development impacted by internal and external factors. Its formation in the scope of new regionalism is undoubtedly a success, as the semi-institutionalised Visegrád cooperation has survived all of its crises and contributed to the Euro-Atlantic accession and the integration of the partner states. The compromising attitude of the group about the topical issues of NATO and the EU, their lobbying within the scope of the EU and the single representation of regional interests contributed to the formation of the Visegrád identity.

Defence cooperation is an unexpected profit from the V4 development. The V4 NATO membership has always been a stabilizing factor which strengthens cohesion on the bumpy road of EU cooperation as the concept of common and indivisible security is shared by all member states. The Common Security and Defence Policy has brought further cohesion for the Visegrád countries, as the changing security environment (the Ukrainian crisis, migration crisis, terrorism) has given new impetus to the V4 defence cooperation.

The Visegrád countries face the same difficulties in the practical dimension of defence cooperation, as in general and sectoral cooperation. Yet the cooperation and its defence consultations served rather the formulation of a joint security perception, than the development of a deeper, conscious level of regional military integration. All programmes after NATO and EU accession have had allied, multilateral or bilateral features instead of the regional ones.

From 2012/2013, the new defence cooperation programme started under the Polish presidency, which has been continued by the subsequent presidencies. Because of this process the long-term vision and the action plan were created in 2014. It has been confirmed that the development requires ambitious and complex programmes (like V4 BG, VJFT or permanent modular force) which are able to improve all elements of the cooperation. Without a central reference point, the different programmes and projects cannot be coherent and would provide only sporadic results. The successful standby of the V4 Battlegroup has raised the level of ambition of the Visegrád countries. They have already undertaken the next V4 EUBG in 2019, and the NATO VJTF in 2020 and planning to establish permanent modular force by 2030. It looks like the V4 countries are changing their policy approach: instead of further cooperation in the framework of the EU and NATO they aim towards achieving a deeper level of integration.

However, the problems of Visegrád cooperation and new dimensional repetitive failures are urging us to show caution. The joint statement of the prime ministers on the 25th year anniversary has forgotten to determine

NATO cooperation in future destinations.[25] At the same time, in a new competitive and uncertain world stronger international military cooperation is required. If the V4 approach to this new world will be more politically inclusive and mutually strengthen their individual approaches, they can more easily cope with the challenges and threats of regional and national development. Then maybe the Visegrád tourism cooperation slogan – European quartet, one melody – will also be true of the defence cooperation.

Notes

1 Visegrád is an old Hungarian historical town, which is located in the Danube bend 30 kilometres northwest of Budapest. In 1335 Charles Robert, Hungarian king, John the Blind, the King of Bohemia and Casimir III the Great, King of Poland signed an economic and commercial agreement against Vienna whereby they established a long-lasting economic cooperation in the Middle Ages.

2 http://www.worldometers.info/population/countries-in-the-eu-by-population/ (accessed 11 February 2017).

3 http://www.tradingeconomics.com/european-union/gdp (accessed 11 February 2017).

4 http://ec.europa.eu/eurostat/documents/2995521/7573561/2-22072016-AP-EN.pdf/16cdaec5-3f1c-4cab-a8cf-954b917e04a9 (accessed 11 February2017).

5 The study rated the strategic documents of the 27 EU member states on the basis of five criteria: (1) The comprehensive evaluation of security environment; (2) The approach which is necessary for achieving future goals; (3) The unity of goals, means, execution and methods of implementation; (4) The identification of concrete goals; (5) The identification and schedule of the resources of the planning period. On the basis of the results, the study placed the EU member states into six categories (grand strategists, strategists, globalists, localists, abstentionists and drifters) and argued for the implementation of a new EU security strategy.

6 Building the Shield. European Nations Cooperate with US, NATO Allies on Missile Defence. Defence News, 26 November 2013. http://www.defensenews.com/article/20131126/DEFREG01/311250029/Building-Shield

7 The command of the Lithuanian-Polish-Ukrainian Brigade (LITPOLUKRBRIG) achieved operability on 24 July 2016. The basic tasks of the brigade include peace support operations and crisis management, but it also prepares for undertaking combat tasks. Every contributing nation sends a battalion into the brigade manned by 4,000 servicemen. The Ukrainians offered 550 and the Lithuanians 350 soldiers. The rest are Poles. Logistical forces and support structure are provided by common effort. Available from: http://litpolukrbrig.wp.mil.pl/en/85.html (accessed 4 August 2016).

8 Security Strategy of the Czech Republic, MFA, September 2011. Available from: http://www.army.cz/ images/id_8001_9000/8503/Czech_Security_Strategy_2011.pdf (accessed 25 July 2016).

9 The Defence Strategy of the Czech Republic. Ministry of Defence, Prague, December 2012. pp. 7, 10–12.

10 AWACS (Airborne Warning and Control System) is a flight deck early warning system of NATO, which has 14 Boeing E-3A planes. In 2006 Hungary, in 2007 Poland and in 2011 the Czech Republic joined the units deployed at the German Geilenkierchen and the English Waddington airbases. Slovakia has not joined the programme yet.

11 AGS (Alliance Ground System) is the terrestrial intelligence system of NATO in the scope of which the Global Hawk fleet, which consists of five planes, will be deployed at the airbase of Sigonella in Sicily. The founders of the programme are the Czech Republic and Slovakia. Poland joined at the end of 2012. Hungary is still thinking about it.

12 A kormány 1035/2012 (II. 21) Korm. Határozata Magyarország Nemzeti Biztonsági Stratégiájáról (Governmental Decree on the National Security Strategy of Hungary). Magyar Közlöny, 2012. 19. Available at: http://www.kormany.hu/download/f/49/70000/1035_2012_korm_hatarozat.pdf.
13 A kormány 1656/2012 (XII. 20) Korm. határozata Magyarország Nemzeti Katonai Stratégiájáról (Governmental Decree on the National Defence Strategy of Hungary). Available at: http://www.kormany.hu/download/d/05/c0000/2012_1220_NKS.PDF
14 Based on 42 indicators (human resources, military technological potential, oil, finances, logistics, and geopolitics) it evaluated 133 states of the world militarily (without nuclear weapons). Available at: https://www.globalfirepower.com/countries-listing.asp (accessed 04 October 2017).
15 Joint V4 Declaration: 'Responsibility for a Strong NATO'. 18 April 2012. http://www.visegradgroup.eu/joint-v4-declaration (accessed 4 October 2017).
16 The V4 states were right regarding the situation of CSDP as they determined similar tasks at the meeting of the European Council on 19 and 20 December in 2013: (1) increasing the influence and efficiency of CSDP, (2) increasing capability development, (3) strengthening the European defence industry. Available from: http://www.european-council.europa.eu/home-page/highlights/security-and-defence-policy-high-on-the-agenda-at-the-european-council?lang=hu (accessed 24 July 2016).
17 See: http://www.consilium.europa.eu/uedocs/cms_Data/docs/pressdata/en/ec/140245.pdf. p. 4. (accessed 18 July 2016).
18 Five Countries to Set Up Joint EU Battle Group, 24 April 2014 Available at: http://2010-2014.kormany.hu/en/ministry-of-defence/news/five-countries-to-set-up-joint-eu-battle-group (accessed 22 December 2016).
19 Program of the Polish Presidency in the Visegrád Group. July 1, 2016- June 30, 2017. Chapter 3, task N.5 http://www.visegradgroup.eu/documents/presidency-programs/program-of-the-polish (accessed 4 October 2017).
20 V4 Battle Group Command in Cracow. 20 November 2015. Available from: http://www.defence24.com/ 273579,v4-battle-group-command-in-cracow (accessed 21 November 2015).
21 Megkezdte tevékenységét a visegrádi harccsoport. (V4 BG started performing its duty) Magyar Idők, 18 November 2015. Available from: http://magyaridok.hu/kulfold/megkezdte-tevekenyseget-a-visegradi-harccsoport-159994/ (accessed 12 June 2016); OPH-Csehországban tárgyaltak a V4 országok vezérkari főnökei. (The Chiefs of Defence from V4 countries meet in the Czech Republic). Available from: http://orientpress.hu/cikk/csehorszagban-targyaltak-a-v4-orszagok-vezerkar-fonokei (accessed 11 June 2016).
22 Member states have offered five Operation Headquarters to the EU (Paris, Northwood, Ulm, Rome and Larissa). In addition, an EU Operations Centre has been created in Brussels with the principal task of directing complex operations. Operation Headquarters (OHQ) have been used by the EU since 2012. Available from: https://eeas.europa.eu/csdp/missions-and-operations/eunavfor-med/pdf/eunavfor_med_-_eu_italian_operation_headquartes_rome.pdf (accessed 5 August 2016).
23 Joint Communiqué of the Visegrád Group Ministers of Defence. Niepołomice, 2 February 2017. Available from: http://www.visegradgroup.eu/calendar/2017/joint-communique-of-the (accessed 12 February 2017).
24 Bundeswehr Multinational Forces Operations Command for EU Battle Groups. Epitoma for Militaris. 8 August 2013. Available at: http://www.phantomreport.com/bundeswehr-multinational-forces-operations-command-for-eu-battle-groups (accessed 21 August 2016).
25 Joint Statement of the Prime Ministers of the Visegrád Group Countries on the 25th V4 Anniversary. Available from: http://www.visegradgroup.eu/calendar/2016/joint-statement-of-the (accessed 12 February 2017).

References

Andersson, J. (2015) If Not Now, When? The Nordic EU Battlegroup. Available from: http://www.iss.europa.eu/uploads/media/Alert_11_Nordic_Battlegroup.pdf (accessed 15 August 2016).

Balogh, I. (2013) *Magyarország és a visegrádi országok biztonságpercepciói: hasonlóságok és különbségek. (Security Perceptions of the Visegrád Countries and Hungary: Similitaries and Differencies)* MKI Studies. [ONLINE] Available from: http://www.kulugyiintezet.hu/pub/displ.asp?id=BRLQHN (accessed 15 June 2016).

Bodnárová, B. (2013) Visegrád Four Battle Group 2016: Run up to Visegrád Four NATO Response Force 2020? CENAA Policy Papers 63/2013. Available at: http://cenaa.org/wp-content/uploads/2013/06/PP-6-2013-Visegrad-four-Battle-Group-2016-Run-up-to-Visegrad-four-NATO-Response-Force-2020.pdf (accessed 21 June 2016).

Csiki, T., Németh, B. and Tálas, P. (2012) A többnemzeti katonai képességfejlesztésről a Közép-európai Védelmi Együttműködési Kerekasztal kapcsán (The Multinational Military Capabilities Development from the Central European Cooperation prospective), *NKE Stratégiai Védelmi Kutatóközpont* 5(5–6), pp. 124–132.

France, O. de and N. Whitney (2013) *Europe's Strategic Cacophony*. European Council on Foreign Relations Policy Brief No. 77. April. [ONLINE] Available from: http://ecfr.eu/page/-/ECFR77 _SECURITY_BRIEF_AW.pdf (accessed 20 June 2016).

Friedman, G. (2011) STRATFOR. Available from: http://www.stratfor.com/weekly/20110516-visegrad-new-european-military-force (accessed 12 July 2016).

Horváth, G., Szenes, Z. and Szép, L. (2007) Az Európai Unió harccsoport – koncepciója, (The EU Battlegroup Concept) *Európai Tükör* 12(4), pp. 97–111.

Madej, M. (2013) Visegrád Group Defence Cooperation: What Added Value for the European Capabilities? Nordica Programme No. 19/13 June. p. 2. [ONLINE] Available from: http://www.frstrategie.org/barreFRS/publications/notes/2013/201319.pdf (accessed 24 June 2016).

Michelot, M., Pomlényi, A., Strázay, T. and Visvizi, A. (2016) The View at 25: Visegrád's Silver Anniversary. [ONLINE] Available from: https://cepa.ecms.pl/files/?id_plik=2854 (accessed 4 October 2017).

Molnár, D. and Szilvágyi, T. (2016) *A szomszédos országok védelmi stratégiái és haderőinek műveleti alkalmazása.* (The Strategic Assesment of the Neighboring Countries of Hungary). Nemzeti Közszolgálati Egyetem, Budapest.

NATO (1994) Partnership for Peace Programme. 11 January. [ONLINE] Available from: http://www.nato.int/cps/en/SID-754332CF-D817A5AC/natolive/topics_50115.htm (accessed 12 June 2016).

NATO (2017) *Defence Expenditures of NATO Countries (2010–2017).* [ONLINE] https://www.nato.int/nato_static_fl2014/assets/pdf/pdf_2017_06/20170629_170629-pr2017-111-en.pdf (accessed 23 January 2018).

Paulech, M. and Urbansková, J. (2014) Visegrád Four EU Battlegroup: Meaning and Progress, in Obrana a Strategie. Available from: http://www.obranaastrategie.cz/en/archive/volume-2014/2-2014/articles/visegrad-four-eu-battlegroup-meaning-and-progress.html#.V8VUy6Lm4qI (accessed 18 July 2016).

Suplata, M. (ed) (2013) DAV4 II: Report: From battlegroup to permanent structure. CEPI, 18 November 2013. Available from: http://www.cepolicy.org/publications/dav4-ii-report-battlegroup-permanent-structures (accessed 6 August 2016).

Suplata, M. and J. Nad (2014) Military Training and Education. An Opportunity for V4 Cooperation. CEPI, 5 November 2014. Available from: http://www.cepolicy.org/

publications/military-training-and-education-opportunity-v4-co-operation (accessed 31 June 2016).

Visegrád group (1991) *Declaration on Cooperation Between the Czech and Slovak Federal Republic, the Republic of Poland and the Republic of Hungary in Striving for European Integration*, 15 February 1991. [ONLINE] Available from: http://www.visegradgroup.eu/documents/visegrad-declarations/visegrad-declaration-110412. (accessed 12 June 2016).

Visegrád group (2013) *Declaration of the Visegrád Group Foreign Ministers 'For a More Effective and Stronger CSDP'*. [ONLINE] Available from: http://www.visegradgroup.eu/documents/official-statements (accessed 12 February 2017).

Visegrád group (2014) *Budapest Declaration on the New Opening in V4 Defence Cooperation*. [ONLINE]Available from: http://www.visegradgroup.eu/calendar/2014/budapest-declaration-of (accessed 11 February 2017).

Visegrád group (2015) *Visegrád Group Defence Cooperation*. [ONLINE] Available from: http://www.visegradgroup.eu/about/cooperation/ visegrad-group-defence (accessed 8 August 2016).

Visegrád group (2016) Program of the Polish Presidency in the Visegrad Group. July 1, 2016- June 30, 2017. Chapter 3, task N.5. [ONLINE] Available from: http://www.visegradgroup.eu/documents/presidency- programs/program-of-the-polish (accessed 4 October 2017).

Visegrád group (2017) *Meeting of the Visegrád Group Ministers of Defence; Niepołomice – Joint Statement*. 2 February. [ONLINE] Available from: http://www.visegradgroup.eu/calendar/2017 (accessed 12 February 2017).

Weiss, T. (2012) *Visegrád Battlegroup: A Flagship That Should Not Substitute for Real Defence Cooperation*. 4 June. Available from: http://visegradrevue.eu/visegrad-battlegroup-a-flagship-that-should-not-substitute-for-real-defence-cooperation/ (accessed 18 July 2016).

Unequal World. London: European Bank for Reconstruction and Development (EBRD). [ONLINE] Available from: http://www.ebrd.com/documents/oce/pdf-transition-report-201617-english.pdf (accessed 6 October 2017).

Galgóczi, B. (2009) Boom and Bust in Central and Eastern Europe: Lessons on the Sustainability of an Externally Financed Growth Model, *Journal of Contemporary European Research* 5(4), pp. 614–625.

Galgóczi, B. (2016) The Southern and Eastern Peripheries of Europe: Is Convergence a Lost Cause? In: Magone, J.M., Laffan, B. and Schweiger, C. (eds) *Core-Periphery Relations in the European Union: Power and Conflict in a Dualist Political Economy*. Oxon: Routledge, pp. 130–146.

Genov, N. (2010) *Global Trends in Eastern Europe*. Abingdon: Routledge.

Giddens, Anthony (2014) *Turbulent and Mighty Continent: What Future for Europe?* Cambridge: Polity Press.

Markiewicz, M. (2013) The Development of the Banking Sector in Latvia, Lithuania and Estonia in the Context of Concentration and Competitiveness. In: Pfannkuche, A. (ed.) *Recovery of the Baltic States After the Global Financial Crisis*. Bremen: Hochschule, Fakultät für Wirtschaftswissenschaften. [ONLINE] Available from: http://www.ssoar.info/ssoar/handle/document/33466 (accessed 5 October 2017).

Myant, M. and Drahokoupil, J. (2011) *Transition Economies: Political Economy in Russia, Eastern Europe and Central Asia*. Hoboken: Wiley and Sons.

Porte, C. de la and Heins, E. (2017) The Aftermath of the Eurozone Crisis: Towards Fiscal Federalism? In: Dinan, D., Nugent, N. and Paterson, W.E. (eds) *The European Union in Crisis*. London: Palgrave, pp. 149–166.

Sikorski, R. (2011) *Poland and the Future of the European Union*. Speech delivered in Berlin, 28 November. [ONLINE] Available from: http://www.mfa.gov.pl/resource/33ce6061-ec12-4da1-a145-01e2995c6302:JCR (accessed 25 July 2017).

Schlipphak, B. and Treib, O. (2017) Playing the Blame Game on Brussels: The Domestic Political Effects of EU Interventions Against Democratic Backsliding. *Journal of European Public Policy* 24(3), pp. 352–365.

Schweiger, C. (2014) Nad rámec otvorenej metódy koordinácie. Sociálny rozmer Európskej únie v krízových podmienkach'(Beyond the open method of coordination: The EU's social dimension under crisis conditions). In: Blaha, Luboš (Hg.) *Euròpsky Sociálny Model: Čo Ďalej? (The European Social Model: What next?)*. Bratislava: Slovak Academy of Sciences, pp. 138–173.

Index